About Island Press

Since 1984, the nonprofit organization Island Press has been stimulating, shaping, and communicating ideas that are essential for solving environmental problems worldwide. With more than 1,000 titles in print and some 30 new releases each year, we are the nation's leading publisher on environmental issues. We identify innovative thinkers and emerging trends in the environmental field. We work with world-renowned experts and authors to develop cross-disciplinary solutions to environmental challenges.

Island Press designs and executes educational campaigns in conjunction with our authors to communicate their critical messages in print, in person, and online using the latest technologies, innovative programs, and the media. Our goal is to reach targeted audiences—scientists, policymakers, environmental advocates, urban planners, the media, and concerned citizens—with information that can be used to create the framework for long-term ecological health and human well-being.

Island Press gratefully acknowledges major support of our work by The Agua Fund, The Andrew W. Mellon Foundation, The Bobolink Foundation, The Curtis and Edith Munson Foundation, Forrest C. and Frances H. Lattner Foundation, The JPB Foundation, The Kresge Foundation, The Oram Foundation, Inc., The Overbrook Foundation, The S.D. Bechtel, Jr. Foundation, The Summit Charitable Foundation, Inc., and many other generous supporters.

The opinions expressed in this book are those of the author(s) and do not necessarily reflect the views of our supporters.

FIRESTORM

Firestorm

How Wildfire Will
Shape Our Future

Edward Struzik

ISLANDPRESS

Washington | Covelo | London

Island Press is a trademark of The Center for Resource Economics.

Keywords: Alaska, Alberta, Arctic, arsenic, asbestos, Banff, biodiversity,
boreal forest, British Columbia, California, Canada, carbon bomb,
climate change, Colorado, Denver, drought, fire ecology, fire management,
fire suppression, FireSmart, First Nations, Fort McMurray, Horse River Fire,
hydrology, Montana, mountain pine beetle, oil sands, Ontario, permafrost,
resilience, Royal Canadian Mounted Police, Slave Lake, spruce budworm,
water quality, watershed, Wood Buffalo

Library of Congress Control Number: 2017940667

All Island Press books are printed on environmentally responsible materials.

Manufactured in the United States of America
10 9 8 7 6 5 4 3 2 1

To my wife, Julia; my children, Jacob and Sigrid;
and to firefighters and first responders everywhere.

And to the First Nations people of Canada and the
North American native people of the United States, with
apologies for our failure to view wildfire the way you once did.

Contents

Introduction

On May 3, 2016, a rapidly spreading wildfire around Alberta's oil sands capital in Fort McMurray sent 88,000 people fleeing their homes, offices, hospitals, schools, and seniors' residences. The people left so quickly that they were gone before the government declared a provincial state of emergency. Thick smoke turned day into night. Embers rained down on cars and trucks as people headed south to the city of Edmonton or north to the safety of oil sands camps and First Nations communities.

By the time rains and cooler temperatures helped firefighters contain MWF-009, as the ninth regional blaze of the season is officially called, 2,800 homes and buildings were destroyed. Nearly 1.4 million acres (566,168 hectares) burned. Insurance losses were expected to amount to $3.77 billion. The total cost of the fire, including financial, physical, and social factors, is likely to be $8.86 billion. Firefighters referred to the enormous conflagration as the Horse River fire or "The Beast." The second was an apt name, as the fire ended up being the costliest natural disaster in Canadian history and one of the most destructive North American wildfires in modern times. Police and firefighters fully expected to find hundreds if not thousands of bodies in burnt-out cars, trucks, and homes. It was a miracle that, except for two young people who were fatally injured in a car crash on the drive south, no one died.

That so few people perished is exceptional, especially given how much went wrong with the management of the fire and the painfully slow decision making that went into the evacuation process. There was no shortage of heroics. But egos got in the way. A unified command that would have been able to reconcile inherently different approaches by wildland and structural firefighters took too long to come together. A provincial state of emergency, which would have given the government of Alberta clear, concise, and far-reaching authority to deal with the fire, wasn't called until two days after most everyone was gone. Unhappy with how the fires were being managed, oil sands companies hired their own independent experts to evaluate the magnitude of the risks to their operations.

Megafire, a relatively new word used to describe wildfire, is by one definition a fire that burns at least 100,000 acres (40,468 hectares). These fires routinely occur in Alaska, the Yukon, the Northwest Territories, and throughout the forests of western Canada, northern Ontario, most of Quebec, and the northern United States. On occasion, they burn in the soggier East Coast and Pacific Northwest regions. The Carlton Complex fire burned more than 250,000 acres on the eastern slopes of the Cascade Range in Washington in 2015. There is a reason for such fires: coniferous trees that grow in the montane, subalpine, Columbian, and boreal forests are ecologically programmed to burn.

The Horse River fire was not an anomaly as some people have suggested. Fires in Alberta have burned bigger (Chinchaga 1950), hotter (Chisholm 2001), and faster (Vega 1968). The difference between what is happening now and what was happening in the 1980s and earlier is that megafires are occurring more often, displacing more and more people, and reshaping forest and tundra ecosystems in ways that scientists don't fully understand.

What made the Horse River fire unique is that it created its own lightning storm, which set off many more fires several miles ahead of its path. What made it rare is that it burned in the so-called urban/wildland interface, where millions of people live, work, and recreate in and around the forests. Catastrophic fires like this one are going to happen more often because urban and industrial developments are encroaching on undeveloped wildlands at a record pace. Humans start wildfires, as they did in Fort McMurray and Gatlinburg, Tennessee, in 2016, Slave Lake in 2011, Kelowna in 2003, and Hayman in Colorado in 2002. In Canada, a little over half the wildfires are started by humans. In the United States, human-started wildfires account for 84 percent of all wildfires, and nearly half of all area that is burned.[1]

When the Horse River fire was finally under control on the fifth day of July, I was in a burned-out area in the boreal forest just north of Fort McMurray, catching nighthawks with Elly Knight, a graduate student from the University of Alberta in Canada. The Common Nighthawk is a small bird that is not a hawk, nor is it strictly nocturnal. Because its population has plummeted in North America, it is also no longer common. Nonetheless, it thrives in postfire landscapes, as Knight had discovered in the weeks before I arrived on the scene.

The nighthawk is a mottled gray, brown, and black bird with white patches, big black eyes, and a mouth that opens almost as wide as its head. More often than not, you hear its sharp, electric *peent* before you see it snatch its prey—a fire beetle or moth—with a graceful swoop.

It was 11 p.m. on a moonless night as I followed Knight through the dusky forest, systematically checking to see if any nighthawks had flown into her strategically placed nets. Along the horizon of the ebony sky, we could see a faint glimmer of light pulsing from Imperial Oil's oil sands plant in the Kearl Lake area many miles to the south of us. The $7.3 billion project pumps out 220,000 barrels of bitumen per day.

Stumbling along in the dark, waving off mosquitoes, I came within an inch of being flattened to the ground when a stubborn, fire-scarred branch I tried to break with my foot rebounded an inch short of whacking me in the head. Just as I bent down to retrieve my hat, one, two, and then four nighthawks swooped down in front of us—not just once, but several times—before they disappeared into the night. It was both utterly charming and completely disarming, like a conjuring of birds in a Harry Potter novel. I could see their big black eyes illuminated by

Figure I-1 Elly Knight holds one of several nighthawks she has been tracking in a burned-out forest north of Fort McMurray and the oil sands. (Edward Struzik)

the glow of our headlamps, looking at us as if to ask, "Who are you? Why are you here?"

It was in that intersection that I saw how these two distinct worlds are colluding and colliding. In front of us fluttered a charismatic, threatened bird thriving on fire beetles and other insects that follow fire so that they can feed and lay their eggs on dead trees. (The warmer the tree, the better for some of the insects.) Behind us glowed the lights of fossil fuel–driven human activity that was both displacing the forest habitat these birds thrive in and emitting greenhouse gases that are warming the climate and triggering atmospheric disturbances, driving wildfire to burn bigger, faster, hotter, and more often.

You would think that the nighthawks would benefit from an increasing number of wildfires, just as insects, woodpeckers, Clark's nuthatches, moose, elk, deer, bears, and other creatures do when scorched trees decay and insects move into a burned area, when wind-blown seeds fall to the ground, and when a new crop of trees, berry bushes, grass, and wild rooted vegetables rise up around them in sequential order. Indeed, they do. With a few notable exceptions such as grosbeaks, goshawks, and endangered spotted owls that thrive almost exclusively in old-growth forest, most of the five billion birds that nest in the northern forests of the continent fare well in postfire conditions as insects and seed-bearing plants begin to recolonize the disturbed landscape.

The wildfire paradigm we are moving into is not what it was when Europeans began settling in North America, however. Nor is it the same as it was before that, when North American indigenous people lit up the forests to promote the growth of berries, to attract wildlife, to clear trails, and to build up firewood supplies.

In this new paradigm, humans, climate, and weather-driven conflagrations are taking center stage in transforming much of the boreal and northern forests on the continent into something that will be quite different by midcentury or even sooner. The bigger, faster-moving wildfires that are likely to occur more often will change the structure of the forests and the vegetation on the tundra, affect the wildlife that live in them, and compromise the quality of water that flows through them and the quality of air people breathe, both immediately downwind of a fire and in places much farther away. Increasingly, industrial activity in these regions will be temporarily shut down, and more towns will have to be evacuated. Like the Fort McMurray fire and the record-breaking fire season of 2015 in the United States and Canada, big wildfires will have a negative effect on national, state, and provincial economies.

The detrimental impacts of wildfire are accelerating at a time when oil sands, hydraulic fracturing (fracking), logging, mining, hydroelectric developments, and ever-expanding townsites are voraciously consuming the northern forests. In the boreal forest, which accounts for most of the trees found in the northern forests and 30 percent of the forested area in the entire world, more than 180 million acres of trees and wetlands have already been consumed by industrial activity. Thirty percent of the boreal forest in Canada is slated for some form of future development. In the United States, there are now more than 46 million single-family homes, several hundred thousand businesses, and 120 million people living and working in and around the country's forests. The pace of development is most pronounced in the American West, where 70 percent of the wildlands are managed by a patchwork of state and federal agencies for a mix of uses: fish and wildlife, forests, water resources conservation, and, increasingly, residential development.

As more people move into forest environments, wildfire tends to loom as a killer, not as a magnificent spectacle that promotes biodiversity. That further complicates the stakes of fire management.

Darby Allen, the man who led firefighting efforts in Fort McMurray, likened the fire he fought to a wild animal that could not be tamed. "It seemed that whatever we did, it just kind've laughed at us and did something else. It was a beast," he told reporters during one of his almost-daily briefings.

It is true that there is no stopping these fiery beasts, as many people in Fort McMurray unrealistically expected before the fire made three runs into town while they were at home, work, or school. The energy of these conflagrations is as powerful as the energy of hurricanes and tornadoes. No one tries to stop those from happening.

When pyrocumulonimbus-driven lightning strikes set off several fires 21 miles (34 kilometers) in advance of The Beast, wildfire scientists were astonished. Wildfire fighters recoiled. Unlike most fires, this one didn't always go to sleep in the coolness of the night.

"This is a really dirty fire," Allen said at one point when it seemed to some like the worst was over. "There are certainly areas within the city which have not been burned, but this fire will look for them and it will take them."

Wildfire scientist Marty Alexander laments that we have a tendency to forget catastrophic wildfire events even when they cause so much despair, death, and destruction. Although there is a museum dedicated to the legacy of wildfire in Peshtigo, Wisconsin, which was struck by tragedy in 1871, it is unusual. There are no major museums dedicated to the legacy of wildfire in Canada or the United States. All there is to commemorate the Great Porcupine fire that sent thousands of people to take refuge in lakes and mine shafts in 1910 is a cemetery monument that pays tribute to the estimated two hundred Ontarians who died. I remember being surprised, almost shocked, when the Whyte Museum of the Canadian Rockies in Banff, Alberta, staged a wildfire art exhibit based on the epic fires that burned in the Rocky Mountains and other regions of Canada and the United States in 2003. It was so unusual.

The 2003 fires were wake-up calls because they demonstrated just how vulnerable we are becoming to fire by encouraging so many people to live and work in the northern forests. But it was not the first time that wildfire demonstrated that it can be a master rather than a servant.

The Miramachi fire in New Brunswick and Maine burned 2.9 million acres (1.2 million hectares) and killed twelve hundred people in 1825. The Peshtigo fire of 1871 burned eighteen towns and 1.2 million acres of trees and killed twelve hundred people in Wisconsin. The 1910 fires in Idaho, Montana, and Washington were so big and devastating that they changed the course of the US Forest Service's approach to wildfire. The 1950 Chinchaga fire complex was the biggest fire incident in North American history. It burned 3.5 million acres of forest in northern Alberta and British Columbia before snow fell and snuffed it out.

In the mid- to late twentieth century, we got good at fighting fires with initial attack crews, helicopters, air tankers, chemical retardants, sprinklers, and wildfire managers who, thanks to science, had books and calculators in hand with equations that could tell them how a wildfire would spread in a particular forest and how it would behave in various weather conditions. It's not that this kind of understanding is bad. Wildfire science has saved tens of thousands of lives and averted ecological and economic disaster in many places. But in suppressing so many fires for so long, we have created a surplus of mature trees in our northern forests, trees that are just waiting to be either burned by wildfire or killed by disease and insect infestations. Letting these trees burn to allow a younger forest to take over is an obvious solution, but doing so is a challenge because we have encouraged so many people to turn wildlands into real estate and private property. Many of us have also convinced ourselves, rightly in some cases, that old-growth forests must be preserved to save wildlife.

When Fort McMurray burned, there was an inclination by many environmentalists to blame it on climate change, but that played into the hands of the deniers and a skeptical media. It is difficult, if not impossible, to attribute one single extreme event to climate change, according Francis Zweirs, a renowned climate change scientist and director of the Pacific Climate Impacts Consortium at the University of Victoria. Far too many variables—such as the El Niño Southern Oscillation, the North Pacific Oscillation, and the retreat of sea ice in the Arctic—can derail the rhythm of the weather-controlling jet stream. Zweirs and his colleagues tried connecting the Horse River fire, the Calgary floods of 2013, China's devastatingly hot summer of 2013, and record low sea-ice cover in the Arctic in 2012 to climate change. The only absolute connection they could make to climate change was record low sea-ice cover in the Arctic.

In drawing the link between wildfire and climate change, what's important is the framing of the answer to the media question. Including the Horse River fire in a pattern of extreme events that are connected to climate change is a good way of informing decision makers and a public tuned in to news and updates in 20-second sound bites and 140-character messages. Canadian scientist Mike Flannigan might have had the best answer for the media when he was widely quoted as saying, "The Horse River Fire is consistent with what we expect from human-induced climate change."

With his almost daily press conferences, Darby Allen may have been the play-by-play host for the Horse River fire, but to get an informed assessment of what was happening and why, the world's media went to behind-the-scenes analyst Flannigan. At one point, Flannigan was on the phone from 7 a.m. to 11 p.m. daily, doing interviews with the *New York Times* and *Washington Post*, Canada's *Globe and Mail*, *Toronto Star*, and CBC, and foreign news organizations such as the BBC and *Le Figaro*.

No one was better qualified to play the role. Flannigan's fascination with fire started at a very early age when he nearly burned down his grandparent's town in rural southern Alberta while playing with matches. The last-minute intervention of a relative saved the day. Since then, he's been redeeming himself with a career that began as a meteorologist, followed by graduate degrees in atmospheric sciences from Colorado State and plant sciences from the University of Cambridge in England. While working as a research scientist for the Canadian Forest Service, he was the *International Journal of Wildland Fire*'s editor in chief and a task leader for the International Geosphere-Biosphere Programme. The US government called on him to lead a group working on wildfire for the National Assessment Program on Global Change. Now a professor at the University of Alberta in Canada, he counts people in government as former and current students.

The facts tell the story, according to Flannigan. On average, more than seven thousand wildfires burn in Canada each year. The area burned has doubled since the 1970s when global temperatures began to rise in earnest, far faster in northern climes than in temperate regions.

Figure I-2 Wildfire made three runs into the city of Fort McMurray before a mass exodus of 88,000 people followed. (Courtesy of RCMP, Fort McMurray)

As the climate continues to warm, he said, the area burned is likely to double again by the middle of the twenty-first century and possibly triple by the end of it. Another Horse River fire, he suggests, is inevitable in a warmer, drier forest environment with more fuel on the ground and more people living, working, and recreating in that landscape.

The future looks just as daunting in the American West, where wildfire is expected to double and possibly triple the area burned in places by 2050. In Montana, temperatures are expected to rise by as much as 5°F (2.7°C). There may be as many as fifteen more summer days in which temperatures exceed 95°F (35°C) by then. It will be a lot drier in summer.

David L. Peterson, a research scientist with the US Forest Service, closely watched the Fort McMurray situation unfold because it came on the heels of a record-breaking fire season in the United States. Like many wildfire scientists, Peterson lives in the forest. He's viewed fire from both a personal and a professional perspective. He has written more than two hundred peer-reviewed papers and has served on the board of the Intergovernmental Panel on Climate Change.

Keeping up with the scientific information on climate change and wildfire, he says, is like drinking from a fire hose. The volume of scientific literature makes it challenging, if not impossible, to sort through and evaluate evolving concepts and interpretations of how climate, wildfire, insects, drought, flooding, and invasive species are going to change our forests.

Peterson allows that you don't have to be a rocket scientist to figure out that fires are more common when it is hot and dry. "If the climate modelers are right, wildfire seasons like the one we had in 2015 when 10 million acres of forest burned could become the new normal by midcentury," he said. "Increasing temperatures coupled with increased wildfire are going to result in complex ecological and social challenges for federal resource managers. This cannot be resolved by simply pouring more money into fire suppression."

No one knows when and where the next Fort McMurray will occur. Fire experts have their own long lists of candidates. Mike Flannigan has Prince George in British Columbia and Timmins in northern Ontario on his list. Ken Till, former deputy fire director for the Western Region of the US National Park Service, fears that a catastrophic wildfire in and around an Environmental Protection Agency Superfund site watershed that flows into Lake Coeur d'Alene in Idaho could result in soil erosion and flooding that liberates toxic materials. Wildfire scientist Cliff White suggests that Sulphur Mountain in Banff could burn, endangering thousands of tourists. Minnesota, Michigan, and Maine are also likely to burn big sooner rather than later. So are the forests of New Jersey, a state not known for making wildfire headlines. A wildfire risk assessment conducted by that state compared the boreal-like Pinelands to "an inch of gasoline covering all of south and central New Jersey."[2] Ten major fires have burned in the Pinelands since the 1950s. The thirty-seven fires that burned in the United States in 1963 are often cited as a benchmark for wildfire/urban interface comparison. Nearly 200,000 acres of forest were torched that year.

The growing cost of fighting wildfires is already overwhelming the ability of governments to manage wildfire and the forests they burn. For the first time in the US Forest Service's history, more than half the agency's annual appropriated budget was devoted to wildfires in 2015, up from 16 percent in 1995. Nowadays, the US Forest Service's annual firefighting budget routinely runs out of money before the fire season ends. With this trend of increasing costs for fighting wildfires expected to continue, two-thirds of the agency's budget will go for this kind of work by 2025. That will take money away from forest management, maintaining parks and recreation areas for hikers, campers, hunters, and anglers, and habitat restoration for threatened and endangered species.

In Canada, where investment in wildfire science has been mercilessly gutted since the 1980s, wildfire, parks, and forest managers are having an equally difficult time keeping up. In 2016, Parks Canada's budget was about a third short of what is required to manage fire in the national park forests. In 2003, there were so many fires burning in British Columbia that the provincial firefighting authority went into triage mode, fighting only those fires that were burning where humans were most vulnerable. For the first time, the government of Alberta couldn't fight all the fires it wanted to fight in 2015, even though it brought in help from Mexico and Australia when some oil sands operations were in danger of burning. Wildfire management costs in Canada topped the $1 billion mark that year. That had never happened before.

Some politicians are beginning to take note. On August 14, 2015, when there were sixty large fires burning in thirteen states and nearly 20,000 people fighting them, Tom Vilsack, US secretary of agriculture at the time, stated bluntly, "We are at a tipping point. Congress must change the way it pays for wildfires by providing a fiscally responsible way to treat catastrophic wildfires more like the natural disasters that they are, end fire transfers, partially replenish our capacity to restore resilient forests, and protect lives and property against future fires."[3]

It is difficult to argue that Vilsack was wrong. But, as David Peterson contends, pouring more money into wildfire suppression is not the answer. The boreal forest, and many of the northern forests that border it, is truly a pyrogenic forest that is designed by nature to invite fires. It is born to burn.

The size of the fires that inevitably come will depend on how high the temperatures are, how dry it is, how fast the wind is blowing, how old and expansive the forest is, and what breaks and barriers there may be on the landscape. These breaks could be a wetland or swamp, a gulch with few trees, or a stand of aspen. In contrast to conifers, aspen stands are less likely to catch fire, and when they do, they tend to burn more slowly. Lakes and rivers like the Athabasca that flows through Fort McMurray are the most common type of fire barrier.

The problem for forest and wildfire managers fighting fires in remote places such as Fort McMurray is that there are not enough up-to-date and reliable vegetation maps. These tools are needed to accurately describe where natural fire breaks are located, where the dead and dying trees are, where fire is most likely to burn quickly, where endangered species are vulnerable, or where fire islands or refugia—parts of the forest that tend not to burn during a fire—are located. Scientists and scientific institutions such as the National Aeronautics and Space Administration (NASA) are developing conceptual frameworks that will inform forest harvest, fire operations, landscape restoration, and conservation about the role that wildfire will play in liberating carbon from northern lakes and the frozen ground.

"The cynical view is that the boreal forest doesn't matter because so few people live there," said Peter Griffith, chief support scientist for the agency's ten-year, $100-million Arctic Boreal Vulnerability Experiment (ABoVE). With government and institutional partners in Canada and the United States, ABoVE had more than one hundred organizations and nearly five hundred investigators on the ground, in the air, and working on satellite data in 2017 trying to answer many of these questions.

"There are more people living in a borough of Manhattan than there are people living in all of Alaska and northern Canada," said Griffiths. "Those who hold that view might not care that many of these people who rely on caribou and others animals for food will suffer as a result of the transformations that are taking place on the tundra and in the boreal forest. Or the fact their water supplies might be affected. But the implications are global. I was in Yellowknife in the Northwest Territories of Canada in the summer of 2014 when there were record-breaking fires burning. Smoke from those fires affected air quality in New York and Chicago, and ash from that fire blackened some parts of the Greenland ice cap. Instead of being reflective, the glaciers were absorbing more sunlight and warming as a result."

It's difficult to overstate the challenge at hand. In the boreal, montane, and subalpine forests of Alaska, the northern United States, Canada, northern Europe, and Russia, which ring the treeless tundra regions south of the Arctic Circle, there is currently an abundance of trees to burn and an extraordinarily large area of forests that needs to be preserved for conservation purposes.

In the right conditions, a wildfire can travel for hundreds of miles, smolder beneath the snow during the winter, and flare up again the next year. That's why in the spring of 2017 the Alberta government had drones in the air and people on the ground literally patting the earth, feeling for heat that might be emanating from smoldering roots and peat that burned during the Horse River fire.

Since 2011, boreal fires in the United States, Canada, and Russia have been burning more trees than all that were burned by fire in the rain forests of the world during the same time period. Canada and the United States now rank second and fourth among countries with the greatest amount of fire-related tree loss. Russia, which is home to the world's biggest boreal forest, tops the list. The conflagrations that are mercilessly commonplace and costly in California are now extending their reach to the frozen Arctic tundra. If the fires continue to move into the Arctic, it promises to turn climate change into a runaway freight train if the carbon frozen in the peat burns.

Mike Flannigan says there are three simple things we need to know to understand why this unfolding wildfire paradigm is going to be such an enormous challenge.

First, the warmer the temperatures are, the drier the northern forests become. That is because the atmosphere is capable of holding more of the moisture that would normally go toward quenching the thirst of highly stressed trees. More precipitation could compensate, if that's what happens. But for every 1.8°F (1°C increase), 15 percent more rainfall is needed to restore the initial balance.

Second, the warmer it gets, the more lightning there will be. Lightning accounts for a third of the fires in the boreal forest and 85 percent of the area burned.

Finally, the warmer it becomes, the longer the fire season will become.

Factor all three into an emerging wildfire regime that includes invasive species, drought, disease, and millions more people working, living, and recreating in and around the northern forests, and you have, according to Brian Rice, the director of the US Office of Wildland Fire, challenges that are almost insurmountable. Something has to give, he said. It may be a series of shock-type wildfire events that result in many lives lost and many buildings destroyed. Or it could result in a fundamental restructuring of federal, state, and provincial wildfire agencies.[4]

On the initial drive north to the nighthawk site, I stopped in Fort McMurray to survey the damage. The images that haunted me were the same ones that haunted everyone who saw them on television, in photographs, and in YouTube videos: burned-out cars and trucks; houses burned or bulldozed to the ground so that others could be saved; and trees, fire-scarred but still standing. Inexplicably, a child's plastic slide was left untouched while the rest of the neighborhood had burned to the ground. A few houses survived among many others that were flattened.

On the nighttime drive south toward home, I passed the Syncrude oil sands plant. The smell of gas and chemicals in the air was so thick and acrid inside the car that I instinctively opened the windows, foolishly thinking there would be fresh air flowing in.

It's been said that the United States and Canada do not have a wildfire problem; rather, they have many wildfire problems. Institutions, governments, and nongovernmental organizations are sometimes burdened with an almost unfathomable array of policies, laws, and jurisdictional oversights—and in some cases the absence of such—or the unwillingness to act on a clearly articulated approach to prevention, unified suppression, and evacuation protocols. The overlap of private and public forests in the United States makes it even more complicated there than in Canada, where most forest lands are owned by government.

It is tempting to blame governments and the oil sands industry for climate change, which is contributing to wildfires burning bigger, faster, hotter, and in more unpredictable ways, but many other triggers are driving us into uncharted territory. Wildfires are a meteorological response to what northern forests need to be resilient to disease, insects, and climate change. We're simply overfeeding and facilitating fire's lust for fuel and causing it to react in increasingly unpredictable ways. We also refuse to make ourselves resilient to the fires that will inevitably come. Some forest towns like Fort McMurray have done some work to create firebreaks and to make themselves resilient to fire. But homes within a stone's throw of a forest continue to be built with highly combustible cedar-shake shingles and flanked with ornamental cedars. Too many towns either can't afford or ignore the idea of thinning forests around them or of creating buffer zones that can help stop or slow the advance of a fire.

Without a new, evolving plan and the resources that are needed to deal with the new paradigm unfolding in the northern forests, year-round and runaway fire seasons will overtake our ability to manage forests in a way that serves our best interests. Of course, changing course is much easier said than done, but the chapters that follow attempt to create a clear-eyed look at the challenges we face.

Wildfire touches on nearly everything important to humans, on both a personal and a national level. Fires are an integral part of many ecosystems where we live. We love the scenic beauty of towns like Whitefish, Montana, and Banff, Alberta. We need clean air to breathe and clean water to drink, both of which can be impacted by a vast wildfire. Increasingly, natural resource development is taking place within northern forests, without a plan in place to counteract the economic ramifications of the threat of fire. Decades of forest suppression have made the task of managing future fires more difficult. Contending with the challenge of wildfire and the risks it requires is not for the faint of heart. We can only find hope, however, in understanding the problems we face in figuring out how to live with wildfires.

Chapter 1

The Beast Awakens

A mighty flame follows a tiny spark.
— Dante Alighieri, *The Divine Comedy*

On Sunday May 1, 2016, helicopter pilot Heather Pelley was on standby with a small firefighting crew at the Grayling Creek Fire Base, 22 miles (35 kilometers) south of Fort McMurray in northern Alberta. Shortly after 4 p.m. that day, Pelley was playing her guitar on the patio deck when the "dispatch alert" came in with notice that smoke was detected in the region. Once a call like that comes over the radio, or satellite phone, the pilot is expected to be in the air with a four-person helitack crew in 10 minutes.

Pelley had seen it coming weeks earlier when the Alberta government had deployed pilots and contract firefighting personnel across the province a week earlier than usual. The relatively mild winter had produced almost no snow. Spring followed with temperatures that were almost twice the average. With dry grass, brittle shrubs, and a never-ending forest of spruce, pine, poplar, and aspen trees thirsty for rain, everyone expected it to be an early fire season.

It was. Even before May arrived, 281 wildfires had burned in the province. Many more were burning to the west in British Columbia and to the east in Saskatchewan.

As hot, dry, and extremely windy as it was that day, Pelley still expected this call to end up being the "one-tree wonder" that initial attack crews often deal with when lightning, an abandoned campfire, broken power line, an arsonist, or the scorching hot exhaust pipes of an all-terrain vehicle (ATV) ignites a fire in the forest. But when the helicopter cleared the trees that surround the base at the Grayling Creek station that day, she realized how wrong she had been to think that.

"I thought 'holy shit.' How long has this fire been burning? It was more than 50 kilometers away and we could see this big plume of white smoke in the distance. There was no need for the dispatcher to give us the coordinates, as they usually do for an initial attack, so we pointed the nose towards it and off we went," she said.

The Bell 407 that Pelley flies is one of the fastest, most maneuverable helicopters on the planet, easily capable of reaching speeds of 130 knots (150 miles per hour). In the short time it took Pelley and the helitack crew to get to the fire with hoses, hand tools, backpack pumps, and a bucket capable of scooping up to 180 gallons of water, the fire was candling, bending with the wind, billowing black smoke over a high-power transmission line, and pushing west and southwest with winds that were gusting up to 21 miles (33.7 kilometers) per hour. The Abasand and Beacon Hill residential neighborhoods on the south side of Fort McMurray were less than 5 miles (7 kilometers) away.

It was Pelley's third year fighting fires. She had been involved in sixty fires the year before. Both she and veteran helicopter pilot Dave Mulock, whose helitack crew discovered the fire and who was still on the scene, knew right away that there was nothing they could do to stop this one. It was too big and growing too fast. A call had already been made to bring in an air tanker, which was based 155 miles (250 kilometers) to the south at the airport outside of the town of Lac La Biche.

Rather than putting anyone near harm's way, the pilots dropped the helitack crews on the blackened ground at the tail end of the fire close to where tall grass was burning beneath the transmission line. "One foot in the black, one foot in the green" is a lesson that every firefighter learns during training. The black is where firefighters can retreat to if the fire becomes too dangerous to engage. The black (or "good black" as it is sometimes called) is considered a safe haven because the area can generally only burn once.

Pelley and Mulock tried dropping buckets of water they scooped from nearby Horse River to reinforce protection of the helitack crews on the ground, but it was futile. They had to hover high above the smoke and the power lines, struggling against gusty winds. "Before any of the water got anywhere near the ground, it evaporated," Pelley said. "I thought to myself: 'This is useless. Nothing is going to stop this one.'"

The Electra air tanker that was on its way from Lac La Biche carries 1,750 gallons of chemical fire retardant that can slow the momentum of a fire. Traditionally, it is guided in by a lead aircraft, or bird dog, like a Turbo Commander 690. The bird dog flies twice as fast as Pelley's helicopter. There were two people on board this flight: a specially trained pilot and a government-employed air attack officer who decides when and where the retardant is to be dropped. Once a bird dog arrives at a fire, the air attack officer takes charge of everything, including the helicopter pilots. It was not as simple as that. Complicating the situation was another wildfire that had ignited almost simultaneously in the TaigaNova industrial district of Fort McMurray.

"The bird dog that came in to deal with this fire was super calm," recalled Pelly. "But you could tell by the urgency in his voice over the radio that he was really concerned. Right away, he informed the radio room that this was a priority fire."

By the time Pelley arrived, smoke was curling over the people on the ground who were throwing buckets of water on the flames. Fort McMurray firefighters were there as well, doing all they could to contain it.

One of the things Pelley remembers most about that day is how quiet everyone was in the chopper when they were flying back from Horse River. She recalled, "Usually at the end of the day, the helitack crew is pumped and talking about what happened on the ground. But all I saw and heard was the four of them looking back at the fire in silence. It was spooky."

Before packing it in at the base camp for the night, Pelley texted all her friends and her boyfriend with the same message: "Pack and get ready to leave. This fire is coming to town." She—and pretty much everyone who was on the front lines of the fire on that Sunday—was convinced that an evacuation of Fort McMurray was imminent. So were a lot of other people who were monitoring weather reports and satellite data. If strong winds pushed the fire toward Fort McMurray, they knew it could easily override the town in two days or even less.

A small number of people, in fact, were told to leave their homes after a local state of emergency was declared around 10:00 p.m. that Sunday. More were told to go at 3:30 a.m. on Monday. The orders to evacuate most of the 88,000 people who live or work in the unofficial capital of the oil sands industry, however, didn't begin in earnest until Tuesday afternoon, when the fires made three runs into town. Children were still in school. Some parents weren't able to pick them up because the Royal Canadian Mounted Police (RCMP) had blocked the roads into some neighborhoods to allow residents and school buses to get out and fire trucks and paramedic vehicles to get in. Many of the sick, the pregnant, and the elderly were still in the hospital and in nursing homes. Some residents refused to leave, even after the RCMP and firefighters knocked on their doors and told them they had to go or risk death if they decided to stay.

By then, it was almost too late. With smoke, flames, and embers raining down on houses, schools, churches, stores, city trees, and wooden fences, the cars and trucks that headed out on the only highway of escape were literally bumper to bumper on all four lanes going in and out of town. To expedite the evacuation, the RCMP, along with peace officers and local sheriffs, redirected thousands of cars to the oil camps north of town. Some of the more panicked drivers ended up in ditches. Mercifully, they and other drivers who ran out of gas were able to hitch rides in cars, trucks, and buses that were passing by. RCMP officers in patrol cars made sure that no one was left stranded on the side of the road.

Lorna Dicks, the acting commander of the RCMP detachment, had nearly all 136 of her officers on the streets, directing traffic, knocking on doors, and helping local sheriffs and public health officials evacuate the hospital as the firefighters poured water over it. She was so sure that the entire town was going to be leveled that night that she and her team considered where they might set up a makeshift morgue.

Figure 1-1 This skyscape was the scene many people in Fort McMurray saw just hours before all 88,000 residents were forced to flee the city. (Courtesy of RCMP Fort McMurray)

She is not alone in suggesting that it was a miracle that only two lives were lost as a direct result of the evacuation. Fort McMurray fire chief Darby Allen told the media that when the sun rose on the day after Tuesday's evacuation, he thought he was being optimistic in thinking that maybe only a few thousand people had died.[1]

By the time the fire was finally brought under control, more than 2,500 homes were destroyed. Twelve thousand cars and trucks were badly damaged. Nearly 1.5 million acres, an area twice the size of Rhode Island, burned. It was the costliest natural disaster in Canadian history. Insurance claims were expected to reach the $3.77 billion mark, twice the cost of the 1998 ice storms that brought down trees and power lines along a narrow swath from eastern Ontario and southern Quebec to Nova Scotia. One study pegged the total economic cost to be $6 billion; another estimated it to be as high as $8.86 billion.[2] Neither study factored in the prospect that the local economy was not likely to recover for a long time to come, even once the rebuild of the city was completed. Thousands of people decided not to go back to Fort McMurray because they had no jobs or homes to return to. Those who stayed had to acknowledge that the sky-high prices they had paid for their homes wouldn't be recouped if they decided to sell.

Fort McMurray may have been the costliest wildfire in North American history, but it was not a one-off event. Since the turn of the twenty-first century (and one might argue that it started well before that), wildfires have been burning bigger, hotter, faster, and more often in places where people live, work, and recreate. By most accounts, Fort McMurray was at medium risk for a catastrophic event such as the one that occurred in 2016. The prospect for more fires in the future was underscored in the months that followed when the Great Smoky Mountains burned around Gatlinburg in Tennessee. Like Fort Mc-Murray, no one saw that one coming, other than climatologists and wildfire experts who had been literally screaming about the potential for more fire in more populated places for years. Fort McMurray was in many ways a bellwether of what to expect in the future as the climate warms and dries out the northern forests and as more people live, work, and recreate in them.

~

On Tuesday, May 3, the day the wildfire entered the residential neighborhood of Beacon Hill at the south end of Fort McMurray, Lucas Welsh was at the Suncor oil sands plant, an hour's drive north of town. He and a group of industrial firefighters who work for the oil sands giant were sitting around the lunch table when they were abruptly dispatched to Beacon Hill to help fight fires that were burning in and around the area.

Before the fire crew left, Welsh called his wife, Adrien, at home to let her know what was happening and to pack a bag just in case.

"I told her not to worry because I was pretty sure that everything would be okay," he said. "But once I saw this Armageddon-like cloud hanging over the city as we crested the hill that goes into town, I knew this wasn't the case. It was like the beginning of the end of the world. Still, I thought that my wife and two sons would be okay because Dickinsfield, the neighborhood we live in, is on the north side of the

Athabasca River. The fire we were dispatched to was burning on the south side. It's a big river. There was a lot of space between the fire and our home."

Before the Suncor fire crew got to Beacon Hill, Fort McMurray firefighters were already on the scene and engaged in what was quickly turning out to be a losing battle. A radio call came in telling Welsh and his colleagues to abandon the plan because it was too late to save those homes. Welsh recalled the sinking feeling he had when he passed a row of burning houses in Abasand Heights, the neighborhood north of Beacon Hill. "Firefighters are meant to fight fires, not drive by them," he said. "This was not right."

When the four-person crew was told instead to go to Dickinsfield, the neighborhood Lucas grew up in and now lived, he phoned his wife to let her know what was happening.

~

Adrien Welsh came to Fort McMurray via Arkansas when she was sixteen years old. She hated it from the get-go until she met Lucas at the church her family had joined. That was the beginning of a long hello. Lucas was in every one of her high school classes, and they hit it off quickly. When Adrien's family went back to Arkansas, she moved into his parent's house after Lucas set himself up in apartment with a friend. They married soon after, involving themselves in church affairs and outreach programs. Lucas became a part-time pastor. Adrien became the director of communications. Life was good in the city she once hated.

Adrien knew on Sunday night that there was a fire near Fort Mc-Murray. It was on Facebook, which along with Twitter became the main source of both news and rumors over the next two days. First, it was the horse owners who were boarding their animals at the Clearwater Horse Club south of town. They were told that they would have to come and relocate them. Then a local state of emergency was called, and people in the residential neighborhood of Gregoire and Centennial Park, a mobile home park, on the south end of town were told to leave.

When the city became shrouded in smoke the next day after a clear, sunny start, Adrien still wasn't fazed by what was happening.

"In Central Arkansas we have tornadoes," she said. "In northern Alberta we have wildfire and lots of smoke. You get used to it."

That calm, however, turned to genuine concern on Tuesday morning when thick smoke once again turned a clear day into night for a brief time.

"I took a picture and sent it to Lucas," she said. "He told me to start spraying the roof with water. I didn't realize he was joking until he started laughing."

Adrien doesn't get rattled. Lucas says she's one of the toughest people he knows. But what followed on that Tuesday afternoon shook her to the core. She was at home with Kamille, a four-year old Congolese boy she and Lucas had recently adopted. Justice, her six-year-old, was at school. After seeing pictures of the fire on Facebook and the television news, Lucas's sister called from out of town, urging Adrien to leave.

Adrien wasn't going anywhere.

"Kamille had gone through a lot before we finally brought him to Fort McMurray in March," she explained. "The adoption procedure had not gone well. His English was not good. He was having a tough time adjusting. I didn't want to worry him all over again by moving away. Home, I thought, is forever. And this is where he needed to be."

Adrien still didn't appreciate the perilous nature of the situation until the school called, telling her to pick up Justice. On the way there, she saw people gassing up cars packed full with personal belongings.

" 'These people are crazy,' I thought. I was convinced this was not going to be a big deal. I didn't know that some parts of town were under an evacuation alert."

At the school, teachers were openly talking about the city burning down. Adrien still didn't think it was as big a deal as that, but decided to go home and start packing just in case.

"As soon as I started to put things into bins, Kamille had a meltdown and started to cry. I didn't know what to do except to put my mom on the computer so she could talk to him and calm him while I packed. I then called Lucas just as he was trying to call me and told him that it looks like we will have to evacuate. 'Yes, you should—right now,' he told me."

Adrien assumed they would only be gone for a day, but decided to pack for three days just in case. Along with clothes and toys, she brought plenty of food and snacks, including peanut butter and packages of Kraft cheese dinner, the kids' comfort food. In the car, she looked around and figured that things didn't look so bad. Once again, she wondered whether she might be overreacting.

"I called our friend Matt Miniely, who is a pastor at our church. He told me not to even consider staying. He insisted that we meet him at his sister-in-law's place in Timberlea, which is close by, so that we could all leave town together."

Just as she was about to pull out of the driveway, a neighbor advised Adrien to go right instead of left on the street because she was likely to run into a firefighting crew blocking the way. Had she not done what he had recommended, she and the kids would have seen Lucas and his crew trying to save homes that were burning in their neighborhood.

"I think we would have all had a meltdown if that had happened," she said.

Justice, however, did break down as they started to drive down the street. "I thought that with the fire, and leaving home like this had got to him. But when I asked what was wrong, he told me he was crying because he realized that he was going to miss the soccer practice that night," Adrien said.

As Adrien drove, Lucas and his colleagues were running up and down the street and kicking down burning fences to stop the fire from spreading. "We'd put one fence out and then turn around and see another burning," he said. "It was relentless." Lucas's boot caught fire at one point. Buoyed by knowing that they had saved all but two homes in the neighborhood, they dashed to another residential neighborhood. Dozens of homes were on fire, and there was little they could do except stay away from exploding propane tanks and try to save the houses that were not burning.

By this time, the gridlock that characterized the mass exodus from Fort McMurray was already well under way. Adrien and her friends had already made the decision to go south to Edmonton rather than north to the town of Fort McKay or one of the oil sands camps. Kamille, she thought, would have had a tough time adapting to what was, for all intents and purposes, going to be another refugee camp.

Fortunately, the RCMP wasn't yet diverting cars north. Traffic, however, was terrible, and it appeared for one brief moment that no one was going to let her merge from the city into one of the highway lanes.

"And that's when I see this guy sitting in the back of his van playing a guitar," she says. "It was a *Titanic* moment. 'We're all going down,' I thought to myself. 'Everyone is going down.'"

Lucas felt much the same way when he collapsed on a pile of fire suits on the concrete floor of the local fire hall that night. "I felt totally defeated," he said. "The city I grew up in was burning down. The home that my wife and I had made for our children was being destroyed. I have never experienced such darkness."

~

In the world of wildfire science, there is a fire triangle that is defined by the type of fuel (anything that will burn), the weather (the higher the temperature, the lower the humidity, the more volatile fuel becomes), and oxygen. On Tuesday, May 3, the temperature was a record-breaking 91°F (32.8°C). The relative humidity reached rock bottom when it descended to a low of 13 percent. The winds were gusting more than twice as hard as they were on Sunday when Pelley, Mulock, and the helitack crews had first arrived on the scene.

Cliff White, the wildfire scientist who helped orchestrate wildfire management strategies in Canada's national parks for more than thirty years, says that the fire triangle is actually a square because of another side that no one likes to talk about publicly. Politics, he says, often plays an oversized role in the development of wildfire strategies and the execution of wildfire management.

Politics played a role in the lead-up to the Fort McMurray fire, in the way it was managed, in the timing of the evacuation, and in manners in which the damage might have been minimized.

Everyone knew that a dangerous conflagration was going to happen somewhere in the northern forests years before the 2016 fire season started. Glen McGillivray, managing director of the Toronto-based Institute for Catastrophic Loss Reduction, said so in 2014 when he put Fort McMurray, along with Vancouver, Victoria, and Jasper, high on a list of likely places that would burn. Fort McMurray, he wrote at the time, narrowly missed being burned in 2011 when the Richardson fire tore through the boreal forest north of town.[3]

That was not the first warning, however. There were many before that, going back to the Big Burn of 1910 and up to 1998 when the Virginia Hills fire resulted in two evacuations of the Alberta town of Swan Hills. The real wake-up calls, though, began in 2002, when three western states had their largest single wildfires on record: the Hayman fire in Colorado, the Rodeo-Chediski fire in Arizona, and the Biscuit fire in Oregon. The following year, nearly 50,000 people were evacuated from national parks and communities in Montana, Oregon, Idaho, Alberta, British Columbia, and Quebec. Firefighting resources were so tapped that some jurisdictions went into triage mode. They did not have all the resources they needed to fight all the fires they would have ordinarily fought.

Political opportunities lie, unfortunately, in the aftermath of devastation. In a report to the British Columbia government, an expert review committee led by former Manitoba premier Gary Filmon suggested that governments have a "once-in-a-lifetime opportunity to implement risk reduction policies and legislation while the devastation of Firestorm 2003 is fresh in the public's mind and the costs and consequences of various choices are well understood."[4] Even so, in a scathing report issued two years later, the auditor general of British Columbia noted that only seventeen of the seventy-four recommendations of the expert review committee were fully implemented.[5]

Another more distant warning came in 2004 when 4 percent of the Yukon Territory and 6 percent of Alaska suffered through the Arctic's biggest wildfire season in modern times. While the Canadian West and the US Northwest caught a break with wet, relatively cool weather in 2005, firefighters in Ontario and Quebec were overwhelmed by wildfires that burned during a record hot summer that year. In northern Quebec, a wildfire near the town of Chibougamau forced the evacuation of 200 residents. Another in the James Bay area resulted in 650 hydro workers being airlifted to safety. The province of Quebec experienced its biggest fire season since 1932.

Many people had seen the writing on the wall by then. In 2004, the US Departments of Agriculture and the Interior brought together five of their natural resources agencies to evaluate the new and emerging wildfire paradigm. The Canadian Council of Forest Ministers did the same when it met in October that same year. The Canadian political leaders put into play a core group of experts to come up with a vision for an innovative and integrated approach to managing the risks of wild-fire across Canada and along the US border. The members included Brian Stocks, who had retired from the Canadian Forest Service a few years earlier, and his former colleagues Mike Wotton, Sen Wang, and Kelvin Hirsch. Rounding out the team was Wally Born from Alberta and Peter Fuglem and Phil Taudin-Chabot from British Columbia.

The Canadian Wildland Fire Strategy they put pen to was by all accounts the best way to move forward in Canada. The strategy called for a restoration of wildfire research funding that was in steep decline; more protection for First Nations communities, which account for a third of the wildfire evacuations in Canada; the mapping of assets that needed to be protected; and the identification of those areas where wildfires might be left to burn themselves out. It called for more pre-scribed burning and a more integrated approach to wildfire manage-ment. Communities, they said, needed financial help and expertise to protect themselves with fuel breaks, fire-resistant buildings, and land-scaping. In short, Canada needed to ramp up the FireSmart program, which was similar to the Firewise program in the United States. Both were established to reduce the risk of wildfire destroying property and endangering the safety of people living or working in areas that were vulnerable to wildfire.

The Canadian panel recommended a lot more, but, as was the case with the Filmon report, very little of it was acted on in any appreciable way, even as data poured in from scientists like Mike Flannigan who pointed out that climate change was largely responsible for a doubling of area burned in Canada since the 1970s. He, along with fire scientists in the United States, were predicting a doubling or tripling of north-ern forest area burned by the end of the century if, as most everyone expects, the climate continues to heat up.

In 2007, Flannigan was still with the Canadian Forest Service. In the fall of that year, he and seventy wildfire managers and wildfire scientists from across North America met in Victoria, British Colum-bia, to discuss the impacts that climate change was going to have on wildfire in the future. Lamenting the absence of traction on almost everything the Wildland Fire Strategy had proposed two years earlier, they all expressed fear that no one was prepared for what was coming to the north half of the continent.

"We're exceeding wildfire thresholds all the time," said Flannigan, when summing up that meeting. "We'd better start acting soon."

"We let 150 wildfires burn each year, and we need to be more transparent about that," said Judi Beck, manager of Fire Management for BC Wildfire Management Branch. "The public needs to know what we can and can't do."

Gordon Miller, a senior manager in the Canadian Forest Service, summed it up succinctly, saying, "More fires mean more communities will be at risk."

Remarkably, no one seemed to know which communities he was talking about.

When British Columbia suffered through another devastating fire season in 2009, the minister of Forests and Range admitted that he couldn't list the communities in the province that were considered at risk for wildfire. Nor, when asked, could he provide a ministry definition of what factors would be considered in determining a community's risk.[6]

In the absence of a national strategy, something had to give. In 2011, it did so, suddenly and tragically at Slave Lake in central Alberta.

On May 15, all 7,000 people in town were forced to evacuate just hours before a wildfire torched a third of the city, leaving 732 people homeless. No one saw it coming so fast, and no one was prepared for it. Until the Fort McMurray wildfire came along, the Slave Lake fire was the most damaging wildfire in Canada in nearly a century.

Still, little was done to address the increasing threat of wildfires. The fire season was getting longer. The weather was getting warmer, and that warmer weather was producing about 12 percent more lightning with every 1.8°F (1°C) temperature increase.

In both Canada and the United States, funding to reduce the risk of fire in forests wasn't keeping pace with the amounts that were required to deal with the new wildfire paradigm. Increasingly, monetary resources for prescribed burns and other forest management strategies were being diverted to fire suppression. In 1995, fire made up 16 percent of the US Forest Service's annual appropriated budget. In 2015, more than 50 percent of the Forest Service's annual budget was dedicated to wildfire. That reallocation of resources had never happened before.[7]

Most everyone expected that the decision makers would finally take the situation seriously in 2015. That year, California burned like it always seems to do. But so did Idaho, Oregon, and even the soggy region of western Washington. Alaska had its second worst fire season ever. Across Canada, 15,000 people were forced to evacuate from 125 communities. The three western provinces experienced two to three times the number of fires they would expect to see in a given year based on a twenty-five-year average. In the natural parks region across the country, the area burned was four times the ten-year average.[8]

By the time the 2015 fire season was over in both countries, most everyone in the world of wildfire was physically and emotionally spent. The US Forest Service was looking more like a national fire agency than a steward of the nation's forests and watersheds. Robert Schmoll, the man who manages regional firefighting efforts for the Fairbanks area of Alaska, summed it up best when he described to me how it felt when the fire season finally ended with rain: "We got our butts kicked," he said matter-of-factly.

He was not alone in thinking that. At the end of the 2015 fire season, Toddi Steelman and her colleagues at the School of Environment and Sustainability at the University of Saskatchewan sent email surveys to 345 fire managers across Canada, asking them how they were holding up under the pressure of dealing with the new fire regime. Seventy-five percent of the fire managers responded.

Virtually every one of them expressed some degree of vulnerability to chronic budget cuts, staffing problems, climate change, drought, insect infestations, megafires, and the increasing number of people who were living or working in the fire-prone areas of the forest of Canada. It was no surprise to Steelman that fire managers in Alberta, Manitoba, Saskatchewan, British Columbia, and the Northwest Territories expressed the greatest degree of concern. That is where the boreal forest reigns supreme, and that is where the really big fires burned in 2014 and 2015. "It was pretty clear that the stress levels were high," Steelman told me when we met at a wildfire conference the following year. "Some of the responses may have been biased by all that happened in 2015. But I think this survey gives us a clear sense that many managers were feeling the pressure."

The Alberta government's answer to this increasing level of stress and vulnerability, and to everything that had unfolded between 2002 and 2016, was to cut the wildfire prevention and management budget by $14.6 million. This cut was announced just months before Fort McMurray burned. Around the same time, British Columbia premier Christy Clark and Saskatchewan premier Brad Wall supported the idea of a national fire strategy that was being revisited, but they refused to accept that something needed to be done to address climate change. Being a socialist, Premier Rachel Notley was compelled to be sincere about addressing climate change, but not at the expense of ramping up oil sands and fossil fuel production, which is driving climate change. The Wildland Fire Strategy seemed to be dead in the water. Fort McMurray would pay the price for that.

~

The Horse River region is a popular destination for recreational ATV riders in Fort McMurray. On the weekend of the fire, there were dozens, possibly hundreds of them, in that part of the backcountry. No one keeps track, but observers saw them lined up at entry points, waiting to get in. On the same weekend, the air tanker that the Alberta government uses to fight fires was stationed 155 miles (250 kilometers) away in Lac La Biche. Fire crews were still in training or getting organized, even though the month of May produces the most wildfires and more forest area burned than any other month.

Science and common sense suggested that ATVs should not have been where they were that weekend and that it may have been prudent to have an air tanker stationed in Fort McMurray and have fire crews at the highest state of readiness..

A month before the Horse River fire ignited, the National Oceanic and Atmospheric Administration (NOAA) issued its monthly drought monitor for North America. The drier and hotter it is, the more likely it is that a wildfire will start if there is something there to ignite it. On April 15, NOAA identified the Fort McMurray region as abnormally dry and on the verge of being classified as a severe drought. Around the same time, Agriculture Canada produced a report that showed that snowfall from November 1 to the end of March was as low as 60 percent of normal. According to Environment Canada, what little snow there was on the ground was quickly melting. Temperatures in the region were as high as 100 percent above normal, a record 81°F (27.2°C) on April 18 when the lakes in the region were still frozen. On the day the fire started, Kerry Anderson, a wildfire research scientist with the Canadian Forest Service, rated the fire danger in northern Alberta as very high.

Summing it all up, Mike Flannigan suggests that the fire danger was almost off the charts the day the Horse River fire ignited. "The relative humidity was as low as 15 percent. The wind was gusting at speeds of 33 kilometers per hour. The fuel on the ground had a moisture rating of 4 percent. Anything—a spark or lightning strike—that looked at this forest sideways would have resulted in a fire," he explained.

Because there was no sign of lightning anywhere on May 1, it was assumed that the Horse River fire was started by a careless person tossing a cigarette butt or by an ATV. ATVs cause wildfire fires; all it takes is dry grass or twigs coming into contact with a roasting hot exhaust pipe or muffler. That was confirmed in a 2002 study initiated by the Alberta government, which concluded that at least eighty-three wildfires were started by ATVs in the previous twelve years. The study suggested that spark arrestors and heat-dispersion shrouds could be added to ATVs to reduce the possibility of ignition by keeping the fine fuels on the ground out of contact with the exhaust system.[9] The government of Alberta never acted on that recommendation other than to advise drivers of the potential for fire.

Whoever it was who made their way into Horse River forest on the afternoon of May 1 probably got there on an ATV. The least the Alberta government could have done heading into May was to close the forests off to ATVs, to hikers, and maybe to the oil and gas and timber industries as well. The ban on ATVs, however, wasn't imposed until the day after Fort McMurray was evacuated.

Once again, denial played into politics and the decision-making process. It seemed as if an "it can't happen here" attitude prevailed in setting up another community to face catastrophe.

~

Darby Allen was the fire chief for the regional municipality of Wood Buffalo and the man who became the face and voice behind the firefighting efforts. Allen was fifty-nine years old. He had come to Fort McMurray by way of Hampshire, England, and the city of Calgary, where he rose from the ranks of training officer to assistant deputy chief of operations. He joined the Fort McMurray Fire Service in 2009 and became the regional fire chief of operations in 2013. His English accent, his tendency to describe the fire as an animal that had a brain— The Beast—and his precautionary, no-nonsense responses to media questions all added authority to everything he said.

Allen was home alone on Sunday, May 1, when Bernie Schmitte, the provincial wildfire manager for the Fort McMurray area, called to say that the Horse River fire was out of control and could be heading toward town if the winds shifted. Given the weather conditions, Allen knew that it might prove to be a big challenge. So, he drove to the Regional Emergency Operations Centre and phoned the head of Fort McMurray's municipal law enforcement, Dale Bendfeld, asking him for assistance. The two men organized a meeting for about twenty people that evening. Melissa Blake, the mayor of Fort McMurray, attended. A representative from the RCMP was there as well.

Given that wildfires can easily travel 6 miles (9.6 kilometers) in a twenty-four-hour period and given the benefit of hindsight, an evacuation order probably should have been called that night after Schmitte had done a flyover and saw that the fire wasn't going to sleep as most do once the cooling effect of darkness comes. No one would say it publicly, but several high-level government officials told me that there were economic considerations to account for. Evacuating the town would have effectively shut down local commerce and dramatically slowed or shut down operations at the multi-billion-dollar oil sands industry. An evacuation would also have resulted in a public outcry if the fire did not enter the town.

At 8 p.m., the municipality's emergency response group would only go as far as to advise people in Centennial Park and Prairie Creek on the city's south side to leave their mobile homes. The nearby neighborhood of Gregoire was put on alert. A refuge center was established at the MacDonald Island recreation complex in town. Everyone else in Fort McMurray was allowed to stay.

A month before the fire, the RCMP assessed the possibility of losing one or more of its buildings in the event of a disaster. Realizing that a police presence would be critical in the event of an evacuation, Lorna Dicks, the acting superintendent of the RCMP detachment, formed her own response team that Sunday night to determine how police resources would be deployed in the coming days, with or without a building for a command center to work from. Preparations began to bring district and provincial RCMP experts into the loop to offer advice and logistical support. Ways of communicating with 136 officers on the streets and in dispatch centers had to be found. Radio and police cars were in short supply.

"In the absence of a plan to deal with a situation like this, we needed to get up to speed," Dicks told me when we met several months later. "None of us had ever confronted anything like this before."

~

When the sun rose on Monday, the skies over most of Fort McMurray were shrouded in smoke. The forest was on fire less than a mile away from the one highway of escape. Bulldozer drivers were spending an inordinate amount of time trying to cross a pipeline corridor to create a break between the wildfire and the city. In the absence of the availability of remote sensing technology that would have allowed managers to identify the perimeter of the fire, an air tanker was dropping retardant in the relatively smoke free area between the tip of the fire and the highway. Bernie Schmitte and his team considered the possibility of lighting a back-burn in between the main fire and the evolving firebreak to remove the fuel that lay along the fire's path. He and his colleagues decided against it. A sudden shift in winds could turn the fire back on the city. All told, there were seven rotary aircraft, two air tanker groups, and twenty-eight firefighters at work. A heavy helicopter and an additional one hundred firefighters were on their way.

After he surveyed the scene in a chopper that morning, Jody Butz, deputy chief of fire operations, was convinced that the fire was well under control and was not a threat to the town. "Didn't look so bad," he told fire captain Damian Asher. "Fire's got about a click, two clicks from city limits, but it's manageable . . . it's still west of the Athabasca. Long as that river stays put, I think we're fine."[10] Schmitte echoed those sentiments later in the afternoon when he told reporters: "We have some good news. Our guys are feeling pretty good after today."

The weather forecast, however, pointed to a potentially worsening scenario. With afternoon winds turning from east to west toward the Athabasca River and blowing at almost 20 miles (31 kilometers) per hour and temperatures rising to 81°F (27.4°C) later that day, the threat to Fort McMurray had begun to escalate dramatically rather than diminish. The forecast did not look good. At a 5 p.m. meeting, Alberta fire behavior specialist Dave Schroeder told fire managers that, in addition to more hot weather and light winds that he expected for the next day (Tuesday), a high-pressure cold front was going to whip up winds, first from the southwest and then from the north, in sustained fashion by late Wednesday or Thursday.

Throughout that Monday, Jamie Coutts, chief of the Lesser Slave Regional Fire Service, was following the fire updates with great interest. He had been through this type of scenario five years earlier when a wildfire had destroyed a third of his town of 7,000 people. His crew and equipment were just a four-and-a-half-hour drive away, and he was expecting a call for advice and equipment. "We were lousy at dealing with fire before that event in 2011. Now we're pretty good, but only because we learned some hard lessons. I thought we could help," he said.

When the call finally came in at 10 p.m. on Monday night, it was not a plea for advice.

"Do you have a structure-protection trailer?" Coutts was asked. "How much do you charge per day?"

"I told them we could leave in 30 minutes. I waited another 30 minutes to get the answer."

Coutts recounts, " 'How much will you charge per day?' they asked. 'I'll give you a deal—$350 per day and I'll bring two men up with me to do the training,' I told them. 'We don't need the training, just the trailer,' I was told. 'How many do you have?'

"The conversation went back and forth like that for an hour. I was kind of shocked that there didn't seem to be much of a worry," Coutts said.

By that time, white ash was falling like snow on the south side of town. Thick smoke blocked the sun as it began to descend over the horizon. Adrien Welsh took a photo of the eerie orange glow that hovered in the southeast sky and sent it to her husband.

Still, there seemed to be no reason for residents to worry too much. At a dinner-hour news conference that evening, Mayor Blake advised people not to return to their mobile homes in Centennial Park. She informed residents of Gregoire and Prairie Creek, however, that they could go home under a voluntary "shelter in place" order, which compelled them to stay where they were. "You should have your bags and be ready to go," she said.

"It's been a great day for us," said Allen, referring to the progress that fire crews and emergency personnel were apparently making. "We're certainly very happy that no one's had their properties damaged, no one's been hurt, and we hope that continues."

Allen's optimistic words may have been bolstered by Jody Butz, who reportedly assured Allen that there was nothing to be concerned about that evening, just as he had assured Captain Asher earlier that day. Allen apparently had his doubts. "Jody's like, 'It's fine, it's not that big a deal,'" Allen told Marian Warnica, a reporter from CBC news in Edmonton. "'These guys [the forestry division of the Alberta government] have got a handle on it.' I was not that convinced about that. But I don't say anything to Jody. Because it's not like we're going home. We're still dealing with this thing 24/7." (Allen later told CBC that he didn't recall saying this.)

Feeling confident the worst was over, Jody Butz went home at around 11 p.m. "The fire went away," he was quoted as saying to his wife that night.

Allen wasn't so confident. Neither was Coutts.

~

The 2011 Slave Lake wildfire that Coutts and his colleagues had to contend with was a jaw-dropping event that once again underscored just how fast and unpredictably fire can move and behave. There were more than a hundred fires burning in Alberta that weekend in May. When the wildfire that eventually marched into Slave Lake started on May 4, it was 10.5 miles (17 kilometers) south of town. Within three hours, it grew to 1,235 acres (500 hectares). Fire managers weren't all that concerned until all hell literally broke loose the following day when winds gusting up to 62 miles (100 kilometers) an hour swept the fire toward the community.

The residents of Slave Lake have had a long history of wildfire. The 1968 Vega fire burned more than 133,550 hectares before stopping just south of town thanks to cooler, wetter weather that moved in at the last minute. Weather also stopped the Chisholm fire when it got to within 5 miles (8 kilometers) in 2001. In 2008, the community of Wagner just west of Slave Lake was nearly destroyed.

Like most other boreal forest communities, Slave Lake had made some effort to make itself resilient to the threat of fire, but not nearly enough. Wildfire experts working for the provincial government knew that the potential for an extremely catastrophic fire in the area was exceptionally high in May 2011, but they were handicapped by budget cuts that had resulted in an erosion of staff, crew, and aircraft resources. A 20 percent turnover rate of seasonal firefighters didn't help when experience on the ground was crucial. Neither did the structure of the Incident Command System, which had trouble dealing with the extraordinary weather conditions in the multiple fire situation that ensued.

The strong winds made it impossible to deploy aircraft to suppress the fire. The smoke from the fire forced the closure of some highways in and out of the region. Water, electricity, and telephone service began to fail. Some firefighters couldn't tap into hydrants, and those that could had a tough time standing up against the wind. For some people, the decision to evacuate only came when they saw smoke and flames approaching. As hundreds of cars headed out of town bumper to bumper, the main source of communication was via social media, which was not always accurate in revealing what was going on. Because of the road closures, drivers weren't sure where to go. In a few instances, police at roadblocks weren't allowing some firefighters from outside of town to come in.

To make matters worse, clear, concise lines of authority that are critical in dealing with a dangerous fire like that one were lacking. There were thirty separate entities and thirty-eight fire departments involved in dealing with the wildfire. Because the Alberta government had not fully implemented a new incident command system, creativity and quick thinking were therefore required. It was quick thinking that led Coutts to give the order to start bulldozing some houses so that others could be saved.

All these shortcomings were summed up in two reports: one by the auditing firm KPMG and the other by a government-appointed review panel. According to Dennis Quintilio, a member of the review panel, Slave Lake was a "forerunner of future fire seasons." Quintilio echoed the views of his colleagues when he suggested that the government should adopt "an early alert system" that would warn citizens when they should be ready to leave on a moment's notice.

Looking through the lens of that fire in 2011, here's what happened five years later in Fort McMurray.

~

On Tuesday morning, the third day of the Horse River fire, it appeared to most everyone in town that the worst was over because the skies were blue and there was no sign of smoke. The only reason it was clear was because an inversion prevented the smoke from rising. With more hot weather in the forecast, it was shaping up to get much worse. No one in town fully appreciated that the winds were shifting and would gust to speeds of 25 miles (40 kilometers) per hour and blow the fire toward town.

Based on all that he had experienced in 2011, however, Coutts feared for the worst. When he got the call from the Regional Emergency Operations Centre at 7 a.m., he assumed that he was going to be asked to send equipment and a trained wildfire urban interface crew to Fort McMurray. Before the caller had a chance to ask a question, Coutts offered to do an orientation for the firefighters and the emergency response team.

" 'Don't need any orientation, just drop the trailer off and head home,' " Coutts said he was told.

"I'm thinking to myself, what's going on here? We'd been down this road before and no one was asking us for advice or support. They wanted nothing to do with us."

Coutts, Patrick McConnell, and Ryan Coutts (Jamie's son)—all fire specialists in Slave Lake—decided to pack a bag and fire gear just in case.

"We were on the road by 8 a.m. and drove straight to Fort McMurray, tuning into the broadcasts about the fire and changes from the previous night as we went," he recalled. "There were so many similarities to the Slave Lake fire that we started to talk about what deploying the gear would look like and what challenges we would face from all the people and organizations involved. We discussed the fact that we would be heading into a situation that people still felt was under control and that we would have to sell our way in."

Just as Coutts and his colleagues began heading north, Heather Pelley was in the air with Mike Milner, a wildfire prevention officer with the Alberta Forestry Division. Halfway through that flight, they saw what Coutts and others had anticipated and what most everyone on the emergency response team had failed to come to grips with: the wildfire had jumped the Athabasca River and was heading toward several residential neighborhoods.

By this time, the RCMP was floating the idea of calling in the military to help with an evacuation, but because the municipality of Wood Buffalo was in charge—there was still no provincial state of emergency—it was not the RCMP's call to make. In the meantime, no one in other positions of authority was willing to go that far. At a news conference later that morning, Mayor Blake gave the impression to some that the situation was under control. She talked as much about garbage disposal (the landfill was closed down due to the threat of fire), recycling pickup issues, and World Asthma Day as she did about the crisis that was unfolding. Blake allowed that the forecast for more hot weather could be bad for the firefighting efforts. Instead of telling people to pack up and leave, however, she said she was "delighted" to announce that in addition to the mandatory evacuation order that had been lifted for the neighborhood of Gregoire at 3 a.m. earlier that day, the residents of Prairie Creek were being allowed to go back home. A "shelter in place order"—a notice that an evacuation might occur—was put into place instead.

At that same press conference, Bernie Schmitte acknowledged that the fire had jumped the river. But he described it as small spot fire and said that ten firefighters and an air tanker were en route to take care of it.

Darby Allen followed Schmitte at the news conference. He didn't sound as optimistic. He told people to be vigilant. "Don't get into a false sense of security," he said. "We're in for a rough day. And it (The Beast) will wake up, and it will come back."

Shortly after the press conference ended, Coutts and his colleagues arrived on the scene only to be told to go home before the highway heading south was blocked. "We weren't going anywhere," Coutts told me. By chance, Darby Allen and Jody Butz came along and greeted them warmly.

Allen listened to what they had to say and asked them to offer operational insight.

At an orientation meeting, they spoke to forty firefighters. "We talked briefly about being prepared, having lookouts, anchors, communications, escape routes, and safety zones," Coutts said. "I talked about what could be saved and what couldn't if the fire hit the city, and what the conditions might be like. From there Patrick and Ryan did a quick orientation on equipment, setup, and systems."

Following the meeting, Coutts caught up with Allen as he was walking back into the emergency operations center.

"I told him he will be under immense political pressure—evacuate, don't evacuate, priorities will be shifting. Follow your heart, follow your gut, and do what you know is right."

For Coutts though, it was becoming increasingly surreal to see the smoke rising over town and hear the radio traffic buzzing. The heat was stifling. The relative humidity was bone dry. The winds were picking up speed. "I could tell that this was going sideways pretty fast. The wind was going to push the fire past the city limits and slam into the southern neighborhoods. We needed to act fast. But no one was mobilizing."

$\sim$

Officials at the government-run Alberta Health Services did, in fact, do some mobilizing by then. To make room in the hospital, some patients were sent home or put up in a hotel in town. A strike team was deployed to the MacDonald Island evacuation center. Hotel rooms were secured for logistical purposes. Like most everyone else, though, hospital workers began work on Tuesday as if it were a normal day. (A birthday cake event was scheduled for 1 p.m. that afternoon.)[11] They had nothing else to go on. The intensive care unit was full. There was one child in pediatrics, twenty-one people in surgery, seven women in maternity, and more than forty more patients bedded down in other wards.

The RCMP had also been planning for the worst as a core group worked around the clock in the detachment's meeting room on the north end of town. But like hospital officials, as well as officials at the Regional Emergency Operations Centre, Dicks had no idea that the fires would get there as quickly as they did. She found that out on Tuesday afternoon while she was on a conference call with colleagues trying to figure how to mobilize their forces in the city and from across the province. In the middle of that call, she got a text message from her sister-in-law, along with a photo of a big fire burning behind a row of houses.

" 'What do you think I should do? Should I get Sam (her daughter) out of school?'" Dicks said her sister in-law asked her.

Puzzled, Dicks asked her where she took the picture.

" 'From the front steps of the house,'" Dicks said was the response.

Dicks was flabbergasted because no one had told her that the fire had entered town. She was given the impression that the stands of aspen that stood between the southside neighborhoods and the forest would slow or stop the fire. Aspen tend to be more resilient to fire than conifers are, but not necessarily when a big fire is burning severely in extremely dry conditions.

"I told her to get Sam—Samantha's my niece—and get out of town right away," Dicks said.

Minutes later, Inspector Mark Hancock, her colleague and coleader, got a similar message with photos of the subdivision of Abasand burning.

At that point, Dicks and Hancock looked out the window and saw what was a normally quiet street at that time of day rapidly filling up with cars heading to the highway.

"Clearly something was happening and it was happening fast," said Dicks. "From that point on, we went into full-court press. It was chaotic. We went from going zero miles per hour to one million miles per hour. I made a call to district headquarters for mandatory overtime and got it right away. We deployed almost all of our 136 police officers, making exceptions for married couples who had kids. One of the parents was allowed to make sure they were safe. We had our officers on the street directing traffic and going door to door."

Some officers were asked to use their own vehicles because there

Figure 1-2 The RCMP and other first responders did not realize the fire had entered town until they received photos from friends and relatives via email and smartphones. (Courtesy of RCMP Fort McMurray)

were not enough police cars to get everyone on the street. Sergeant Jonathan Baltzer, normally on duty in the forensics section, was one of them. An hour before he was assigned to direct traffic on the highway—"traffic duty is never fun, even on a good day," he told me—he was out walking his dogs. Smoke and a big orange glow were rising up from the forest on the edge of town. As someone who suffers from asthma, Baltzer would have been within his rights to decline to go out into the smoke without a mask. There were not enough available officers because the truck that was bringing them in had broken down. But the thought of bowing out to do desk duty instead never crossed his mind.

"It was surreal being out in the middle of the two and a half lanes of highway directing traffic. Most people I talked to were calm, but you could see in their eyes that they were in a panic. Some of them had lost track of their husbands and wives and children. They were asking questions that I couldn't answer. They were counting on me to assure them that they would be okay in this chaos. It was a nightmare because all I could do really was tell them to calm down and drive south or north."

Constable Andrew Brock was dispatched farther up the road to the four-lane highway intersection at the neighborhoods of Beacon Hill and Gregoire to direct traffic so that residents such as Dick's sister-in-law and niece could get out quickly. The toughest part, he said, was stopping worried parents from going in to pick up their kids in school. "Imagine what you would say if I told you that you couldn't go into a burning neighborhood to get your kids?" he asked me as we stood at the intersection to review what had happened that Tuesday afternoon. "You could see from where we're standing how the smoke and flames were burning trees and buildings around the school up there. I'm telling the parents that they can't go in because I need to get everyone out and to let the fire trucks in. I ask them to trust me that their kids are being loaded onto a school bus and being driven to Anzac south of town. The thought occurred to me more than once that I would be run over. I'm not sure I could have blamed them if they did," he said.

In the half hour or so that followed, Brock watched in disbelief as the sky went from blue to black in minutes. The flames were 50 feet high. Fire whirls kicked up dust, smoke, and embers all around him. All he had for protection was a pair of sunglasses. It was, he said, akin to a Middle East dust storm that one would see on television. "I watched as the Super 8 hotel over there burned to the ground in 45 minutes," he said. "I was concerned this gas station on the corner here was going to blow up. Then the fire jumped the four-lane highway right before my eyes. It lit up the grass and fence over there. There was a heavy loader parked nearby. I figured those buildings were going to burn next. Then some guy comes along, gets out of his truck, starts up the heavy loader, and knocks down the burning fence to save the buildings. He came out of nowhere and disappeared just as quickly."

By this time, Coutts was already heading up the road into Beacon Hill with firefighters from Station One. Many of them were young firefighters who had not yet graduated from training. Barbecue tanks were exploding. Fire hydrants were losing pressure. The new recruits weren't sure what to do or how to do it. They were also operating on a different radio frequency from the one the forest firefighters were using and therefore were unable to ask for and direct air tanker support. All they could realistically do by this point was help evacuate residents,

Figure 1-3 RCMP officers directed traffic out of town. In some cases, they had to stop parents from going into school neighborhoods to get their children. (Courtesy of RCMP Fort McMurray)

round up pets that were left behind or trapped in burning buildings, and set up pumpers in places where they could still get water. Coutts figured that if they had been there an hour earlier, they might have been able to save more homes.

Instead, the winds picked up, transporting embers everywhere and driving wildlife such as moose out of the forest and into the burning subdivision. At one point, Coutts was struck by the realization that he was living through the Slave Lake fire all over again. "I told the firefighters to forget about the houses that were on fire and save those that haven't burned. For a firefighter, that's tough to accept. We put house fires out, period," he explained.

The looks from some of his unit—all members of the new recruit class—were haunting, according to Coutts. "Were these the looks on our faces when Slave Lake burned? I could hear and see all around us that like Slave Lake, this was turning into several small battles across a huge battlefield."

He was right. Abasand and Centennial Park were also burning at this time. Everyone in Grayling Terrace and Beacon Hill was told to leave at 2:30 p.m. At 4 p.m., residents of Gregoire, Waterways, Terrace, Draper, Saline Creek, downtown, Thickwood, Wood Buffalo, Dickinsfield, and the lower townsite were told to leave as well.

A mandatory evacuation order for all Fort McMurray to leave was finally issued at 6:25 p.m.

Well before that happened, the highway was jammed with cars and trucks. It wasn't so much the sinking of the *Titanic* as Adrien Welsh had expected; rather, Chrys Byrne, a local media personality, suggested that it was more like "going through Mordor," the fiery hell in *Lord of the Rings*.

"Everyone called it The Beast because it was so unpredictable," said Baltzer. "You see what happened in the aftermath of the fire and you can only conclude that it had a mind of its own. It would pick off two dozen houses and then it would leave three. It did that everywhere it went. It was like it was taunting us, flaunting its power at will."

Constable Brock felt the same way. Thoroughly spent and suffering from a bloody wrist that was lacerated when he smashed a window to get into an apartment building, he spent a few minutes toward the end of that night sitting on the hood of his cruiser, trying in vain to make sense of what was happening around him.

In the day that followed, the little sleep that he, Baltzer, and many other RCMP officers got was in a jail cell at the southside station. In the next five days, the RCMP had to move its emergency operations center four times because of the threat of fire. "It was like a game of battleship," Dicks told me. "The fire made a move, and we responded by moving. In ninety-six hours, I got nine hours of sleep. All the guys on the team did the same."

If there was one moment of lightness, it came when Coutts went back to the fire hall that night to get some water and a bite to eat. "As I was walking to the washroom, I ran smack into the ass end of a horse. 'A horse!' I thought. What was horse doing here? Apparently, the owners could not get to their trailer to evacuate their animals, so they brought their two horses to the fire hall. That was a first for me."

∾

The media came from all over the continent. CBC, the public broadcaster, and other media in Alberta did a great job informing refugees where they could get food, money, gas, shelter, and support. "Thank God for the CBC," people kept telling me. For safety reasons, however, the media could not match what appeared on the internet. Nothing could describe the fires and the evacuation better than the videos that were posted on YouTube. This fire was a social media disaster like no other. In one video recorded from a dash cam on Fort McMurray resident Michel Chamberland's pickup truck, trees are candling by the side of the road, with embers glowing and raining down on cars and trucks. Traffic is bumper to bumper on all four lanes. Day is night because of the smoke blocking out the sun. Chamberland would have been still sleeping had a friend not woken him up and told him that the town was being evacuated.

"Oh my God, I can feel the heat!" he says at one point in the video. "I don't know where to go," he says as a police officer—Constable Brock it appears to be—directs him to keep driving south. "The house is gonna be gone."

In another video, Fort McMurray resident Erika Deker is sobbing uncontrollably in a vehicle as she, her husband, and children flee the Beacon Hill neighborhood that Lucas Welsh and his crew were first called to. "Oh my God," she says to her husband. "Our house is going to burn down. . . . Is Mom out?" she screams.

Sixteen-year-old Jada Polem became an instant internet sensation when a picture was posted of her riding across town on one of the horses she was trying to rescue. After a long ordeal riding along and through bumper-to-bumper traffic, she ended up getting picked up on the highway at 1 a.m.

No part of town, it seemed, was safe, no matter how far away it was from the fire. In one video where there is no sign of fire or smoke, an apartment balcony suddenly explodes into flames after being ignited, presumably by embers transported by the fire burning more than a mile or so away. In that video, people are freaking out, wondering if there is anyone inside.

Some people drove over lawns and along ditches to get out of town ahead of others. But you can tell from most of the videos taken that people were trying as best they could to make the evacuation an orderly one. The heat, however, was too much for one motorcyclist—a Hells Angel look-alike—who was patiently following a pickup truck. When it appears that the heat and the fiery scene begin to overwhelm him, he speeds up, goes around the pickup truck, and disappears.

The most unnerving is the home security cam video that James O'Reilly watched on his phone as he was heading out of town that night. The living room in the video looks like any other, with a red wall, a leather couch, and a glowing fish tank. Through the window on the left you see black smoke moving toward the house. The sounds of several pops follow. The window smashes. Bright flames lick at the side of the house as smoke fills the room. The fire alarm does not go off until the room is dark with smoke.

In the days that followed, just about everyone from Fort McMurray had a sad story to tell. Inspector Dicks's brother and sister-in-law lost their home. They took refuge at their cabin near Wandering River and played host to about ninety people who followed them there. Brian Jean, the political leader of the Wildrose Party of Alberta, lost his home in Beacon Hill. Fifteen-year-old Emily Ryan, a daughter of deputy fire chief Cranley Ryan, died in a car crash along with her nineteen-year-old cousin Aaron Hodgson as they were heading south to Edmonton. Twenty firefighters, including Scott Germain, the acting fire captain of Fort McMurray, lost their homes while trying to save others.

Lucas Welsh told me that at one point he questioned his faith.

"You'd think that saving five houses in one day would make you feel good," he said, "but when you see a dozen houses burning a block away you don't feel much a winner. I didn't feel God, because I thought at the time that this was a godless event."

～

In the days that followed the evacuation of Fort McMurray, some of the pats on the back gave way to grumbling that the orders to leave came so late. In the absence of an emergency alert system and a predetermined evacuation plan, the largest emergency airlift in Canadian history had been dependent on creativity, quick thinking on the part of health officials, and the support of the RCMP, airlines, and the oil sands industry.

There were more than a hundred patients at the hospital when the final evacuation ordered had been issued. Among them were newborn babies and people in intensive care. Seniors had been just as vulnerable.

So were children who were still in class, in some cases just hours before fire burned in the neighborhoods their schools served.

"They evacuated us so late," Fort McMurray resident Crystal Mercredi told a CBC radio host. "So late that people were stuck in traffic and people were calling the radio station, saying . . . 'We're bumper-to-bumper. We can't move. Come and save us. . . . We're sitting ducks.'"

It wasn't just the public that was looking to blame someone. Expressing complete surprise that a mass evacuation was necessary, Jody Butz suggested to CBC that the provincial forestry officials weren't giving him the up-to-date fire information he needed. "We were starting to receive reports, not from forestry, but from citizens, from social media, that they could see flames from Beacon, from the Shell station in Beacon Hill. . . . "I did not realize the fire was that close to the city," he said.[12]

Jaimie Coutts heard a lot of complaining about the Alberta Forestry Service. "We kept hearing people asking where the Alberta Forestry people were," Coutts said, but he attributes that to lack of understanding about what the Forestry people could do and what structural firefighters should be doing. "At no time did I feel that anything I saw or heard from Forestry was not right," he said. "They were calm, professionals doing a terribly difficult job with people that don't understand their operations."

As flawed as the lines of communications were between Alberta forest firefighters and municipal firefighters, no amount of air power was going to stop this blaze. That was made by clear early on by Mike Flannigan, who likened efforts to suppress a big fire like this one to spitting on a campfire. A provincial wildfire official also made it abundantly clear six days into the fire when there was a veritable army of men and women on the ground and in helicopters, air tankers, fixed-wing plancs, and bulldozers fighting it.

"Air tankers are not going to stop this fire," said Chad Morrison, senior manager of wildfire prevention for the government of Alberta. "This fire is an extreme fire event. It's going to continue to push through these dry conditions until we actually get some significant rain to help us. The air tankers will help protect the community, but I expect this fire to continue to grow over the next number of days."

The command structure in a firefighting regime is a militaristic one. Depending on the size of the fire, teams can be made up of between ten and twenty managers who formulate a plan or a series of plans. These plans are contingent on what meteorologists and fire behavior specialists tell them.

The analysts also rely on computer modeling programs such as Prometheus to predict the movement of a fire. Humidity, wind speed, topography, fuel types, and other elements are factored into the equation.

Formulating a wildfire management plan is as much an art as it is a science, according to Marty Alexander, a fire behavior specialist who worked for the Canadian Forest Service for thirty-five years. "There can be no substitute for actual 'hands-on' experience in observing and fighting fires in understanding how fires behave in a forest environment. Insights that come from experience are just as important as computer models are. Fort McMurray was particularly complicated because you have forest and buildings burning at the same time," Alexander said.

According to Jaimie Coutts, the command structure was divided in two districts. North command was run by fire officials from the county of Parkland and the city of Edmonton. South command was run by four battalions from the Regional Municipality of Wood Buffalo based in Fort McMurray. Calgary helped as best as it could. Crews tended not to be catalogued by South Command, according to Coutts. No one could tell how many trucks, types, or crews there were available. Egos often got in the way. "It was not what we were used to, so we tried to get it under control," he said.

At one point, South Command, which ran its own show, stopped in at North Command and said, "It's our fire and our city and if you don't like it, leave," Coutts confidentially said at a government debriefing. "Add f-bombs where applicable. This went on for quite some time."

The confusion and chaos, according to Coutts, was underscored on Wednesday, May 4, when South Command moved into the town of Anzac, which had opened its doors to about 250 Fort McMurray refugees the day before. Now Anzac was under the threat of fire. "South Command went in without a plan, without the resources that were needed, and without proper communication," said Coutts.

"We understand this was an unusual fire—we definitely understand that—but basic principles still apply," he said. "We were there when the wind shifted. We tried to tell the Regional Municipality of Wood Buffalo what was happening, but the Regional Emergency Operations

Centre had too many things on the go and not much time to deal with everything. For us it was so clear. Weather conditions changed, which changed fire—bad wind, wrong direction, and no belief that it would actually enter the city. We tried to help them understand but just couldn't."

In the absence of a unified firefighting plan, clear lines of communication, and an advanced, well-thought-out evacuation strategy that outlined what everyone was supposed to do in an emergency such as this one, efforts to get people out of Fort McMurray went as well as could be expected, just as they did in the Slave Lake fire five years earlier.

Heroic is the only way to describe how firefighters, paramedics, the police, sheriffs, teachers, doctors, nurses, hospital staff, water treatment plant employees, utility workers, and ordinary citizens instinctively responded to the crisis, acting on instinct, common sense, and compassion.

An hour before the evacuation, several teachers personally took responsibility for children whose parents were unable to pick them up. School principal Lisa Hilsenteger tacked a note on the school door with her name and cell phone number on it to let parents know that she was bussing children to another local school where they would be safer. All but twelve of the children got picked up there. Once the evacuation was ordered, she and the bus driver had no choice but to drive north to one of the oil sands camps. Before they headed out, they picked up a family of four whose car had run out of gas and two restaurant workers who had no other way of getting out.

That evening, all the patients—including the newborn babies in intensive care—at the Northern Lights Regional Health Centre were evacuated. Staff, sheriffs, and the RCMP worked through the night to get everyone out safely.

In the days that followed, the Red Cross deployed 2,630 volunteers and staff to reunite families, issue cash cards and vouchers, and provide clothing, transportation, and referrals for those who were stressed or overwhelmed. Oil sands companies, churches, synagogues, mosques, universities, and colleges in Edmonton and the Northlands Centre opened their doors to the wildfire refugees. In all, thirteen cities and towns responded.

In the meantime, to make sure that the firefighters had the water they needed to fight the fires, senior water treatment operator Guy Jette and his colleagues stayed behind in Fort McMurray while fire raged outside the building.

Renne Charbonneau, a female biker who calls herself "Belt Drive Betty," stood out among the thousands of volunteers. Betty was the editor of the online Busted Knuckles Chronicle (BKC), which serves the biker community with news and advice on a wide range of topics. She was watching the early morning news the day after Fort McMurray was evacuated and decided then and there to do something to help. Lynda Klouth, the contractor who runs the BKC News Bytes in the city of Grande Prairie, agreed to drive her there.

Along the way, they picked up Jessy Kappel, a firefighter from the town of Grovedale who wanted to join her seven brothers on the front lines of the fire.

At Anzac, they were stopped by the RCMP roadblock. The officers on scene told them that they hadn't eaten anything in ten or twelve hours. Beltdrive Betty and Lynda gave them sandwiches, fruit, vegetables, and water.

As they waited for an escort to come, the Anzac Fire Command Centre went up in smoke. The RCMP moved Betty, Lynda, and Jessy to the other side of the highway. It was almost midnight when they were finally escorted to the MacDonald Island refuge station in Fort McMurray.

"The very first firefighter we served was a big man who anchored out his rig and got out of the fire truck just vibrating with fatigue from head to toe," Betty wrote on her online blog. "He asked if by chance this food was for them and when I told him that yes, we motorcyclists of Alberta were here to serve them, he picked me up and crying told me I was his angel, that he hadn't eaten in 62 hours. He'd been surviving on Ritz Crackers and granola bars.

"And story after story was the same—OMG Coffee, I haven't had coffee in two days . . . this sandwich is the best thing in the world—I haven't eaten in two days or 24 hours. . . ."

Jessy Kappel wasn't the only firefighter who wanted to offer her services. The Alberta government knew that Fort McMurray didn't have the resources needed to prevent the entire town from burning down.

So, on Tuesday evening, an appeal was made to firefighting units across Alberta for help, and they came in droves. Thirty-seven towns, cities, and counties responded.

Those who were first on the scene were flabbergasted by what they saw. Calgary firefighter Danny Freeman likened it to the aftermath of an atomic bomb. St. Albert firefighter Greg Harvey was reminded of scenes from the *The Walking Dead*, where abandoned cars are littered along the side of the road.

When I asked Harvey why he volunteered to put himself into harm's way just two weeks after he and his colleagues were almost killed or seriously injured fighting a grass fire, he answered as if that was a stupid question. "I'm a firefighter," he said. "We live to fight fires."

Coutts expressed a similar sentiment when he told me that despite the absence of a unified command, the giant egos, the insults, and the tendency for firefighters to blame the Forestry Division when the division was doing all it could, he had no regrets.

"There is no place on Earth I would have rather been on this day trying to save Fort McMurray with my brothers and sisters in the fire community," he explained.

~

Hours after the first group of firefighters arrived in Fort McMurray late on that Tuesday night, the fire breached the intersection of Highways 63 and 69. That meant that no one could come or go, including supply convoys. On the afternoon of Thursday, May 5, Alberta premier Rachel Notley declared a level 4 state of emergency. It was only the second time in history that the government had taken that extraordinary measure. Doing so allowed the provincial government to enact centralized control in a crisis, enact emergency plans, and order the evacuation of people, livestock, and personal property.

By this point, the cold front that Dave Schroeder saw coming had come in with a change in wind direction that then turned the flank of the fire into the front. It would get worse before it would get any better. Sleep-deprived firefighters in town carried on, putting out spot fires, saving pets, and feasting on granola bars and dry sandwiches before better supplies of food arrived. Some of that food came from preauthorized break-ins of grocery stores.

The Fort McMurray fire had become an international event. The Queen of England sent her condolences. Pope Francis offered a prayer for the displaced and a blessing to those who helped orchestrate the evacuation. Even the Russian government, at odds with Canada over the Crimean invasion that especially infuriated Canada's large Ukrainian community, offered to send in planes.

It wasn't just Fort McMurray burning in the days that followed the evacuation. There had been were twelve new starts across the province the day before, adding to the twenty-eight that were already burning. More than 1,200 firefighters, 110 helicopters, 295 pieces of heavy equipment, and 27 air tankers were fighting those fires. They were losing the battle in several cases because of winds that were gusting up to 25 miles (40 kilometers) per hour, however.

The following weeks offered little relief even as more firefighters arrived from various parts of the world. British Columbia firefighters were not immediately among them, though, because they were too busy dealing with their own fires. It was reminiscent of the 2003 fire season, when many jurisdictions had to go into triage mode.

As the Horse River fire continued to grow, it became increasingly clear that the oil sands plants might be overrun by the wildfires that were moving north. Unhappy with the way the fires were being managed, some oil sands companies took independent action to protect their assets. As a precaution and to protect their employees from hazardous smoke, officials at Syncrude evacuated 1,500 employees and shut the facility down.

On Tuesday, May 10, two of the biggest fires that were burning around Fort McMurray joined and were moving east toward the Saskatchewan border. By this time, the fire had grown to about 618,000 acres (quarter million hectares).

The bad news just kept piling up over the next six days as more oil sands and oil and gas sites and small communities were added to the growing list of places placed under evacuation order. By the end of May, the firefighting effort looked more like a war zone than anything else. There were 2,197 firefighters on the scene, along with 77 helicopters, 20 air tankers, and 269 pieces of heavy equipment. There were firefighters from South Africa, Mexico, the United States, and almost every province and territory in Canada.

The only good news was that the danger in Fort McMurray had passed by the first week of June. Emergency services had been fully restored. Food stores, pharmacies, and banks were ready to open their doors. Those who still had homes drove north by the hundreds. They were greeted by firefighters and police officers waving welcome banners on the overpass leading into town.

Adrien and Lucas Welsh made the drive on June 10. "I thought I'd be emotional," said Adrien. "I had at one point come to the conclusion that we no longer had a home. But as we drove into town we had the Flo Rida song playing. 'Welcome to my House.' You know how it goes. I knew everything was going to be okay."

That wasn't the case for many other people. By summer's end, some 20,000 people—more than a fourth of the population of Fort McMurray—were asking for some form of psychological help. Many of them were joining churches they had given up or never joined. Thousands of others decided not to come back because they had lost their homes after losing jobs to a recent downturn in the energy industry.

~

In the weeks that followed, I talked to many firefighters, police officers, and wildfire experts who told me in confidence that detailed plans for evacuation should have been made earlier. No one would go on the record, though, because there were two provincial reviews in play and lawsuits pending.

Most everyone acknowledged that luck was one reason no one died directly as a result of the fire and most of the buildings in town were left undamaged. But luck was not the only reason the wildfires didn't turn out to be as destructive as they might have been.

The winds that brought the fires to town also shifted in a timely fashion. Had the oil sands economy not been in a downturn, the camps that accommodated thousands of evacuees who headed north wouldn't have had enough lodging or food for them.

Having all four highway lanes available to move people south helped as well.

RCMP Constable Brock is convinced that demographics also played a role in the outcome. Fort McMurray, he points out, is a town of young, mobile people. Few people retire there. Otherwise, it would have been a nightmare trying to get elderly people on the road in cars, even if they could sensibly drive them through flames and falling embers.

Sergeant Baltzer is convinced that 95 percent of the people listened and took directions from officers like him because of the mandatory safety training that most oil sands employees go through. "In a safety training exercise, you're told to listen and do what you're told in an emergency, even if you think it is wrong," he explained. "That worked in our favor. It's why the big burly guy in the pickup truck that was trying to get his kid out of school in a burning neighborhood didn't run me down when I told him that he couldn't go in."

Others attribute the orderly evacuation to the rural, outdoors mentality that prevails in places such as Fort McMurray. The tendency to panic is trumped by an inherent understanding that it is better to be calm.

The important thing is that no one died in the fire, people keep telling me over and over again. They are right, of course. But they are also wrong, because loss of life is not necessarily the best way of measuring success. Fort McMurray was the worst natural disaster in Canadian history. It could have been much worse if so many things—wind, demographics, safety training, quick and creative thinking, heroism, and luck—hadn't aligned in the manners they did. The town dodged a lot of bullets.

If there was a lesson to be learned, it is that a wildfire like that one is going to happen again. The next time, those in the line of fire may not be as fortunate as those in Fort McMurray, Slave Lake, and other places where the loss of many lives was narrowly averted.

Chapter 2

Inside the Mind of a Wildfire

To get back up to the shining world from there My guide and
I went into that hidden tunnel, . . . Where we came forth, and
once more saw the stars.
— Dante Alighieri, *The Divine Comedy*

Eight days into the Fort McMurray wildfire, Bruce Mayer, the
assistant deputy minister of the Alberta government's Forestry
Division, sent Cordy Tymstra and a small team of wildfire
science specialists to size up The Beast. Their job was to figure out
what was driving this inferno to burn as big and as uncontrollably as
it did, before the rains came and washed away the evidence. While the
ground was still warm in some places, the team took samples from the
duff, measured soil moisture, identified the age and type of trees that
burned, mapped out the topography, and considered how a massive
infestation of spruce budworm in the region between 2007 and 2010
may have played a role in how the fire behaved. Tymstra was surprised
by how quickly the vegetation was regenerating in some of the burned
areas.

It was an enlightened investment in wildfire science because the
Horse River fire was unique in one way, mind-boggling in others, and

breathtaking for the way it behaved in its first week. Meteorologists, public health officials, the media, and people all over the world viewed it like a sports car enthusiast watching a daring new model on a test run. Many people had read about big fires burning so severely in the populated areas of California and Australia, but few imagined being able to view on social media anything quite as powerful as this one racing through so much human traffic.

For the Canadian Forest Service, which operates the Canadian Wildland Fire Information System, Horse River was a ratings hit, worthy of a new television show. Its technical website informs firefighters, wildfire behavior specialists, police, and public health officials about fire danger, smoke, and weather that drives fire. It's not must-view TV for most people, but at the peak of the Horse River fire, more than 400,000 people tuned in. Brian Simpson, one of the forest analysts and modelers who feeds and maintains that system, says that interest in what was happening in Fort McMurray was so far off the charts that the system overloaded and temporarily failed before a recovery system kicked in.

The Horse River fire is the kind of wildfire that scientists expect to see more of in the future as the climate heats up and as more and more people live, work, and recreate in and around northern forests. It is the kind of wildfire that underscores the need for scientists to better understand big fires that burn near urban and industrial settings. Lessons they learn can inform police, firefighters, foresters, national park managers, tribal governments in the United States, First Nations governments in Canada, and public health officials about what to do before and when the next big fire occurs.

Cordy Tymstra is the supervisor of wildfire science for the province of Alberta. He has seen a lot of big fires in his time, many of them in this part of Alberta where the boreal forest is an unending stand of tightly spaced aspen, poplar, and coniferous trees that are designed by nature to burn in hot, dry conditions. He wrote a book about Chinchaga, the biggest one of all that burned northwest of Fort McMurray in 1950.[1] The Horse River fire, however, impressed him beyond measure.

"On May 4, a number of new fires ignited in a cluster 35 kilometers [21.7 miles] southeast of a pyrocumulonimbus cloud that had formed from the hot air rising from the fire," he told me shortly after he returned from the trip. "It was a lightning storm generated by that fire cloud that was responsible. This does happen. But I have never heard of lightning causing new fires so far in advance of the main fire."

The physics behind pyrocumulonimbus clouds, or pyroCbs, are complex and continue to puzzle meteorologists. What we know is that the heat of an intense fire creates an updraft that sucks smoke, ash, burning materials, and water vapor from lakes, streams, burning vegetation, and the atmosphere high into the sky. They then cool and form fire clouds that look and act like those associated with classic thunderstorms. One by-product of the combustion process, vegetation burning, is the water vapor that adds energy to the development of pyroCbs.

In extremely rare cases, these fire clouds can help put out the fire below with rain. The heat and the particulates in the smoke almost always trigger a chemical reaction that arrests the ability of the cloud to produce precipitation. What's then left is a lightning storm that stokes the surrounding landscape, triggering more fires. That's exactly what happened near Fort McMurray in 2016.

In any case, a form of meteorological chaos ensues. The cooler air that rushes in to replace the rising hot air causes the fire to shift in unexpected directions, often with powerful gusts that can literally roll over incoming winds or speed up those that are pushing the fire forward. Updrafts can also collapse, sending hot, ember-drenched air downward, where it hits the ground and spreads in all directions. It's akin to what angry dragons do on fantasy television shows like *Game of Thrones*.

In extreme conditions, such as those that helped drive the Fort Mc-Murray fire forward, these collapsing columns and rapidly spreading bursts of hot, ember-filled air can cause fires to advance a mile or more in just a few hours. The 2014 King fire that galloped 10 miles across the heavily forested area of Pollock Pines, California, in less than two days moved at a pace that *National Geographic* magazine described as one that would be talked about by firefighters for years to come.[2] It was no match for the Vega wildfire that burned near Slave Lake in Alberta in 1968, however. That fire set a record when it made a 39.7-mile (64-kilometer) run in just ten hours.

Megafires such as the Great Peshtigo fire that killed 1,200 to 2,400 people in 1871 often produce fire-induced winds and whirls that are as destructive as the towering tornadoes that routinely blow up in the American Midwest in advance of a cold front on a hot, humid evening. Fire-induced wind that grew out of the Mann Gulch fire in Montana in 1949 behaved like a poltergeist with pyrotechnic powers. It lifted one of the surviving firefighters off the ground three times during the time it took the main fire to pass over him in a small burned-out area.[3] He was lucky to be where he was. Thirteen other firefighters didn't make it.

A bigger puzzle is how these high-energy conflagrations affect regional weather, stratospheric chemistry, and global climate. In 1983, astronomer Carl Sagan, atmospheric scientist Richard Turco, and others published a paper in the journal *Science* describing what might happen if the Soviet Union and the United States engaged in an all-out nuclear war. According to their "nuclear winter" scenario, the explosion would result in massive forest fires raging across the continent. Smoke from these fires would block out the sun over the entire planet for months and possibly years. Temperatures would cool dramatically. Farmers would be unable to grow crops. Millions of people would starve. Many more millions would be stricken with radiation sickness.[4]

It was not the first time scientists had suggested that global cooling might take place following a nuclear war. In 1982, Paul J. Crutzen of the Max Planck Institute in West Germany and John W. Birks of the University of Colorado proposed a similar scenario.

This theory, however, lost traction when skeptical scientists concluded that the most likely targets were too far from forests that were big enough to fuel anything close to a nuclear winter. Even if that happened, others argued, the trunks of the trees, which contain 80 percent of the biomass, would have to be reduced to ashes. That rarely happens, even in an intense fire. In addition, the inner part of a tree's trunk absorbs more heat than the outer layers produce. That would mute the effect of thermal radiation. In a 1990 *Science* article, Turco and his colleagues eventually conceded that that they had overestimated the severity of a nuclear event.[5]

Still, many questions about the dynamics of megafires remained unanswered. Maybe the exhausting debate over the nuclear winter theory was to blame, but for a time it seemed like the scientific community couldn't appreciate how much energy there is in a firestorm.

Research meteorologist Mike Fromm saw a bit of denial when he began working for the US Naval Research Lab (NRL) in Washington, DC, in 1993. The NRL provides the advanced scientific capabilities required to bolster the country's position of global naval leadership. In pursuit of this mandate, some its scientists explore the physics behind hurricanes, volcanoes, and wildfire.

The NRL had sent a satellite into space that same year. Fromm used data from the Polar Ozone and Aerosol Measurement instrument monitoring the stratospheric clouds and plumes in the first papers he wrote.

Fromm's interest in pyroCbs began in the summer of 1998, when the satellite instruments he was using were homing in on weird-looking clouds in the stratosphere. They were weird because clouds like those only form in winter. It wasn't the first time that scientists had seen summer clouds in the stratosphere. From 1989 to 1991, puzzling images of aerosol clouds had periodically appeared over the boreal regions in the summers.

At the time, though, the scientists who identified them concluded that the clouds must have come from volcanic eruptions. That was because, like everyone else in the scientific community, they believed that thunderclouds didn't have the energy to get past the troposphere, which contains half of Earth's atmosphere and is where weather occurs. There was, however, just one problem, according to Fromm. There was no documentation of a volcano erupting anywhere in the world during that time.

Try as hard as he did, Fromm could find no evidence of volcanic activity to account for what he was seeing in the stratosphere. Nor could he convince his colleagues that something was amiss.

So, he began doing some detective work to determine whether pyroCbs might be responsible. Among the first people he called was Canadian meteorologist René Servranckx of the Canadian Meteorological Centre in Dorval, not far from Montreal. Servranckx's support of the idea, according to Fromm, was crucial to making the case for the pyroCb explanation. As plausible as that seemed to Fromm, it was not easy persuading others.

"Many scientists who saw our early presentations scoffed," he recalled. "One actually chuckled at the idea. That might have been a seminal trigger to get to the bottom of this wild weather story."

Fromm presented his theory to Brian Stocks of the Canadian Forest Service. Stocks had been conducting research on fire behavior in the boreal forest since the 1970s. When Stocks asked Fromm at what height the stratosphere began in the boreal zone, Fromm told him that it was between 25,000 and 30,000 feet. Stocks replied that he had measured many columns of smoke that traveled higher. That was the start of some great collaboration among Fromm, Stocks, Servranckx, and many other wildfire and atmospheric scientists.

Using satellite image data, satellite-based profile data, and ground-based lidar data, Fromm eventually linked those weird-looking clouds in the stratosphere that summer to extreme pulses of smoke from the Chisholm fire in Alberta. The smoke from that fire drifted completely around the world more than once.

The most powerful insights occurred in 2008 when Fromm, Stocks, and more than a hundred scientists from around the world descended on a NASA-led research base site at Cold Lake, Alberta, to track smoke from wildfires that were burning in western Canada. In a research plane, a small group of them made the first-ever flight into an active pyrocumulus cloud to get measurements in the updraft core.

Unlike conditions found in the core of any other cloud, this one produced total darkness, courtesy of the vast abundance of smoke and small cloud droplets.

The possibility that wildfire could send smoke from the troposphere, where the pollution it generates is a regional problem, into the stratosphere, where it becomes a global problem, was underscored on July 4 of that summer. Flying into a suspected pyroCb that day, Fromm could smell forest fire smoke at 34,000 feet inside the NASA aircraft.

The more Fromm and his colleagues looked, the more links they discovered. The 1988 fires in Yellowstone, the 1989 fires in Manitoba and Saskatchewan, and the 2003 Connibear fire in the Wood Buffalo National Park in the Northwest Territories of Canada all produced pyroCbs with enough energy to pass through the troposphere into the stratosphere. One of the most impressive was the 1998 Norman Wells fire that produced four enormous pulses of smoke just south of the Arctic Circle. Another was the 2002 Hayman fire in Colorado that was started by a US Forest Service employee who was allegedly burning a letter from her estranged husband.

"PyroCbs from the Circle Fire in Alaska explained the stratospheric anomalies that were reported in 1990," said Fromm. "We also now know that the Yarnell Fire in Arizona in June of 2013 spawned a pyroCb that was active at the time nineteen men were killed fighting that fire."

In contemplating the nuclear winter scenario, it's true that pyroCbs may result in some short-term cooling, but Fromm doubts that they can influence climate in the dramatic ways that major volcanic eruptions like Mount Pinatubo have done. Aerosol pollutants from that eruption in the Philippines reduced global temperatures by as much as 3.6°F (2°C) over a period of one to four years, depending on the area of the globe. The sea ice in western Hudson Bay lingered for so long the following winter that polar bears got extraordinarily fat with the few extra weeks they had to hunt seals. In a research paper explaining the cause for the weight gain, Ian Stirling, a Canadian Wildlife Service scientist, dubbed them the "Pinatubo bears."[6]

Before making conclusions about how fire will contribute to climate change, a great deal still needs to be learned, but the evidence points to wildfire transforming the northern forests and peatlands from an ecosystem that absorbs and stores greenhouse gases to one that adds greenhouse gases to the atmosphere. A big wildfire season such as 2015 has the potential to liberate a decade's worth of stored carbon in a single year.

Understanding how megafires behave is also important because the firestorms they create produce erratic winds, whirls as well as those iconic mushroom-shaped updrafts that can be a nightmare for firefighters on the ground and for helicopter and air tanker pilots. Just a year before the Fort McMurray fire, an air tanker pilot assigned to a fire near the Air Weapons military range at Cold Lake, Alberta, was coming out of his third drop of fire retardants when he encountered severe turbulence. The aircraft went nose up and then rolled left before pitching nose down. The plane was too low to the ground for the pilot to make a recovery.

According to the Canadian Transportation Safety Board report, the pilot could not see the fire whirl because it had not yet ingested enough loose debris to make it visible. Because the pilot had not experienced any difficulties on the previous drops, the report noted, he likely would not have anticipated what was in the flight path. The investigation found that if fire-behavior training is not provided to personnel involved in fire-suppression activities, there is a risk of aircraft being flown into unsafe conditions. The investigation also found that not all types of restraint systems adequately protect pilots from the effects of severe turbulence, although this fact did not contribute to the accident.[7]

Mark Heathcott, a wildland fire specialist who once orchestrated fire management for Parks Canada, recalled one harrowing moment in 1996 when he and his colleagues dropped some fuel from a helicopter to burn stands of trees ahead of the Klewi fire north of Fort McMurray so that it had nowhere to advance. "We really stoked it [with fuel] and created this rotating column, which anviled out, spitting out new fires kilometers away," he told me. "I saw this a few times up there on various fires when it really was brewing up. Nothing like flying under the curtain of one of these monsters, door off and backfiring. A real Mutual of Omaha moment for sure."

Although large fires greater than 494 acres (200 hectares) in size—megafires—account for only 3 to 5 percent of the fires that start in the boreal forest in a given year, they represent more than 95 percent of the area burned and most of the damage that is done to communities. Still, for most of the past century, efforts to understand how big fires behave have taken a back seat to fire suppression.

~

When the US Forest Service was established in 1905 to manage national forests—which were located almost entirely in the Rockies and the western United States up until that point—fire management was an afterthought, just as it would be in the National Park Service when that agency was created eleven years later. "Light burning"—a controlled burning of a forest such as that practiced by First Nations people—was being done in some national parks, but the main goal of the National Park Service was to attract as many people into the backcountry as possible. The goal of the Forest Service was to protect watersheds as well as merchantable timber. Officials in both agencies ignored the direct connection between the increase in backcountry traffic and an increase in wildfire.

That way of thinking began to change when a series of big fires, many of them started by steam-driven locomotives, miners, loggers, slash-burning farmers, and campers, began to overwhelm the ability of the US National Park Service and the US Forest Service to manage their forests. The biggest of these conflagration events occurred in the summer of 1910, when 1,737 wildfires fires burned through 988,000 acres (400,000 hectares) of forests in Montana, Idaho, and Washington.

The Big Blowup, also known as the Big Burn or the Great Fire of 1910, ignited on April 29 along the southern edge of the Blackfeet National Forest in northwestern Montana, which has since been divided between the Kootenai Forest and Flathead Forest. Fires burned off and on along the Canadian border until August 20, when hurricane-force winds fanned the smoldering fires back to life all across the Rockies. Eighty-five people died. Nearly 8 million board feet of timber burned. Several small towns were destroyed. Trains carrying 9,000 troops were sent in to help. In the town of Wallace, according to eyewitness accounts reported by the *Idaho Press*, prominent men fought with women to get on the train that came in to rescue them. One man, "a fat gambler," was forced off at the end of a bayonet belonging to a soldier trying to maintain some semblance of order.[8]

Firefighters on the front lines of these fires didn't stand a chance of slowing these fast-moving firestorms. One crew of forty-three firefighters dispatched to the wilderness outside of Wallace was forced to flee under orders of Forest Service ranger Ed Pulaski. They barely made it to the shelter of a mineshaft. Exhorting the men to lie down on the tunnel floor while he hung wet blankets over the entranceway, Pulaski threatened to shoot anyone who tried to make a run for it. All but five of the men survived.

Stephen Pyne, the prolific American wildfire historian, suggests that virtually every story of fire protection on public lands in the United States can trace its modern origins to all that happened in 1910.

In assessing the damage that was done by the Big Blowup as well as by fires that burned in Yellowstone and Glacier National Parks and from California to Washington that year, Henry Graves, the newly appointed chief of the US Forest Service, began championing the need for a more aggressive approach to fighting fires. Ferdinand Silcox, head of the region's quartermaster corps, called for science, technology, and manpower to help fulfill Graves's request.

That way of thinking continued when Colonel William Greely, the man who directed one of the many firefighting efforts in 1910, became

Figure 2-1 The Coeur d'Alene Hardware warehouse in the town of Wallace, Idaho, lies in ruins after the fire of August 20, 1910. In Wallace, prominent men fought with women to get on the train that came in to rescue them. (PG 8, Barnard-Stockbridge Collection, University of Idaho Library Special Collections and Archives)

forest service chief in 1920. Greely regarded wildfire the way a military commander would view the enemy. He considered everything, including the use of airplanes and dirigibles, aerial grenades, gas bombs, cloud seeding, lightning detectors, and even electrified sand dropped from the sky to fight or retard fires.

"Fire prevention is the No. 1 job of American foresters," Greely declared. "And 'smoke in the woods' should be the yardstick for American progress."[9]

During Greely's tenure, the protocol of fighting all fires that were burning bigger than 10 acres was put into play. When Silcox took over the US Forest Service in the 1930s, that policy was upgraded with the 10 o'clock rule, or goal that ordered firefighters to have a wildfire under control by 10 a.m. the next day. Taking the lead from the Forest Service, John D. Coffman, the National Park Service fire expert, dispensed with the "light burning" ideas that were being tested in California and replaced them with a strategy that dictated that all fires be put out.

Under President Franklin D. Roosevelt's New Deal in the 1930s, there was no shortage of resources and manpower to get the job done. Both the US National Park Service and the US Forest Service became the recipients of Depression-era work crews, such as the Civilian Conservation Corps (CCC). In operation from 1933 to 1942, the CCC was a public relief program that put young men to work. These men built a huge network of firebreaks, lookout towers, and roads and trails that allowed firefighters to get to a backcountry fire.

Although the US Forest Service established a research branch in 1916, very little was done to advance wildfire science and technology. Like action on climate change in the twenty-first century, an enlightened approach to the understanding of fire behavior moved forward glacially in the early twentieth century. One notable exception occurred in 1922, when forest scientist Harry Gisborne was sent to the Priest River Experimental in northern Idaho. Gisborne's approach to the science of wildfire was much less invasive than Greely's philosophy on fire suppression. Each time a big fire burned, Gisborne was on the scene to analyze its behavior and talk with foresters in the field to better understand what they faced when a fire ignited.

In his quest to understand why and how fires burn the way they do, Gisborne refined or invented a variety of bizarre gadgets—such as the Asman aspiration psychrometer, visibility meter, anemohygrograph, double tripod heliograph, and blinkometer—throughout his career. His greatest invention was the fire danger meter that foresters could carry in the field to make relatively simple but accurate fire predictions.

Gisborne didn't live to see that system developed in a more sophisticated way; he died of a heart attack in November 1949 while investigating the Mann Gulch fire in the Helena National Forest of northwestern Montana. In the 1950s, however, John J. Keetch and his colleagues at the Division of Fire Research further developed Gisborne's fire danger meter into the first National Fire Danger rating system. The legacy of that system lives on to this day in color-coded postings in national parks and national forests that rank the threat of fire with an arrow pointing to a scale of low, moderate, high, very high, and extreme.

The Mann Gulch fire, as it came to be known, was a fire that aptly demonstrated how the typical response of trying to suppress all wildfires was insufficient in dealing with the bigger problem of fire in a forest landscape. Twelve of the fifteen smokejumpers and one fireguard died as a result of mistakes, misinformation, miscommunication, and a lack of understanding of how fires behave. Their deaths underscored that there was much to be gained from putting resources into wildfire science.

The fire started in a fir and pine forest on the ridge of the north-facing side of Mann Gulch on August 5, 1949, when air temperatures reached 100°F. It was not a big fire by any measure. In fact, the smoke-jumpers likened it to a "10 o'clock fire." Hours after the fifteen Forest Service smokejumpers were parachuted in to put the fire out, a powerful updraft sent flames marching up toward them from the bottom of the gulch. R. Wagner (Wag) Dodge, the crew's leader, realized that they were sitting in a deathtrap, so he ordered everyone to head to the south-facing Plains side of Mann Gulch, where there was abundant grass and far fewer trees.

The fast-moving gulch fire sent the crew scrambling up the impossibly steep hillside looking for shelter or an escape route. That's when the fire blew up, exploding into whirls and a 2,000°F wall of flame that was 200 feet high. Hampered by the steepness of the terrain and slippery soils, Dodge lit an "escape fire" in the grass in hopes of creating a burned-out area that was big enough to protect them from the heat and big enough to provide them with oxygen that fires typically inhale in large gulps.

Whether the men ignored Dodge or did not hear him beckon them is unclear, but none of the crew members or the US Forest Service fireguard they met along the way answered him. Instead, they continued to run up the gulch until the fire quickly caught up with them. Only Dodge, the one who was lifted up three times by swirling fire-induced winds, and two other smokejumpers who escaped north into the next drainage survived.

The Mann Gulch fire was made famous in 1992 when *A River Runs Through It* author Norman Maclean wrote a book about it. *Young Men and Fire* uncovered conflicting stories about how the fire behaved and how it overran the smokejumpers. In researching the book, Maclean approached fire scientists Richard Rothermel and Frank Albini to help him reconstruct the behavior of that fire.

An aeronautical engineer with no background in forestry, Rothermel advanced research into fire behavior to a new level at the Intermountain Fire Sciences Laboratory in Missoula, Montana, which was established in 1960 by Jack Burrows, the man who succeeded Gisborne. Rothermel and his colleagues used the wind tunnel, combustion chambers, and other technologies at the lab to determine how fires spread under varying speeds of wind, temperature, humidity, and slope conditions. Their observations were then translated into mathematical equations that gave firefighters a much better idea of what to expect in a real-world environment. All the firefighters had to do was punch numbers into a specially designed calculator to get the answers they were looking for.

Rothermel used this technology to determine the Mann Gulch fire's rate of spread, its intensity, and its flame length. Much of what happened in the final moments of those men's lives, he concluded, couldn't be explained entirely by the fire catching up with them. Embers, which had likely fallen around them, may have started new fires. Still, the men would have had to run at a sustained speed of 6.5 miles per hour uphill over rocks and grass with packs on and with heat and smoke working against them to make it. Without understanding how and why fires behave in this way, Rothermel suggested, the smokejumpers ended up in "a race that couldn't be won."[10]

Had fire managers known what we know now about the science behind wildfire behavior, the tragedy that unfolded at Mann Gulch might have been averted.

~

Up until the 1960s, Canada had embarked on a path that was almost a carbon copy of the one the United States had followed since the early 1900s. Like the Big Blowup of 1910, Canada had its own share of big fires, such as the Fernie fire that killed 22 people in the Rockies of southwestern British Columbia in 1908, the Baudette fire that killed 43 people while burning in the boreal forest along the Ontario/Minnesota border in 1910, the Great Porcupine fire that killed as many as 200 people near Cochrane in 1911, the Matheson fire in Ontario that killed at least 223 people in 1916, and the Lac La Biche fire of 1919 that killed relatively few people, but only because all 300 residents jumped into the lake with wet blankets covering their heads.

Like the United States, Canada poured money and resources into fire suppression in hope of avoiding future catastrophe. First Nations people who routinely ignited fires to attract wildlife and grow berries were unceremoniously kicked out of national parks such as Banff and Jasper. Roads, trails, and fire towers were built so that fires could be detected and acted upon quickly. The 10 o'clock rule was as much a goal for firefighters in Canada's national parks as it was in the United States. When World War II ended, Canada used surplus airplanes in earnest in the detection and suppression of wildfires.

At one time, Canada also had its own national forest service, which was established in 1899. But it suffered from too many name changes, constantly shifting departmental oversights—a remarkable twelve in total—funding problems, and institutional and political pushback from the western provinces, which greedily protected their forest interests after the federal government transferred natural resource ownership to them in the 1930s.

Canada had its own Gisborne and Keetch in James G. Wright and Herbert Beall. In 1933, after figuring out how weather influenced moisture content in trees, shrubs, grass, litter, and duff that led to the ignition and spread of fires over the Canadian forest landscape, Wright and his protégé Beall created their own fire danger tables.

Wright had initiated a federal forest fire research program in 1925 that had focused on fire danger measurement. Despite government indifference in the ensuing decades, beginning in 1928 Wright, Beall, and their successors created a series of four increasingly sophisticated fire danger rating systems to help the provinces, territories, and national parks to deal with fires.

The one thing that distinguished fire research in Canada from fire research in the United States was the means by which the end goals were reached. Homegrown scientists such as Charlie Van Wagner believed that the "answers to predicting fuel moisture and fire behavior would never be found in expensive laboratories or through sophisticated complex maths and physics."[11] He and other Canadian fire scientists believed that the best approach would come from the kind of

Figure 2-2 Two men who were injured in the forest fire of 1910. (PG 8, Barnard-Stockbridge Collection, University of Idaho Library Special Collections and Archives)

fieldwork that started in the 1930s with 2-minute test fires lit by a match and grew to the much larger experimental fires that began in the 1960s.

Van Wagner was a pioneering member and a technical leader of the federal forest service's so-called Fire Danger Group. The group included John Muraro, Jack Turner, and Bruce Lawson from the Pacific

Research Centre; Dave Kiil and Dennis Quintilio from the Northern Forest Research Centre in Edmonton; Al Simard and Dave Williams from the Forest Fire Research Institute in Ottawa; and Brian Stocks and John Walker from the Great Lakes Forest Research Centre in Sault Ste. Marie. They all had analytical skills and extensive experience working in the field. Muraro, who many say was the best field scientist among them, was the first to experiment with larger experimental burns, such as the 395-acre (160-hectare) prescribed fire he helped orchestrate in a logging slash in the interior of British Columbia in 1963.

The group's effort to turn the Wright-Beall index into one that would take into account the varying range of fire weather in Canada and the sixteen different types of fuel that are most commonly found in the northern forests of Canada succeeded well beyond the expectations of administrators when it came into play all across Canada in 1972 as the Canadian Forest Fire Weather System. Increasingly sophisticated iterations of that index evolved, with the best of old features preserved and new ones incorporated.

Eventually, though, it became apparent to a new generation of fire researchers such as Brian Stocks, Bruce Lawson, Marty Alexander, Timothy Lynham, and Robert McAlpine that the development of an even more sophisticated fire science system was needed. They envisioned one that could predict fire behavior characteristics such as rate of spread, fuel consumption, and frontal fire intensity. This holy grail of fire science, they concluded, could only arise from data collected from experimental fires that were much larger than the small test fires used to develop the Fire Weather Index System. They wanted to burn the forests as North American natives did, albeit with controls in place that would contain the fire and allow them to study fire as Fromm and his colleagues later studied pyroCbs by flying into them.

Those experiments began modestly in the late 1960s and early 1970s. The number of burns grew over the next fourteen years, with a database that included more than four hundred experimental, wild, and prescribed fire observations. The payoff was the Canadian Forest Fire Behavior Prediction System. This system used temperature, humidity, wind speed, precipitation, and an assessment of various fuel conditions on the ground to better understand the eccentricities of fire as it moved through various kinds of forests across the country. The Fire Weather

Index System and the Fire Behaviour Prediction System became the core of the Canadian Forest Fire Danger Rating System, which Stephen J. Pyne describes as "arguably, the outstanding accomplishment of Canadian fire science and one of Canada's most extraordinary cultural achievements."

Not all went smoothly, as one might expect in a boreal landscape that can literally explode into whirls if the conditions are right. Politicians and senior government bureaucrats had an aversion to fire and smoke. Their instincts were the same instincts as those of Greely, Silcox, and Robert Bernhard Fernow. Fernow had been the third chief of the US Division of Forestry before he became the influential dean of the Faculty of Forestry at the University of Toronto from 1907 to 1919. He described wildfire as Canada's "worst enemy" and viewed forests as crops that need to be harvested, not burned to waste.

Marty Alexander recalled a summer in north central Ontario when, at the last minute, the Ontario government told Brian Stocks, the mastermind behind the province's experimental burn program, that he could not proceed with a burn he had been planning for months because suppression resources were not available. "I'll never forget his reaction when he got the news. Brian was so frustrated, he kept shouting 'Gad damn it' while kicking inside a work truck over and over again with his steel-toed boots," Alexander told me.

Alexander is an American-born Canadian resident, the son of a US Air Force serviceman who was stationed for most of his career in various places across Canada. While working on a master's degree from Colorado State University, Alexander was determined to find work in his adopted country. Stocks obliged by hiring him straight out of Colorado in 1976 even before his thesis on fire and lodgepole pine stands was finished. Alexander spent five years at the Canadian Forest Service's lab in Sault Ste. Marie before transferring to the Canadian Forest Service's Northern Research Centre in Edmonton in 1981.

Two years into his new job, Alexander got into the crosshairs of a minor public controversy when an experimental burn he was responsible for coordinating in the remote Caribou Range of the Northwest Territories escaped the control lines and burned 3,500 acres (1,411 hectares) of spruce-lichen woodland. Van Wagner ended up on a national television morning show trying to explain what had happened. Kiil, the director of the lab in Edmonton, gave Alexander an encouraging pat on the back and told him to move forward.

Alexander did, and in doing so, he created, along with others, an advanced national training program for wildland and fire personnel that was merciless in its emphasis on understanding fire behavior. "He ran it old school, stressing the candidates out completely, with many needing time out as they twisted off," said Mark Heathcott, the man who directed Parks Canada's fire operations in western Canada for many years. "I experienced this first as a candidate, then as part of the training cadre, where he really tortured-tested the various agency personnel. Those of us who came out of that training program were grateful for what we learned because it set us up nicely for the challenges we would face in the real world."

The closest Alexander came to putting into practice the lessons he taught was in May 1998 when an El Niño–phase wildfire like the one in Fort McMurray forced two evacuations of the town of Swan Hills. Alexander wasn't there when the first evacuation occurred in the middle of the night. While serving as the fire behavior analyst, though, he made sure that the incident commander had the data he needed to make sure residents were given ample time to evacuate the second time around.

Stocks had his own share of challenges in helping create the Canadian Forest Fire Behaviour Prediction System that was introduced in 1989. Political interest in fire science began to lag in 1979 when the federal government shut down the Forest Fire Research Institute in Ottawa. Funding was increasingly in short supply. The big burns that Stocks and his colleagues wanted to light were coming under scrutiny. The media and environmentalists who were beginning to engage in national and regional campaigns to save the country's forests, which were being clear-cut with almost reckless abandon, were keeping a watchful eye. Burning was not part of their vision.

Then there was Canada's decision in 1982 to allow the United States to test cruise missiles in Canada. This move triggered antiwar sentiment across the country in a way that would, at one point, shut down Stock's experimental burn program in 1985 for a year.

The unlikely chain of events began with the "nuclear winter" theory, which triggered a flurry of controversy and research that tried to verify, discount, or better understand what Sagan, Turco, and their colleagues were proposing. NASA, the Defense Nuclear Agency (DNA) in Washington, DC, the Los Alamos National Laboratory in New Mexico, and many American university scientists got involved. In Canada, the Royal Society commissioned a study on it.

Stocks was made aware of the nuclear winter theory at a meeting in Boulder, Colorado, in 1985 that was organized by the US National Oceanic and Atmospheric Administration. Some of the DNA-sponsored scientists attending that meeting learned then that he was conducting large-scale, prescribed burns in Ontario. They were being done for forest management purposes as well as to better understand fire behavior. During these burns, a helicopter would drop fuel in the center of the slash and, from there, move outward in concentric rings. This way, much like a bonfire, winds moved inward on all sides of the fire, lessening the likelihood of escape. One of the side effects was a massive convection column that reached stratospheric heights. That was the kind of fire that piqued the interest of scientists who were focused on the nuclear winter theory.

Shortly after that meeting, Stocks invited Richard Turco, Frank Fendell, and Richard Small to a prescribed burn in northeastern Ontario that was being conducted by the Ontario Ministry of Natural Resources forest management program. The aim in lighting this particular fire was to find an economically efficient way of preparing logging slash sites for planting and seeding. No studies were being conducted by the visitors. It was simply an opportunity for the scientists to observe.

The burn would have taken place that day regardless of whether Turco and his colleagues had been there. Government officials knew about the guests and assumed no one else did.

The story, however, was leaked to the press by the author of the Royal Academy report on nuclear winter. When the group returned to the nearby town of Chapleau, the media, including several US and Canadian national television news broadcasters, were there waiting. The *Toronto Star* put the story on its August 4, 1985, front page with a headline that screamed "Ontario Inferno Tests Nuclear Theory."

"From that point on, this routine burn quickly became a nuclear winter fire," Stocks recalled. "The US scientists were asked many questions, none about prescribed burning. I ended up on CBC's 'As It Happens' radio show the next day trying to tell the whole story, but no one was interested by then."

Fueled by misinformation and the subsequent public outcry over allowing Americans to conduct nuclear winter tests in Canada, the Ontario government closed the door to the possibility of more collaboration with the Americans. Stocks was as upset as he was disappointed. However, concerns over climate change, spruce budworm diebacks, and smoke chemistry issues in Canada resulted in an Ontario government minister quietly asking Stocks to reengage with the nuclear winter scientists the following year.

Stocks was happy to oblige.

"We ourselves were primarily interested in leveraging DNA funding so we could study mass-fire ignition dynamics from an operational safety standpoint," he said. "As a result, DNA funded a number of subcontractors in the US, along with the US Forest Service, NASA, and NOAA, to come to northeastern Ontario. We conducted aircraft and ground measurements of fire behavior and smoke chemistry in a way we never could with our budget. Between 1987 and 1991 we documented close to ten burns. This was the beginning of the move to international, interdisciplinary fire research. Our lack of budget forced us in that direction, but global awareness of fire as it related to atmospheric chemistry and climate change was growing and we were part of that group. So, nuclear winter was a short-lived bit of serendipity."

The nuclear winter scenario and interest in what Stocks was doing were inspired in part by an enormous fire in northeastern British Columbia and northern Alberta in 1950.

The Chinchaga fire had burned for 222 days, torching a stretch of forest that was 175 miles long. Canadian Weather Bureau officials estimated that at one point the blanket of smoke was 400 miles long, 200 miles wide, and 3 miles thick. Smoke from the fire traveled all the way to Europe and reduced temperatures by as much as 7.2°F (4°C) in some places for a short time.[12]

Like the Fort McMurray fire, the Chinchaga fire made the front pages of the *New York Times* because it turned day into night. In one of those articles, the effects of the Chinchaga fire were compared with the eruption of Mount Krakatau, which killed 36,000 people and sent plumes of fine ash around the world after it erupted in 1883.[13]

It was, of course, a different time. Americans who weren't tuned into the news didn't know what to make of the pall. A Mrs. Dora Gesaman of Wichita Falls "announced gravely that at 4 p.m. when the pall of smoke lifted, her rooster crowed as if it were dawn and the chickens left the roost under the impression that a new day had arrived."[14]

One elderly man in the town of Busti in New York was so frazzled when a relative went in to check on him that he was shaking like a leaf. "Do you think this is the end of the world?" he asked.[15]

The news media didn't help calm fears. One Cincinnati radio station told its listeners that "Canada was on fire."

"Everyone remembers what he was doing when he heard that President Kennedy had been shot, that Pearl Harbor was bombed or that either world war had ended," local historian Norman Carlson wrote in the *Jamestown (NY) Post Journal*. "So too everyone my age and older remembers another event: a Sunday afternoon in 1950 when the sun ceased to give her light and our primitive fears of darkness, mortality and powerlessness rose at least near enough to the surface to etch a lasting trace that belied our outward calm."[16]

Newspapers had a field day with the story.

"Toronto's sky was filled with weird wonder," the *Globe and Mail* newspaper reported. "A great saffron-colored cloud filled the sky. Around it rolled steel grey clouds, shot by blackness and rippled, as water is rippled by a sudden light wind. Far off to the north and east the cold white light of the horizon accentuated the darkness that hung over the city."[17]

The impacts of that fire were much more than "awe and wonder" spectacle. In Buffalo, Pittsburgh, Cleveland, Fort Erie, and many towns in New York state, it was so dark at midday that streetlights and the lights at baseball fields, including those at Yankee Stadium, had to be turned on. Overwhelmed by the power demands, blackouts occurred in Ontario.

Finding themselves in zero-visibility conditions, several aircraft pilots were forced to soar to great heights in what was often a futile effort to escape the dense blanket of smoke. In one case, the US Air Force was compelled to postpone a search for a missing plane. In another, an American Airlines pilot flying from Cleveland to Phillipsburg, Pennsylvania, thought for a few minutes that his plane was on fire when he smelled smoke in the cockpit.

Astronomers were just as astonished as the public in tracking the movements of the smoke that the Chinchaga fire generated.

"Anyone who witnessed it, as I did, the great smoke pall of September 24 to 30, 1950 can never forget the eeriness of the occurrence and the extraordinary gloom," astronomer Helen Sawyer Hogg wrote in the *Journal of the Royal Astronomical Society of Canada*. "The western sky became a dark, terrifying mass cloud of haze, as though a gigantic storm were approaching."[18]

The pall that the fire's smoke cast may be a harbinger of what is likely to come if climate change causes fires in the boreal forest to burn even bigger, hotter, faster, and more unpredictably as the Fort McMurray fire and other wildfires have been doing.

Although the Fort McMurray inferno didn't generate the pall that the Chinchaga fire did, scientists in the United States tracked that plume as it moved into eastern Canada, the central United States, and across the Atlantic Ocean in 2016.

Marty Alexander wonders what might have happened if the rains hadn't come in June to slow the Horse River fire. "If you drew a line around the area the Fort McMurray wildfire eventually covered, it would have been some 1,000 kilometers in length," Alexander said. "Just imagine just how big it might have been if the hot, dry windy weather continued throughout the summer, as it might have. It's hard to envision that enough resources would have been available to try and contain a fire that big under those conditions."

Alexander is not alone in suggesting the possibility of a Chinchaga-like fire occurring in the future and casting a similar pall over parts of the world. Mike Flannigan believes so as well. Flannigan, though, emphasizes that there will be important differences between what happens in the future and what happened in 1950.

In the future, it will not only be warmer and likely much drier, but there will be a lot more mature trees in the forest because of all the fire suppression efforts over many parts of the country in the twentieth century. There will also be lot more people living, playing, and working in the boreal forest than there were in northwestern Alberta in 1950.

As the climate warms, big fires are going to occur with more frequency. People will inevitably get in the way. The thing for policymakers to seriously consider is that Fort McMurray was a medium-risk community. Many other communities in the boreal forest regions of Canada and parts of the American northwest are much more vulnerable than Fort McMurray.

"What we saw happen in Fort McMurray is going to happen again. We need to be prepared," Flannigan told me.

If that past tells us anything about the future, it suggests that wildfires like the one in Fort McMurray will come sooner rather than later and will come much more often. In Canada, wildfire burned more than 494,000 acres (200,000 hectares) of forest only four times between 1970 and 1990. Since then, it has done so twelve times. In the United States, wildfire burned more than 494,000 acres or more three times between 1983 and 1999. Between 2000 and 2016, it has done so eleven times. In the United States, the federal costs of fighting those fires rose from $240 million in 1985 to $2.1 billion in 2015. In Canada, the costs have been as high as $1 billion.

The only thing we don't know with certainty is where the next Fort McMurray will occur.

Chapter 3

A History of Fire Suppression

As is well known to old timers, the Indian fired the forests
with the deliberate intent of confusing and concentrating
game so as to make hunting easier. . . . A bunch of deer
with their heads in the air waiting for a fire presented an
easy mark, even to the Indian's bow and arrow, and it was
this fact, and not any desire for fancied forest conservation,
which caused the Indians to burn the forests.
— Aldo Leopold[1]

On the day the Sunshine Ski Hill in Banff National Park
opened early in November 2016, temperatures skyrocketed,
making it feel more like early summer than late fall. As ski-
ers gleefully headed for the hills for the first time, wildfire specialists
Cliff White and Ian Pengelly took me to the top of Sulphur Mountain, an iconic peak that provides breathtaking views of the wilderness
and townsite below, to show me how a Fort McMurray–like wildfire
might burn one of the world's most popular tourist destinations.

I was intrigued because many wildfire experts are predicting that
another wildfire like the one in Fort McMurray is inevitable. Among
those places mentioned by wildfire experts I talked to were Timmins in

Ontario, Prince George and Whistler in British Columbia, and Redmond, La Pine, and Sisters in Oregon. People in Libby, Montana, are fearful that a fire in the Kootenai National Forest will bring destruction and despair to them soon. Many Alaskans living in the state's interior feel the same. The list that Brian Stocks, a wildfire expert and member of the expert review panel that looked into the Fort McMurray and Slave Lake fires, keeps is a long one. He believes there are literally hundreds of communities at risk on both sides of the border.

California has long dominated the headlines for the wildfires that routinely wreak havoc throughout the state. California currently spends the most money per acre on fire suppression because it is heavily forested in places, hot, and often very dry and because it has so many people living in and around wildlands where it is difficult and expensive for firefighters to suppress fires.[2] Seven of the ten costliest wildfires that burned in the United States between 1990 and 2017 occurred in California.[3]

The new wildfire paradigm that is emerging is a California problem migrating into the northern forests of the continent. There are many reasons for this change, but several developments stand out. Since the 1990s, industry and hundreds of thousands of people have been moving into the boreal, montane, Columbia, and subalpine forests where climate change and decades-long policies of fire suppression have turned thick stands of mature trees into kindling during exceptionally hot, dry summers. When household risk of exposure to wildfire is considered in the United States today, California still ranks high on the list, but so do Montana, Oregon, and Washington.[4]

The situation is similar in Canada. Several years before the fire in Fort McMurray, and just months before a third of the town of Slave Lake burned, the Institute for Catastrophic Loss Reduction warned of a $1 billion wildfire event happening sooner rather than later. At the time, Glenn McGillivray, managing director of the institute, didn't predict fires ravaging Fort McMurray or Slave Lake, but he did warn that fire could bring destruction to Vancouver, Victoria, and Whistler in British Columbia as well as to Jasper and cottage country in Ontario and Quebec.[5]

A hotter, drier climate cycle is not just a problem facing the West, the North, Ontario, and Quebec as many people assume. Climatologists have also been predicting that wildfire will wreak havoc in regions of the American Southeast, such as Tennessee. There, a wildfire in the Great Smoky Mountains killed 14 people, injured 130 others, and forced 14,000 people to evacuate in December 2016. Wildfire is also a threat in the East where boreal and boreal-like forests such as the New Jersey Pine Barrens are located. Wildfire follows people irrespective of where the trees are located. New Jersey is a leader in this regard. Ninety-nine percent of all the wildfires in that state are caused by humans. In the boreal forest, humans cause about 65 percent of the fires.

What distinguishes northern forests from most of those in the East and Southeast, according to Lee Frelich, a University of Minnesota scientist who has been studying fire in the boreal region since the 1980s, is that the spruce, pine, and larch trees that dominate a good part of the northern forests burn much more easily than deciduous trees such as the oaks that mix with pine in the Pine Barrens and the maples that prevail in places such as the Great Smoky Mountains.

Frelich invited me to come see the rich history of fire he has documented in the Boundary Waters Canoe Area Wilderness in northern Minnesota. The Pagami Creek fire in 2011 was the biggest that state had experienced in a century. Frelich has no doubt that there will be more fires like that one and that these future fires will accelerate the dramatic restructuring he has been documenting in the state's boreal forest. As tempted as I was by Frelich's offer, I accepted Cliff White's invitation to come to Banff instead because I knew that countryside as well as anyone who does not live there. If Banff burned, I realized, the world would pay attention because so many people worldwide have been there at one time or have dreamed about going.

The theoretical Banff fire begins on a dry, hot day in late spring or summer when there are 25,000 tourists in and around the town of 9,000. About 1,500 of them are hiking up the trail or riding the gondola that goes close to the top of Sulphur Mountain, an 8,041-foot peak. Down below on the wild west side of Sulphur, a fire ignites in a stand of old-growth coniferous forest that hasn't burned since the last big wildfire raced through this part of Banff in 1889. Like that fire, this one may have been caused by a lightning storm that has come in with a cold front, or perhaps it was caused by people illegally camping in the Spray River Valley below.

With nearly seventy years of fire science and fire management experience between them in the national parks of Canada, Pengelly and White know better than anyone else what might happen next.

"If we had conditions like we had in 2003 when fire threatened Banff, it might take only twenty minutes for a fire like that to reach the mountaintop from the parking lot below," Pengelly said as we gazed up at the mountainside before going up. "That would be a big problem because the trees go right to the top. There is no escaping the fire up there."

Getting a thousand people off the mountain using the gondola, as Parks Canada and the owners of the interpretive center hope would happen, would take possibly three hours, two at best. That process would be extremely risky because the gondola might be hit by a fireball or by a thick plume of smoke that could asphyxiate people inside the cars.

According to Marty Alexander, a wildfire expert who spent nearly thirty-five years with the Canadian Forest Service studying fire behavior, people have only a few options when they are threatened with being entrapped or burned over by a wildfire. If there is no vehicle or building in which to take refuge, they can hunker in place. They can run through the fire edge to a burned-out area, or they can, if they have something to light a fire with and dry enough fuel on the ground, burn out a safety area.

When we get to the top, I survey the site and check out the tourists who are standing on the lookout outside the newly furbished interpretive center. Many are elderly. A lot of them are Japanese or German. Presumably, many of them don't speak or understand much English. Only a handful are making the minor effort it takes to walk the boardwalk steps to the summit. Their city shoes wouldn't get them there comfortably. They would be sitting ducks if a fire were to race up this precipice. I can't imagine them running through the fire to escape or lighting a fire to burn a safety area.

The best option, according to White, would be to herd everyone on top into the interpretive center and hope that the building is resilient enough to withstand the heat and the smoke. "Hikers on the mountainside would likely be toast by then," he says. "And getting people to go inside might prove to be a challenge because humans, like wildlife, instinctively flee rather than stay put when a fire comes towards them.

The best you could hope for is a helicopter coming in with a Parks Canada search and rescue team ordering people to get inside."

As the fire engulfs the forest on the mountaintop, burning embers come raining down on the town of Banff, which lies at the bottom of the valley on the east side of the mountain.

"Being upwind of the townsite, Sulphur Mountain would be like a volcano erupting," says White. "Trees, fences, and rooftops would begin to catch fire just as they did in Fort McMurray in 2016 and Slave Lake in 2011. Outside help would be at least one to two hours away in a best-case scenario. Even then they would have trouble getting into town because there might be 25,000 people or more trying to get out. It's not unusual to have gridlock on the streets of Banff on a busy summer day without an emergency unfolding."

Pengelly suggests that if the wind is calm, the wildfire is unlikely to end up being as bad as the Fort McMurray fire was because the town of Banff has made some progress in making itself FireSmart, which is a not-for-profit program that makes communities resilient to fire. Parks Canada has also done some work to create firebreaks between the town and the forest. Pengelly oversaw a lot of that work.

"That may be true," said White of Pengelly's opinion, "but is that your default position? If there are squirrely winds swirling around, you won't be able to light the backfire that would be needed to steer a fire like that away from town."

While listening, I had to wonder aloud. Even if the conditions were favorable for a back-burn—a fire that is purposely set along the inner edge of a fire line to consume the fuel in the wildfire's path—would the bureaucrats at Parks Canada be brave enough to light one given what happened with back-burns here and elsewhere? Consider Los Alamos, New Mexico, where a back-burn that was set in 2000 got hopelessly out of control and raced up a mountainside toward towns and a national laboratory complex filled with people and underground nuclear weapons

"It could get ugly," Pengelly acknowledged.

~

In 1910, California timber owner George Hoxie caused a stir in the forestry community when he wrote an article making the case for light burning to manage fire in the forest. "We had best adopt fire as our servant; otherwise it will be our master."[6] The stir died down quickly, however, when the Big Burn or Great Fire of 1910 swept through the drought-stricken forests of Montana, Idaho, and Washington that same year, burning huge chunks of Yellowstone and Glacier national parks.

The practice of lighting fires to manage forest environments is called prescribed or controlled burning. It is likely as ancient as the migration of First Nations people from Eurasia to North America during the last Ice Age. British botanist David Douglas found that out in 1826 while traveling through the wilds of Oregon where the Paiute tribes lived and hunted in the Cascade Mountains.

"Most parts of the country burned; only on little patches in the valleys and on the flats near the low hills that verdure is to be seen," he wrote. "Some of the natives tell me it is done for the purpose of urging the deer to frequent certain parts, to feed, which they leave unburned, and of course they are easily killed. Others say that it is done in order that they might better find wild honey and grasshoppers, which doth serve as articles of winter food."[7]

The Paiute of Oregon weren't the only practitioners of lighting fires for selfish reasons.

There is compelling evidence to suggest that Lenape Indians used fire to manage the forests of the New Jersey Pine Barrens just as the Sioux and Blackfeet did on the Great Plains of the West. In the 1840s and 1850s, Oblate missionaries such as Albert Lacombe described how these First Nations people lit up parkland, forests, and prairie shrublands so that lush grass would grow and attract bison. Emile Petitot, an Oblate who preached to the Dene in the Arctic several years later, described a similar practice in the northern boreal forest.

Working with the Salish and Kootenai tribes of Montana and Idaho, wildfire scientists Steve Arno and Stephen Barrett confirmed that those North American native tribes started fires to attract game, to enhance berry growth, to facilitate travel, and to communicate with other tribes.[8]

In the 1970s, anthropologist Henry (Hank) Lewis interviewed Cree and Dene elders living in the boreal regions from Jasper to Fort McMurray and learned that each spring, before the woods dried to tinder

Figure 3-1 Blackfoot men lighting a grass fire in 1918. North American indigenous people routinely lit fires in the grasslands and forest of the continent to attract game and nurture the growth of berries. (Provincial Archives of Alberta)

during a hot summer, they, too, burned meadows to attract elk, deer, and moose. They also burned to enhance fur-bearing populations along wetlands, to encourage berry growth, and to create a supply of wood. "Lighting fires," wrote Lewis, "was simply part of a sound strategy for adaptation in the boreal forest."[9]

As the case for prescribed burning was being made over the course of a century, decision makers refused to be swayed. When the US government first considered the idea of fighting fire with fire in 1882, the commissioner of agriculture bluntly told Congress, "We can't do that." Decades later, William B. Greeley, the man who became chief of the US Forest Service, dismissed it as "Paiute forestry."

"We should no more permit an essentially destructive theory, like that of light burning, to nullify our efforts at real forest protection than we should permit the advertisement of sure cures for tuberculosis to do away with sanitary regulations of cities, the tuberculosis sanitaria, fresh air for patients, and other means employed by medical and hygienic science for combatting white plague," said Greeley.[10]

Both scientists and social scientists also had trouble coming to grips with this strategy of fighting fire with fire to enhance biodiversity and to prevent catastrophic fires from happening in the future. In 1935, Elers Koch, a US Department of Agriculture forest supervisor who was involved in the Great Fire of 1910, wrote a landmark essay in the *Journal of Forestry* questioning the economic cost of fighting fire and making the case for letting forested wildlands burn for ecological reasons. His case was summarily dismissed by an accompanying article written by Earl Loveridge, the man who came up with the policy that advised firefighters to extinguish all fires by 10 a.m. the next day.[11]

That way of thinking persisted for many more decades, most notably in the Smokey Bear slogan: "Remember . . . Only YOU Can Prevent Forest Fires." When anthropologist Omer C. Stewart tried in 1954 to convince his colleagues at a conference that aboriginal burning had a profound impact on forested environments, Alfred. L. Kroeber, the so-called dean of American anthropology at the time, reluctantly conceded that this might have been the case. After thanking Stewart, he then dismissed it with a wave of the hand, saying, "We should all be grateful and leave it there."[12]

"In the early 20th century, the debate was not about whether American Indians used fire to manage landscapes," said Hutch Brown, a US Forest Service policy analyst, "but that they did so much of it, which in the view of early conservationists, violated the precepts of sound scientific forestry."[13]

White is not alone in suggesting that the impact of prescribed or controlled burning by native people in the eighteenth, nineteenth, and twentieth centuries was probably minor compared with what it was before contact with Europeans. The North American native population might have been as high as two million before Europeans arrived on the scene.

According to the Canadian Royal Commission on Aboriginal Health, the native population in Canada declined by as much as 80 percent after the first settlers arrived because of the introduction of infectious diseases such as measles, influenza, and smallpox. The First

Nations people had no immunity and no available drugs. Some northern people such as the Beothuk of Newfoundland and Labrador disappeared entirely. Much more territory would have burned had there had been more people to light fires in the forests.

European settlers frowned on these prescribed burns by First Nations and Metis not only because they were "unsightly," as explorer David Thompson wrote in 1795, but because they threatened livestock, logging leases, communities, and forests in national parks that emerged in the late nineteenth and early twentieth centuries. Government officials on both sides of the border attempted to put a stop to this practice through various draconian measures. The Shoshone and other tribes were discouraged from entering Yellowstone National Park in the late nineteenth and early twentieth centuries. Officials in Yosemite National Park evicted the Shoshone on a number of occasions.[14] When Jasper National Park was created in the Rocky Mountains north of Banff in 1907, First Nations and Metis were summarily forced out.

Edward Wilson Moberly was just eight years old when that happened to his family and to six other families living in the park. In the summer of 1909, a government commissioner handed his father, a Metis trapper, hunter, and part-time farmer, an eviction notice. Moberly's father accepted the compensation that was offered, but only because he would not be able to hunt, trap, fish, or light fires if he tried to stay.[15]

Wildfire historian Peter Murphy first met Ed Moberly in the summer of 1975 when Hank Lewis introduced the two to each other. At the time, Murphy was just beginning his tenure as head of the University of Alberta's Forest Science department. He recalls Moberly describing how and why the Jasper families burned forests in the springtime.

"They burned so that there would be open meadow for horses and cattle to graze on and for the hay they needed to grow to feed their milk cows. According to Ed, they also burned in the uplands to improve mountain sheep habitat. None of us could quite believe it when he insisted that the countryside in Jasper was a lot more open in those days. Now we know that he was right," Murphy said.

In fact, following his fur-trading expedition to Jasper in 1817, Ross Cox described the now heavily forested upper Athabasca Valley as "savannah."[16]

If there were any doubts about how North American native people may have shaped the northern forest landscape with the fires they lit, those doubts have been widely dispelled by recent archaeological and tree-ring research and by repeat photography projects that vividly describe how many parts of the northern forest appear now compared with what they looked like a century ago.

A repeat study that stands out is the one that ecologists Eric Higgs and Jeanine Rhemtulla did in the 1990s when Parks Canada historian Rod Wallace handed them a box of photographs of Jasper that were taken by surveyor Morrison Parsons Bridgland in 1915. When Higgs and Rhemtulla revisited the scenes depicted in Bridgland's superb images, they saw that Moberly was right: the Athabasca Valley had a lot fewer trees then than it does now. Lightning-ignited fires may have been partly responsible for some of it, but because the Athabasca Valley in Jasper lies within the rain shadow, it's clear that humans must have had a hand in the burning, as Moberly and others testified.

Several years ago, Cliff White and historian Ted Hart produced a similar book of repeat photography to demonstrate how much the Banff landscape has changed over time. On Sulphur Mountain that afternoon, White showed me a photo from the book, one that was taken by photographer George Paris in 1898 from the approximate spot where we were then standing. The mountain vista of and around the Banff townsite looks the same in Paris's photo as it does now, with one notable exception: today, there are a lot more trees on the mountainside than there were back then.

Historian I. S. MacLaren, a member of the Culture, Ecology and Restoration Project in Jasper, summed it up best in 1999 when he noted that the loss of the savannahs to which Cox had alluded means the loss of firebreaks that had developed in the Athabasca River valley in epochs when fires induced by lightning—and, presumably, by First Nations people—occurred regularly.

"If," as one Jasper National Park official has quipped, "we're in the business of creating ideal pine marten habitat, we can take a bow; otherwise, we're standing in the middle of an ecological disaster, and we humans are entirely responsible for it."

Cliff White shares that sentiment. "When we pushed First Nations people out of the parks and began suppressing fires, the trees took over," said White. "It may look nice to tourists, but it challenges all of the definitions of what is natural."

~

The realization that all was not natural in terms of the way forests and wildfire were being managed began in earnest in the 1960s when a number of ecologists such as University of Michigan's Stanley Cain lamented the lack of research being conducted in the country's national parks. Some scientists suspected that the decades-long suppression of wildfire was the reason some conifers, such as the 2,000-year-old giant sequoias in Redwood Mountain Grove of Kings Canyon National Park in Nevada, were not regenerating.

Like jack pine and lodgepole pine, sequoias depend on wildfire. The heat they generate opens up the dry seritonous cones that contain hundreds of seeds necessary for new trees to take root. Squirrels and birds are often not enough to disperse all those cones, especially in a thick understory with a large overhanging canopy. Seedlings have a tough time competing in that environment.

Many of these well-founded concerns led to a government inquiry chaired by zoologist A. Starker Leopold, a son of the legendary conservationist Aldo Leopold. The landmark recommendations that he and his colleagues made in 1963 set the stage for a new approach to wildfire in national parks and a series of experimental burns that convinced the US National Parks Service in 1968 and the US Forest Service in 1978 to use prescribed burning as a management tool.

The development of this new relationship with wildfire in the northern forests was fraught with trial and error and pushback from politicians, the public, and plant and animal ecologists who continued to see fire as a destroyer and not a birther. The biggest setback occurred in the late 1980s, when three monumental wildfires surprised fire scientists, horrified decision makers, and rocked the wildfire world in a way that had not happened since the Great Fire of 1910.

The first of those fires occurred in 1987, thousands of miles away along the vast stand of boreal forest that lines the border of Siberia and Manchuria in northern China. The Soviet government let the fire go when it moved in from the Chinese side because the timber that was being burned was of little economic use. China, on the other hand, sent in 60,000 soldiers and firefighters in a vain attempt to contain it with every available resource. Several hundred people were either injured or died in the line of duty. The so-called Black Dragon fire burned more than 18 million acres of trees. It was the biggest wildland fire recorded in several hundred years, one immortalized in articles and a book written by *New York Times* reporter Harrison Salisbury.[17]

No one expected a fire of that magnitude to occur in the United States. That changed on June 30, 1988, when lightning struck a tree in the Crown Butte region of Yellowstone National Park along the borders of Montana, Wyoming, and Idaho. Fire managers initially allowed the fire to burn until it, along with dozens of other fires, quickly spun out of control during a summer that turned out to be the hottest and driest in 110 years.

The 240 fires that burned in Yellowstone that year didn't match the Black Dragon fire in magnitude, but the fires put fear in the hearts of decision makers and a public that had all but forgotten—or had never heard of—the Great Fire of 1910. For weeks, the Yellowstone fires made the front pages of newspapers and magazines all across the country. The *Los Angeles Times* made it the lead story on thirty-two occasions.

Canada had more than its share of fires up until this time, but the 224 fires that lit up nearly 10 percent of the forests in the province of Manitoba a year after Yellowstone burned were unprecedented. More than 24,000 people from thirty-two communities had to leave their homes. At one point, Bill McKnight, Canada's minister of defense, was roused from his bed in the middle of the night to approve military planes and soldiers to be flown in.[18] It was an extremely rare fire season in Manitoba. According to a study done by Mike Flannigan, who was just beginning to make his mark in the Canadian Forest Service, it was a once-in-four-hundred-years event. In a space of just a few months, the amount of forest burned exceeded everything that had been torched in Manitoba over the course of the previous twenty-five years.

Both the Yellowstone and Manitoba fires, and to a lesser extent the Black Dragon fire, made decision makers reluctant to proceed expeditiously with the prescribed burns and the "let burn" policies that were needed to deal with more than eighty years of highly combustible fuel building up in the northern forests. Following the fires at Yellowstone, US president Ronald Reagan dismissed the "let burn" policy as "cockamamie." Donald P. Hodel, secretary of the Department of the Interior, described it as "absurd," and, on July 21, he ordered parks officials to fight all the fires. John Melcher, the Democratic senator from Montana, promised in the *New York Times*: "They'll never go back to this policy. From now on the policy will be putting the fire out when they see the flames."[19]

In the United States, they did go back, but not with gusto. In 1988, the year that Yellowstone burned, fifty fire plans in the 387 designated wilderness areas on National Forest System lands were approved. In 1992, only thirteen fire plans were operational. "The decline in plan numbers probably reflects the apprehensions—both external and internal—that developed after the fires of 1988," Jerry Williams, the national director of Fire and Aviation Management, acknowledged at a fire symposium in Missoula, Montana, in March 1993. "Certainly, 1988 demonstrated the kinds of risks that can accompany the wilderness fire program."[20]

The Americans, however, weren't giving up. Following the fires of 1988, the secretaries of the Departments of Agriculture and of the Interior established a multiagency Fire Management Policy Review, which concluded that the policy of allowing fire to play a role in wilderness resource conservation was sound. What was needed was a better way to mitigate the risks. To back up that conclusion, they put research money on the table. In 1995, the National Park Service came up with a new national fire plan that raised the budgetary ceiling for prescribed burns, accepted the risks that were inherent, and provided for mobile tactical support that was needed in years when the fire season was exceptionally severe.

It was a similar, yet in some ways different, story in Canada. Following the Manitoba fire, the Canadian government's approach to wildfire science was surprisingly muted. In 1991, the National Research Council disbanded the Committee on Forest Fire Management. The position of fire advisor for the government of Canada was eliminated. Research on fire ecology and fire suppression began to play an increasingly minor role.

Even though 1994 and 1995 produced two of the most severe fire seasons on record, political indifference to fire science continued to morph into savage budget cuts. In 1995, the Canadian Forest Service's budget was subjected to a program review that resulted in the annual budget being slashed from $221 million to $96 million. The regional center in Newfoundland was shut down, and everyone was transferred out of Petawawa Forest Experiment Station in northern Ontario northwest of Ottawa.[21] By 2001, the experimental burning that Van Wagner advocated ended with an ambitious project that involved fourteen countries and more than a hundred scientists in eighteen fire experiments in the Northwest Territories. Canada would never see the likes of that kind of fire science again.

Fortunately for Cliff White, Parks Canada adopted a different attitude. Like the US National Park Service and the US Forest Service, Parks Canada once viewed wildfire as an enemy of wilderness. Fire suppression was the main reason the warden service was established; it is also the reason there are so many roads in the mountain national parks that have since been turned into trails. These roads were once used, with limited success, to get firefighters and resources to a backcountry fire.

With an eye on what was happening south of the border in the 1970s, some people in Parks Canada began to realize, as Starker Leopold and his colleagues had done, that the country's parks were not as self-sustaining or as "natural" as previously thought. Even more so than the sequoias in King's Canyon and Yosemite, the spruce, pine, and larch in the boreal, alpine, and montane forests in Canada's national parks are fire-dependent.

Under the guidance of Van Wagner, the senior scientist with the Canadian Forest Service who had led a team that pioneered the art of experimental burning in a real-world environment, Parks Canada came up with a policy statement in 1979 that recognized the role of fire in conservation, as loaded a term as it was at the time even though no one had any idea what was "natural." By coincidence, White went to the United States that year to study wildfire, unaware that he would soon become one of the architects of the wildfire strategy that would eventually unfold.

~

Unlike most Banff national park employees, Cliff White did not have to move to the Rocky Mountains to take the job he got in Banff in 1973. I found that out the night before we went up Sulphur Mountain when he took me to see a movie debut at the Banff International Film Festival. The two hour film was based on the lives and adventures of artists Peter and Catharine Whyte, granduncle and grandaunt of White, who became pillars of the mountain town in the early to middle part of the twentieth century. (The "y" in the Whyte name was an affectation Peter White used to promote his artist profile.)

Catharine Whyte was a rich socialite from Connecticut who once dated John D. Rockefeller III. Peter was the son of an entrepreneur who came to Banff when the railway was built. Catharine and Peter met at an art school in Boston in the 1920s, and she followed him back when he resettled in the mountains.

The legacy of the White family is imprinted on the renowned Whyte Museum of the Canadian Rockies in Banff, but it is also there in the ski hills and an historic lodge in the park. Cliff's grandfather conceived of and built the Mt. Norquay ski hill and Skoki Ski Lodge, the first commercial enterprise to serve backcountry ski enthusiasts in North America. In 1960, Cliff's father bought the now world-famous Sunshine Ski Hill and installed a second lift, which dramatically increased the number of people who came to Banff. He and his wife sold it a few years later when Cliff was just nine years old.

Although White once served on the board of directors of the museum, his main interest was in the outside world. A job with Parks Canada seemed like it might make a good fit. When he was hired in 1973, it was as a firefighter in Banff. As the years went by, he and other Parks Canada staff rapidly specialized to take on tasks such as mountain rescue and prescribed burning. "When I first walked into the Banff warden office, there were forty-five wardens. All of them had the same job descriptions. When I left in 2009, there were thirty-five job descriptions," he said.

White's interest in the science of fire began at college in Missoula, Montana, and then at Colorado State between 1979 and 1985. At

Colorado, he crossed paths with Tom Zimmerman, who would go on to assume senior wildfire management positions in the US National Forest Service and the US National Parks Service. (When White and Pengelly were meeting with me in Banff, Zimmerman was peripherally involved in a government-appointed review of the Fort McMurray fire.)

Cliff's immersion in the policy side of wildfire science got its start in 1986 when Nikita Lopoukhine, the director general for Parks Canada, arranged for him to come to Ottawa to work on a national fire management and prescribed burn program with Stephen Woodley, a forest ecologist. Lopoukhine was an outsider who broke the mold of national park managers traditionally rising up from the ranks of the warden service. A great-grandson of Russian novelist Leo Tolstoy, he grew up in the boreal forest of Quebec, deciding early on that he would make forestry a profession. In university, he studied under Stan Rowe, a noted ecologist who viewed the natural world in the manner of Aldo Leopold.

Lopoukhine never wavered in his belief that fire was a management tool that needed to be used in national parks to promote biodiversity and to prevent really big wildfires like the one in Yellowstone from happening in the future.

It was not easy figuring out when and where to burn or whether to let a wildfire burn itself out in a national park, especially in Banff, which attracted so many tourists. Yellowstone was a testament to that, as were as number of prescribed burns that had grown out of control across Canada and the United States. Firefighters died in the line of duty. Hundreds of homes and buildings were burned unintentionally.

"We were prepared for the possibility that something could go wrong in those early days," White said later that second afternoon as he led me and Pengelly to a small experimental burn he had orchestrated at Two Jacks, near Lake Minnewaka in Banff, in the 1980s. "We had a long line of fire trucks and about 100 people ready to move in the day we lit this fire. It was overkill. But we really didn't know what to expect."

The goal at Two Jacks was to burn the dense stands of pine and spruce so that aspen, berries, and other deciduous shrubs would grow and lure back animals such as deer, elk, and bears. The operational part

Figure 3-2 Elk and other animals thrive in areas that have been burned by fire as this forest in Jasper was the year before this photo was taken. (Edward Struzik)

of the burn went off without a hitch, but not the ecological outcome. Instead of getting aspen regenerating, they got a gorgeous stand of white spruce. The tourists didn't complain, but the burn did nothing for wildlife. Then they tried burning Two Jacks again several years later, this time in spring instead of fall. They got the season right with the right kind of fire. Lodgepole pine seeded back in, but there was no aspen recovery.

White and Pengelly orchestrated many successful burns in Banff, but the most ambitious was one planned for the Fairholme Mountain Range that separates Banff from the town of Canmore, Alberta. Mark Heathcott, the national fire incident commander at the time, called it a "moonshot." The goals in this case were to create a firebreak between Banff and Canmore, a town of about 8,000 people back then, and to restore some semblance of ecological integrity to a wilderness that had been seriously compromised by nearly a century of fire suppression.

The burn was also designed to halt the march of the mountain pine beetle, which had ravaged vast stands of forest in British Columbia, Oregon, and Idaho and was making a big run into the Rocky Mountain parks.

Planning for and getting the go-ahead for the controlled burn at Fairholme was years in the making and was complicated by things continuing to go horribly wrong in places where prescribed burns were lit. Most pertinent to what Pengelly and White wanted to do at Fairholme was a prescribed burn at Bandelier National Monument in New Mexico that got out of control in 2000, a year in which wildfires in the United States burned more than 6.5 million acres, twice the ten-year average.[22]

The Cerro Grande fire was named after the big mountain in Bandelier that rises to a height of 10,199 feet. The fire began on May 4, 2000, with a prescribed burn in a small section of Bandelier. More than 18,000 people were ordered to leave the towns of Los Alamos and White Rock before the fire destroyed 280 homes and threatened nuclear weapons storehouses at the Los Alamos National Laboratory. On two occasions, the fire roared across the lab's underground emergency command center, forcing employees inside to evacuate along with the lab's heavily armed security guards.

With more than $1 billion in damages, the wildfire was the biggest and costliest in New Mexico's history.

Within days, Bruce Babbitt, secretary of the Department of the Interior, took the blame for the government. "The calculations that went into this were seriously flawed," he said at a news conference. A preliminary investigation by his department was hard on those who planned the burn and those who oversaw it. Echoing Babbitt's initial observations, they concluded that virtually every aspect of the prescribed fire was poorly planned and executed.

In truth, fire planners in Bandelier were damned if they did and damned if they didn't go ahead with a prescribed burn. They had inherited a disaster in the making. A century of fire suppression in the region had created a dense, old-growth coniferous forest that was, like Sulphur Mountain in 2017 and the Fairholme Range in 2003, just waiting to be lit up by lightning, an arsonist, or a careless human. Almost everyone knew by then that a sleeping dragon was about to wake up. In

1998, the US Forest Service had warned of the likely possibility of a fire at Bandelier. The Department of Energy concluded a year later that the probability of a fire overtaking the Los Alamos National Laboratory was "not only credible, but likely."[23]

Prior to the Cerro Grande fire, the US National Parks Service's record for planning and managing prescribed burns was stellar. Just 38 of the 3,746 prescribed burns that had been set since 1968 had escaped the boundaries of control. This burn, however, was doomed from the beginning because of hot, dry weather and the failure to follow up on a weather report that inexplicably omitted the prospects of strong winds that could drive the fire out of control. No one asked for the missing data. Bandelier was also underresourced, which may be the reason planners underestimated the number of people and heavy equipment that would be needed if the fire were to get out of control.

It was akin to what happened in Slave Lake in 2011 and Fort Mc-Murray in 2016. Within hours, the prescribed burn became a wildland fire that was in need of additional assistance from federal and state agencies.

To make matters worse, the fire grew out of control at the same time a prescribed burn on the north rim of the Grand Canyon got away from the national park fire managers who had set it. Like Bandelier, the Grand Canyon National Park was overloaded with mature ponderosa pines in a coniferous forest that had been aggressively protected from the ravages of fire. This prescribed fire was also lit in hot, dry conditions. No one had anticipated that a powerful windstorm, which was not in the weather forecast, would come in and blow on fire crews.

None of it mattered to the public or politicians. At the Nankoweap trailhead, tourists were hemmed in by the fires and trees that had fallen down. Search and rescue personnel had to be brought in, further challenging the resources of the incident management team that was badly in need of more resources. Because there were so many fires burning elsewhere, only two interagency hotshot crews were available.

In the end, formal inquiries failed to find any person to be at fault for what happened at Grand Canyon or Bandelier. Reputations were damaged for political reasons, not for ecological ones. Politicians and the public wanted someone to blame, and so did the media, all for good reason in the case of Bandelier. "An out-of-control wildfire. A nuke factory with enough plutonium to wipe out the entire Southwest. A handful of exhausted firefighters. Just how close did we come to annihilation?" ran the headline in *Maxim*.

Roy Weaver, the superintendent of Bandelier, was pilloried in the press. Some wanted him to lose his pension. That he and his team did not know about the possibility of strong winds pushing the fire out of control didn't matter. Nor did anyone care that he and his crew were underresourced.

"I don't want to deny our responsibility for igniting the prescribed fire," he said after remaining silent for a year after the fire. "But we did it with a plan that seemed valid and workable. Things happened that we couldn't or didn't anticipate. And that we couldn't control."[24]

~

In planning for the prescribed burn at Fairholme, White and Pengelly went to Los Alamos and were humbled by what they saw and heard. Wanting to know more, they arranged to have US Forest Service personnel come to Banff to share the lessons they had learned that summer.

"This was as big a project as Ian and I had worked on, and we both knew that the fingers would be pointed at us if something went wrong," recalled White. "We wanted to make sure that we had all the bases covered."

Walking through the Fairholme burn that November day, Pengelly and White showed me what mechanical logging, a method of thinning the forest, and the prescribed burn had accomplished and how predetermined fire lines helped save the day when the prescribed burn that was lit threatened to get out of control. Instead of a thick stand of 120-year-old trees, there are now open meadows with a rich mosaic of aspen, pine, spruce, and poplar growing above a ground cover that includes fescue, blueberries, crowberries, and other fruit that grizzly bears covet. If lightning or a human starts a fire upwind, the firebreak will slow or stop the blaze from jumping into the town of Canmore.

Walking along, we saw the fresh tracks of grizzly bear, elk, deer, and wolves. Had hikers been unaware of what had happened here in 2003,

I thought, they would have been hard-pressed to conclude that the landscape they were passing through was unnatural.

"There were moments that summer when this might have got away," said White. "But if this can be done in a national park with all the regulations, tourists, and threatened and endangered species that are in place, why can't it be done in places like Fort McMurray that are vulnerable to fires. The job in Banff and other national parks across Canada and the United States isn't over—not by a long shot. We need something like this to prevent a fire from racing up Sulphur Mountain. We need to continue to deal with the backlog of old-growth forest that we created over the past century."

~

Jane Park was just a year into her job in Banff when the Fairholme prescribed burn took place. She had taken over from Pengelly when he had retired in 2011. She admits that the prospect of a fire racing up Sulphur Mountain unnerves her. Maintaining a shelter-in-place policy in the facilities on top of the mountain is not the best option, she says. And, with only one helicopter pad available, the prospects of lifting people out are very limited. According to Park, the best option is to use the gondola.

"We've been talking to Brewster's, the owner of the company, and they have a plan in place that can get up to 625 people off the mountain in an hour. We're working with them and the city of Banff to address the scenarios that Cliff and Ian have highlighted. This winter we're going to be conducting some table-top exercises to sort out what can be done in an emergency," she said, speaking of the upcoming 2017 winter.

What happened in Fort McMurray in the summer of 2016, according to Park, has energized existing plans to reburn part of Fairholme and other areas in the park. Those plans, however, are contingent on funding and weather.

What could also get in the way is the "never saw it coming" attitude that is endemic to the way decision makers, firefighters, and the public think about the potential for catastrophic wildfire events. The Black Dragon fire of 1987, the Yellowstone fires of 1988, the Manitoba fires of 1989, and the Cerro Grande and Grand Canyon fires of 2000 demonstrated just how dangerous many forests are becoming in this era of climate change. The real wake-up call, however, didn't come until 2003, when tens of thousands of people were forced out of their homes and communities in a fire season that was like no other in western North America up to that time.

Chapter 4

Visions of the Pyrocene

The world keeps on turning and the bush keeps on burning.
— Common phrase used by firefighters in
Canada's Northwest Territories

In the summer of 2016, I was standing along the banks of Vermillion River in the Canadian Rockies not far from the Burgess Shale, which is home to the fossilized impressions of weird and wonderful creatures that lived half a billion years ago. Paleontologist Charles Walcott discovered this site in 1909, but it was Harvard scientist Stephen J. Gould who made these fossils famous in his 1989 book *Wonderful Life: The Burgess Shale and the Nature of History*. In that narrative on the quirks of evolution, Gould argued that as fit as these soft and hard-bodied animals might have been, fitness did not ensure their survival in a world that was rapidly cooling at the end of the so-called Cambrian explosion.

Standing there with me there on that warm, late-summer day was Rick Kubian, the Parks Canada resource conservation director who oversees wildfire and conservation initiatives in Kootenay and Yoho national parks and in Lake Louise in Banff. I couldn't help but wonder whether something as transformative as the Cambrian explosion was already happening in the vast northern hemispheric forests now that the world has entered a hotter, drier climatic cycle.

The long, punctuated history of wildfire in this part of the world was etched there on the mountainsides in front of us, like a time line that leads to catastrophe, extinction, or, alternatively, to resilience and adaptation. "That's the Mount Shanks fire," said Kubian, pointing to a large swath of scorched tree trunks that are still standing to the northeast of us. "That was a big burn in 2001 that lasted a month. Beyond that is the Shoebox fire that burned in 1994. Over there is the Assiniboine Slide burn of 1984. To the south of us is the Spar Mountain fire that burned in 1991. It was one of the first big fires that was allowed to run its course. That was a big decision to make back them. Above that is the Octopus Mountain prescribed burn that we started in 2011 to do what we wouldn't let Mother Nature do in the national parks for decades. I'm really proud of how that worked out. It's already coming back very nicely. And over there is the Verendrye fire that you witnessed in 2003 when you were here with us. That and the Tokumm fire that burned the same summer was the fire of a lifetime."

Not a lot of forest burned in the United States and Canada in 2003. Nationwide in the United States, it was about half the amount that had burned the year before and less than the average that had burned in the previous eight years.[1] The percentages were higher in Canada, but not by much. What did burn, however, burned big and hot, and it burned severely in places where there were a lot of people and great number of tourists, homes, and businesses standing in the way.

In Montana's Glacier National Park, where only 0.04 inch of rain fell in July 2003, twenty-five fires burned 13 percent of the park that summer. One of the bigger fires moved so fast and unpredictably that diners at Lake McDonald Lodge were in the middle of their meals when they were told to get into their cars and drive out. In relatively short order, the entire Lake McDonald Valley was evacuated. More than five hundred people were forced to flee their homes in East Glacier, Apgar, and West Glacier. The national park headquarters narrowly avoided being destroyed.[2]

In the Salmon-Challis National Forest of Idaho, renowned for hellacious wind and firestorms, two members of the helitack crew were killed fighting fires that exhibited levels of extreme behavior that few had ever seen before.

It was even worse in the Crowsnest Pass on the Alberta–British Columbia–Montana border. There, more than 2,000 people were forced out of their homes and campsites when the so-called Lost Creek fire came within a third of a mile (half kilometer) of the towns of Hillcrest, Blairmore, Bellevue, Frank, and Coleman. More than 850 firefighters, twenty helicopters, four air tankers, thirty-four bulldozers, and twenty water trucks were brought in to contain the blaze that burned 54,363 acres (22,000 hectarees) of forest.[3]

Oregon fared a little better in 2003, but not by much. Some 1,000 people had to be evacuated when two fires—the Bear Butte and Booth fires—in the Central Cascades joined. At one point, there were 2,379 firefighters on scene supported by 112 pumper trucks and fourteen helicopters. More than $40 million was spent on fire suppression in two national forests, in one Native American reservation, and on both state and private lands.

Even the sub-Arctic region along the west coast of Hudson Bay caught fire that year. Dozens of polar bear dens were destroyed along the Hayes River region at the north end of the boreal forest. At one point, fire threatened to burn down York Factory, a historic sub-Arctic fur-trading post that is now managed by the Parks Canada.

The biggest drama, however, played out in the southern interior of British Columbia where more than 45,000 people were forced to flee their homes in the city of Kelowna and the municipal district of Barriere. Three pilots died in the line of firefighting duties, and 334 homes were lost in a season in which 2,500 fires torched 1,000 square miles (2,650 square kilometers). It was the costliest natural disaster in Canadian history before Fort McMurray and a flood along the Rocky Mountains in 2013 came along.[4]

As much as the 1988 Yellowstone fires, the Manitoba fires of 1989, and the Cerro Grande and Grand Canyon fires of 2000 strained the resources of fire agencies, the 2003 fire season was the one that screamed out that fire managers were increasingly unprepared to deal with an escalation of fire in the northern forests during periods of intense drought and in years when climate change, El Niño, and El

Figure 4-1 The 2003 fire season produced a lot of surprises. Fire that swept through polar bear denning sites along the west coast of Hudson Bay was completely unexpected and another sign that fire had no boundaries in the boreal. (Edward Struzik)

Niño–like climatic patterns in the North Pacific were bringing shorter winters, earlier springs, more lightning strikes, and hotter, drier, and sometimes windier weather. After nearly a century of relentless fire suppression, there was just too much fuel on the ground.

The 2003 fire season was the wake-up call that tested the limits of the resources that were needed to keep residents, tourists, pipelines, timber leases, oil rigs, and other assets on both sides of the border out of harm's way. For many firefighters and wildfire experts, it was a fire season like no other, and it was a forerunner to what would lie ahead in the continent's northern forests.

~

The fires in Kootenay in 2003 were not ones for the history books. There was no mass evacuation as there was in Kelowna and in Glacier National Park. There was no major infrastructure damage and no deaths, as there were in the Salmon-Challis Forest of Idaho that summer. The worst that happened was the closure of one of the only three highways connecting the eastern part of Canada to the West Coast. Had a few gutsy, potentially career-ending decisions not been made by firefighting planners and managers, however, the Kootenay fires would have spread into Banff and imperiled the safety of some 25,000 to 30,000 people who were living there or visiting. It might have ended in the kind of disaster that White and Pengelly are warning about. People might have died, and the town of Banff could have burned because no one was prepared for a fire season like that one. To this day, no one really appreciates how close it all came to a disaster.

Kubian recalls the 2003 fire season as if it were yesterday. Well before a violent thunderstorm rolled in on the last day of July, lighting up seven wildfires in the middle of the night, he had known that he and his colleagues were in for trouble that summer.

The first warning came in April in a memo from Mark Heathcott, the national parks fire management coordinator for western Canada. Heathcott was in the habit of forecasting the upcoming fire season on April Fools' Day, using the handle "Charlie Lima" (also known as "Chicken Little when the forecast looked scary"). He sent out a map that spring illustrating how most of Canada, and especially western Canada, had gone through one of the driest autumns and winters on record. The meteorological data that he tapped into made his forecasts sound ominous. So did those that were being issued by other agencies on both sides of the border.

Both the British Columbia Forest Service and the US Forest Service were expecting the 2003 fire season to be one of the most challenging yet. "El Nino," Heathcott added in his memo, "was going to hang in there, until at least the end of summer. . . . Look for an active fire season in Mt. Revelstoke/Glacier, Kootenay and Yoho," he said before signing off.

The second warning came with the passing of spring weather that produced almost no snow or rain in advance of a summer that turned out to be one of the hottest and driest on record in southwestern Canada and the northwestern regions of the United States. El Niño events tend to influence climate and weather patterns in this part of the world, but no one had seen anything quite like the baking that took place in the western forests in June, July, and August. Heading into the summer of 2003, southern British Columbia, Montana, Idaho, and parts of Oregon had gone through their driest three-year period on record. Streamflows in many places were between 10 and 20 percent of normal. Water flow along the mighty Fraser River was at a historic low. Salmon were dying en masse in lethally warm streams. The mountain pine beetle population exploded on a march that would eventually cover more than 45 million acres (18.2 million hectares) of forest, an area five times the size of Vancouver Island. Power companies, utilities, and many towns were on high alert, concerned that there would not be enough water to get them through the hot summer.

With the benefit of hindsight, Parks Canada may and probably should have reconsidered an aggressive plan to thin the forests in Jasper, Banff, Kootenay, Waterton, Prince Albert in Saskatchewan, Riding Mountain in Manitoba, and La Mauricie national parks in Quebec with several prescribed burns that were lit that winter and spring. But almost everyone involved in those decisions expected that the normally reliable June monsoons would come to douse the fires if they threatened to burn beyond the containment zones. This year, however, the rains didn't come and the hot weather didn't let up.

The premonition of trouble arrived on May 22 after an unexpected cold front moved in and a prescribed burn in La Mauricie in the Laurentian Mountains of Quebec took off, with powerful winds whipping up smoldering embers into a wall of flame.

Normally, this kind of situation would not have caused too much concern for experienced fire crews. La Mauricie was the site of the first prescribed burn in a national park east of Manitoba in Canada, and fire crews had done a good job containing it during that spring of 1992. This fire, though, proved to be too much for the local fire crew, which was forced to back off. With La Mauricie being located in the district represented by the prime minister of Canada, all stops were pulled to get this fire under control. To help with the efforts in La Mauricie, Parks Canada sent Steve Otway, one of four national fire incident commanders, to the scene along with Dave Smith, the fire and vegetation specialist at Jasper National Park, and a group of first-string firefighters.

With Smith in the east, Kubian and Rob Walker were brought in from Kootenay to oversee the prescribed burns that had been planned for Rock Creek and the Syncline Ridge area in Jasper. Kubian was an obvious choice because he was once the vegetation and fire specialist in that park. Sending Walker also made sense. He was the man responsible for all aspects of fire management in Kootenay, Yoho, and Lake Louise.

All would have gone according to plan had the fire crew been able to start the Syncline fire in the ignition zone that had been identified in the initial proposal, but the forest floor was too damp to get the flames to spread. So, rather than postpone the effort, a decision was made to light the fire in the containment zone, where the chance of the fire escaping is higher. Everyone was confident that fire crews on standby could deal with the situation if it got out of control. Once again, they were also counting on the June monsoons to help them if it did.

Satisfied that everything was in order, Kubian took some time off and went home to be with his wife and newborn son. When it looked like the June monsoons might not come, however, Walker started getting nervous as he watched the fire danger ramp up in the Rockies and Cascades on both sides of the border.

The trouble started first in Banff, where Pengelly and his team were well into the process of creating a firebreak on the Fairholme Range, which separates the national park from the town of Canmore.

On June 7, ground crews were forced to flee for safety when there was a mix-up in ignition operations. Later that same day, the prescribed fire at Rock Creek in Jasper escaped ignition. Alberta water bombers were called in to prevent it from spreading into the province and other parts of the national park.

Both of those prescribed burns and another at Syncline Ridge continued to smolder into June and July. Walker suggested that Kubian cut short his leave to get on top of the fire management plan for Kootenay.

The big blowup of 2003 got under way in earnest on July 17, when an early morning lightning storm in Montana's Glacier National Park ignited six fires that spread across the park in the following days. Officials in neighboring Waterton Lakes National Park in Alberta were put on high alert.

The next day, a sub-Arctic fire began spreading rapidly toward York Factory near the west coast of Hudson Bay. Heathcott remembers thinking at the time how crazy it was that a wildfire was burning in polar bear country.

At this point, Heathcott realized that the threat of wildfire was spiraling out of control. He sent Cliff White to Jasper to try to gently persuade colleagues there not to rekindle the prescribed burn that was smoldering at Rock Creek. Try as he did, White was not successful.

On July 22, in cooperation with the Alberta government, the Jasper team went ahead with the plan, not anticipating the possibility that the Syncline fire would blow up the next day, race up the Rocky River through the park and potentially toward the town of Hinton on the east side of the national park.

It seemed then that it couldn't get more complicated. But it did.

As Rock Creek smoldered and Syncline burned dangerously out of control, the Fairholme burn began showing some signs of life with several heart-stopping runs. White remembers it well. He had just returned from Jasper. "I was about to go on vacation with my son when I walked into a parks meeting in Banff," he said. "I told them that they needed to back-burn Fairholme before it blew up on them. No one wanted to do that because we promised the business community that we wouldn't burn in summer. They didn't want the smoke to deter tourists from coming."

In the days that followed, Walker got word from Heathcott that Crowsnest Pass was being evacuated and that Wood Buffalo, Canada's largest national park, was burning big, just as it often does when it is hot and dry. The situation in Glacier had also taken a turn for the worse on July 23 when the jet stream dropped, causing the Trapper fire in the park to blow up and the Robert fire just outside the park to grow from 10 acres to 1,945 acres in a few hours. When the Trapper fire made a run for the Granite Park Chalet, park officials closed the road, leaving forty-one people stranded at the chalet for the night. Water bombers from Canada were brought in. Plans to evacuate 3,000 people from the MacDonald Valley were made that night. Mick Holm, the parks superintendent, was also presented with the risky proposition of lighting a back-burn below Apgar Mountain to prevent or slow the fire from engulfing the town West Glacier.

"I remember at one time, my deputy and I went up to Lake McDonald and we were standing on the lake, watching the scooper planes

from Canada pick up water," he recalled. "That was one of those moments where we realized that this was going to be something people
will remember."

By then, everyone in Parks Canada knew as well that 2003 was turning out to be a fire season like no other and that it was time to develop
a new strategy. Because there were so many fires burning on both sides
of the border, resources would be limited, if they were going to be
available at all.

On July 25, Parks Canada formed a geographic area command team
composed of senior managers to develop strategies and priorities for
fires in the national parks of western Canada, dividing the area into
northern, central, and southern zones.

"There were two heavies, Crane and Chinook helicopters, based at
the Banff airport," Heathcott recalled. "We considered the Banff and
Kootenay fires as a single operating area during this time, with additional operating areas in the west at Glacier, Mount Revelstoke, and
Jasper national parks. Wood Buffalo was the park we really stripped of
personnel and resources. The fire management officers there joked with
me that they felt like they were in *Apocalypse Now*, sold down the river."

Wood Buffalo wasn't the only park that got poached. Banff's fire-
fighting team was so badly depleted of experienced fire personnel that
Pengelly dubbed the crew he ended up with in late July and August as
"The Leftovers."

~

In Kootenay, Kubian was feeling confident about the challenges that
lay ahead, especially because a helicopter base had been constructed at
south end of the park the year before. Air power could now be brought
in and kept close by if a wildfire threatened people and important assets. Thanks to Heathcott, who anticipated the big fire season that was
coming, Nikita Lopoukhine, director general of Parks Canada, sent a
memo to all the superintendents of national parks in Canada to place
firefighters and wardens on standby to offer on-the-ground support if
needed.

Still, Kubian, Walker, Heathcott, and Jeff Weir, a fire incident commander who was brought in from Prince Albert to help with the firefighting plans in Kootenay, couldn't help but be humbled when six

lightning strikes lit up the tinder-dry mountain forests in Kootenay during the last three days of July, with the Tokumm Creek and Verendrye fires signaling that they would be the most challenging.

"We suspected then that it was going to be a nightmare season that our national parks overhead team had been talking about for some time," recalled Walker, who is now responsible for wildfire-, vegetation-, and forestry-related issues for the greater city of Victoria on Vancouver Island. "One of these years, we kept telling ourselves, we're going to have a year like this. And we did."

~

No one fully appreciated it at the time, but the 2003 fire season was a harbinger for what a warming climate would do to wildfire activity in the northern forests and was a forerunner to the catastrophic events that unfolded at Slave Lake in 2011, the record 2015 wildfire season that made headlines in Canada and the United States, and Fort McMurray in 2016. It literally begged scientists, firefighters, and decision makers to rethink and critically examine the way wildfire, wildlife, water resources, and trees are managed in a world that is warming as fast as it may have been cooling 500 million years ago.

Johann Goldammer, director of the Global Fire Monitoring Center at Germany's Freiburg University, is widely recognized as the person who alerted the world to the northern forest's inextricable link to the fate of the global environment. Following publication of a research paper in 2006 that documented what he meant by that, he likened the boreal forest to a carbon bomb. "It's sitting there waiting to be ignited, and there is already ignition going on," he wrote.[5]

The link between wildfire and climate, however, had been made by Canadian and American scientists long before that. The media just didn't notice.

Mike Flannigan and Charlie Van Wagner raised the issue of climate change's impact on wildfire in 1990 with a report that suggested a 46 percent increase in fire severity if the climate heated up in the way that was being forecast at the time. "These increases would not necessarily wreak havoc on Canadian forests," they wrote, with perhaps unintended understatement.[6] Without stating it, they seemed to imply that it might.

Brian Stocks was a lot more forthright in a report that he wrote three years later. Early on in a career that began in the 1960s, Stocks was more interested in the pure science of fire research than the policy implications associated with it. That began to change in 1985, however, when he attended a wildfire meeting in Boulder, Colorado, where he met with US Forest Service scientists as well as Richard Turco and other nuclear winter thinkers. The issue of climate change was raised then.

Stocks's eyes widened when he saw what the world's biggest wildfire did when it killed more than six hundred people in China in 1987. That fire, the Yellowstone fires, and the fires that burned 10 percent of Manitoba in 1989 convinced him that the worst was yet to come and that both Canada and the United States were woefully unprepared to deal with the heat that was going to dry out the northern forests in the coming decades.

"It was obvious that a warming climate in the future would require a rethinking of forest fire management priorities and a reevaluation of fire in forest management in North America," Stocks wrote in 1993.[7] There would be no "quick fix solutions," he and Michael Weber noted in another report. "Increased fire activity would strain current levels of fire suppression resources, but may also adversely affect boreal forest distribution with a concomitant reduction in plant and animal biodiversity."[8]

The Canadian government, however, wasn't listening as it was rapidly moving away from fire research. In 1995, the Canadian Forest Service's budget was cut from $221 million to just $96 million. The last experimental burning program ended in 2000. Fire eventually ceased to be a separate research program. By 2012, the annual budget for wildfire research was just $1.3 million, forty times less than the US Forest Service was spending. As well-funded as it was by comparison, the US Forest Service wasn't happy, because an increasing amount of its budget was being diverted to the kind of intense fire suppression that resulted in triaging in 2003.

~

In some ways, there was nothing special about the way things initially unfolded in the northwestern part of the continent in the summer of

2003. Lightning Alley in Kootenay, for example, has always been a magnet for electrical storms, as Kubian pointed out that day we met in the summer of 2016. In Glacier, there has been a big fire every year, except one (1964), since the park was established. The Salmon-Challis National Forest in Idaho is known as the "fire forest" for obvious reasons. It's had more than its share of big, catastrophic fires since the 1910 fire burned a 50-mile swath of forest from the Salmon River to and beyond the Canadian border. One might also argue that the fire seasons of 1994, 1995, and 1998 were even bigger than the one that occurred in 2003.

The 2003 season was different, though. Not only did many of the fires burn bigger, hotter, faster, and in unpredictable ways, they were threatening people, homes, and infrastructure in ways that had only previously played out in firefighters' nightmares.

"The Kootenay fires were the 'holy shit' fire of a lifetime," said Kubian. "Every time we put someone in a helicopter to have a look at it [the Kootenay fire], they'd say 'holy shit.' Every time I flew over it, I would get a lump in my throat looking over between Banff and Lake Louise where there was a near continuous stand of old-growth forest just waiting to go up in flames.

"Only a handful of people know how close things came to lighting up the Banff side where the forest went on forever. At times, the fire had its own mind, doing whatever it wanted to do. Fortunately, we made the right decisions and contained it. But it was awful close. We learned a lot of lessons that year."

∽

The hardest lessons began the first week of August when Paul Holscher, owner of the Kootenay Park Lodge, refused to abandon the historic Canadian Pacific Railway tourist facility that he bought in 1990. He was on hand the night the storm swept in on July 30.

"I've seen quite a few electrical storms pass through here, but never a strike," he recalled. "So I'm always looking. It was around suppertime when I saw one hit very high up, very deep in the Verendrye above us. Initially, the trees candled. Then the fire died down. I thought it was out. But at 11 o'clock, I looked out again and it had flared up. So I reported it to Parks Canada."

Rob Walker was already in a helicopter that night to assess another lightning strike reported at Taylor Lake on the Banff side of the park. "Lightning was flashing all around us," recalled Walker. "It was quite a show. But the storm didn't produce a drop of rain. Given the tinder-dry conditions of the forests, I knew we were going to be seriously challenged at some point along the way."

With virtually every firefighting resource in the western half of the continent tied up dealing with those fires in Jasper, Glacier, Idaho, Oregon, Waterton, the Crowsnest Pass, Manitoba, and Wood Buffalo, the second largest national park in the world, Parks Canada decided to call in firefighters who were on standby in twenty-two other national parks across the country.

The added manpower, which included people from the provinces and the territories, was as much a curse as it was a blessing. Each region and jurisdiction, be it on the Canadian side or the American side of the border, has its own way of dealing with a fire. Americans, for example, are known to be less risk averse and much more aggressive fighting fires. Canadians tend to be more cautious—a sounder approach, they say unabashedly—which is backed up by statistics. Almost no one dies fighting fires in Canada.

The mountain landscape also proved to be a problem for the flat-land firefighters. Fires in the mountains tend to move up a slope fast rather than sideways. So, in Kootenay, Yoho, Banff, and Jasper, being comfortable in the mountainous terrain is important for safety reasons. Those who have never fought a fire on a steep slope are at added risk of getting in harm's way.

Cognizant of this inexperience and knowing that proper training was wanting for some of those who were brought in, Walker was prepared at one point to send the men and women from Newfoundland and the Maritimes home. "In the end, they talked me out of it. The wildfires were such a big news story in Newfoundland and the Maritimes, they didn't want to be seen coming home with their tails between their legs. It was matter of pride. I had bad dreams letting them stay, but in the end, it worked out reasonably well," Walker said.

Even with the added firefighters, no one anticipated how quickly the challenges would mount. That first night, the Tokumm fire flared near the Yoho/Banff border in Kootenay. At first, it covered an area of only 5 acres (2 hectares); by the next morning, it had spread to a little more than 12 acres (5 hectares). By the time Walker returned in a helicopter the second evening to give Michel Boivin, the superintendent for Yoho, Kootenay, and Lake Louise, a bird's-eye view of what they were facing, there was a 15,000-foot column of smoke billowing into the air. In just a matter of hours, Tokumm had grown into a 247-acre (100-hectare) inferno just as three more fires—at Healy Creek, Spray River, and Parson/Beaverfoot just outside the park—were about to be ignited by more late-afternoon lightning.

When a second lightning strike at Taylor Lake was discovered the next day, Banff warden Patrick Langan, a former Alberta Forest Service employee with nearly three hundred firefighting missions under his belt, was on-site at 6:30 a.m. All he found was a single charred tree that was barely smoldering. But when a helicopter dropped a bucket of water on it an hour later, it went from a no-smoke, no-flame situation to one of huge candling and torching in 10 seconds.

"It was outrageous fire behavior," Langan recalled. "It was like we poured a bucket of gasoline on it. What happened, I figure, is that the downdraft that came with the falling water lit it up. Everything around that tree was so dry that the water wasn't enough to put out the fire."

Recognizing the explosive nature of the situation, Langan took the extreme measure of calling in an air tanker on contract to the Alberta government to drop some chemical retardants on the site.

Calling in an air tanker is an extremely costly move. These amphibious flying boat–type aircraft have the capability of scooping water from large lakes and delivering long-term fire retardants from tanker bases. Not only do they a require a tremendous amount of fuel to fly, they also need a "bird dog" aircraft, with an air attack officer on board, to assess and formulate the attack plan before leading the tanker to its target. Before that can happen, the air space in the area has to be cleared.

Although it might have seemed like overkill for such a small fire, Langan's call turned out to have been the right thing to do. Taylor Lake sits in the Bow Valley between the towns of Banff and Lake Louise. All that stood between the townsites was a 29.8-mile-long (48-km-long) stand of old-growth forest that had been saved from thinning by more than half a century of fire suppression. With few natural breaks in the forest for firefighters to work from, a runaway blaze here could easily have turned into what Parks Canada fire coordinator Dave Smith likes to call an "ABC burn." A, in this case, stands for armchair, B, for binoculars, and C, for a can of beer.

"That's about all you can do" Smith told me. "Sit back in an armchair, get out your binoculars, and pop open a can of beer. Contrary to what the public might believe, you can't put out a big fire once it gets momentum."

Helicopters and water buckets may not be able to put out a big fire, but they can steer a fire away from places where it may do harm to people and to infrastructure. Because nearly all the air power available in western North America was tied up fighting fires outside the parks that summer, Walker had to search high and sometimes dry to find the helicopter he needed. Supply was so tight that one helicopter—an aging Hughes 500—broke down twice on the way to Kootenay. When it finally arrived with a pilot who also appeared to have seen better days, Walker knew after a couple of days of flying with him that it wasn't going to work out. He sent the helicopter and the pilot home.

Even with the helicopter base that had been built the summer before, the task of keeping choppers in the air was a challenge. Thick smoke and an extremely narrow air space in Kootenay's Vermillion Valley posed some serious problems. The days were often as dark as the nights because of the smoke. Invariably, pilots were compelled to stick religiously to a predetermined flight path. Some days, weather inversions filled the valleys with so much smoke that the choppers weren't able to take off until afternoon.

Heathcott and his colleagues in the national fire coordination center also faced the challenge of deciding which parks needed the helicopters most. Just a day before the Kootenay fires got started, for example, they made the decision to send four choppers north to Jasper. There, the Syncline Ridge fire was threatening to take another run on the eve of a major folk festival and one of the busiest weekends of the year in Jasper.

～

The Syncline Ridge fire was ignited in May to create a firebreak along the Rocky River, where years of diligent fire suppression had led to an unnaturally dense stand of highly combustible old-growth forest.

If left the way it was, it could have ended up burning all the way to the appropriately named Disaster Point and to the town of Hinton, where some 10,000 people live. Parks Canada was counting on June monsoons to help put the fire out. When the arid conditions persisted, gusting winds that kicked up on July 25 pushed the fire across the Rocky River.

This fire required a lot of airpower to keep it in the Rocky River basin and out of the Fiddle and Athabasca River valleys. Firefighters from Alberta and the Yukon, fire behavior specialists from the Canadian Forest Service, contract crews from Ontario, and national parks personnel were brought in to help.

Back from La Mauricie, Steve Otway, who was based in Elk Island National Park, didn't hesitate when he got the call to lead the suppression effort. As confident as he was about all he had learned about wildfire over the years, he admits that he never felt as much pressure as he experienced over that next week. In an effort to prevent the fire from jumping into the Athabasca Valley, he arranged to drop some fuel in the area to prevent some tourist facilities from burning. That was July 28.

Although the risky maneuver worked, the situation turned critical again on August 1, when an approaching cold front threatened to bring the fire to the Yellowhead Highway. This route is used by thousands of tourists to get in and out of the park.

"At the time, I thought, 'This is it,' " recalled Dave Smith, who was there to help orchestrate the firefighting plan. "With a cold front, you get all kinds of in-flows and out-flows that can push the fire in any kind of direction. And we had a big one going. But then Steve comes up with this plan and says, 'Hey guys, we can do this.' I knew at the time that what he was proposing was the right thing to do. But I also knew that it was risky. If this thing got away on us, there would be hell to pay."

Otway's plan involved dropping twenty-eight barrels of gelled fuel onto the forest above Talbot Lake and bringing the fire down to the Yellowhead Highway in a controlled fashion. To do that, Parks Canada would have stop thousands of cars from coming in on the highway.

"I knew that if we didn't bring the fire to the highway when we were ready, it was going to do it on its own," said Otway. "And it wasn't going to stop at the road. It was going to keep going unless we removed some of the fuel in front of it. Sure, it was a calculated risk. But it was a lot better than the alternative, which was to fight this fire on an even bigger front in the Athabasca Valley where it could have gone in all kinds of directions."

Otway fully understood what they were getting into. If a back-burn like the one he was proposing were to be successful in removing all the targeted trees, the firefighters would end up patting themselves on the back because no one else would ever appreciate what they had pulled off. If it weren't to turn out that way, people would be pointing fingers and blaming them for all that damage that was done.

With Alberta government's air tanker group, the Edson Fire Centre, and two bulldozer groups on standby, Parks Canada closed the Yellowhead Highway and notified the five thousand people who were living in the town of Jasper. The possibility of an evacuation wasn't part of the message, but it was in the contingency plan if the back-burn got away on them.

As traffic backed up for 31 miles (50 kilometers), a helicopter dropped the fuel in the path of the fire. When Smith saw the 2.5-mile-long, 230-foot-high (4-kilometer-long, 70-meter-high) wall of flame with a 25,000-foot (7,620-meter) column of smoke on top of it marching away from the highway, he was uncharacteristically at a loss for words in describing what the back-burn looked like. "At the time, I was in awe. This was Mother Nature in all her fury. It was a humbling sight," he said.

Eight hours later, traffic was moving again on the Yellowhead. "When the road opened at 9:30 at night, it was quite the light show for people that were driving by," said Otway. "They may have been tired and frustrated, maybe even mad, but I think they understood why we had to close the road."

Even with this success, there was no time to sit back and take a breather. Three days later, employees who operate a chalet and boat trips in the popular area spotted a menacing plume of smoke near the shores of Maligne Lake. Had an air tanker and ground crew not been on hand that day to cool things off and contain the fire, the 35-acre (14-hectare) blaze could have easily moved down the valley toward Jasper Park Lodge and the Jasper townsite.

"It was a case of us being in the right place at the right time," said Smith. "Our computer models show that had we not moved in with the ground crew and then called in the air tanker as quickly as we did, that 14-hectare fire would have grown to 1,000 hectares by nine that night. Then we would have had another major fire on the landscape possibly heading toward Jasper."

~

To this day, Rob Walker isn't so sure that the helicopters and ground crews that were deployed in Jasper and elsewhere could have contained the situation in Kootenay, which was worsening each day in August. The Tokumm Creek and Verendrye Creek fires were becoming increasingly vicious.

"To tell you the truth, we had drawn a line in the sand at Vermillion Pass a week or so after Jeff Weir came in from Prince Albert National Park to be part of our core team," he said. "We knew looking at the big picture that this fire had the potential to jump into the Bow Valley and on to Lake Louise or Banff at some point if we didn't get some rain or cooler weather. We had it in the back of our mind that we might have to pull back at some point to see what equipment was available. If there's a really big emergency, then we take it to another level."

The fire situation was serious enough that Michel Boivin, superintendent of Lake Louise, decided as a precautionary measure to shut down west Yoho National Park to the public, plus nearly everything in Kootenay, including Holscher's lodge, and Highway 93 to Radium.

Parks Canada officials used the lodge as a base from which to fight some of the fires. Life at the lodge was nothing short of surreal over the next three weeks, according Walker. Parks Canada put up pilots and some of its support staff at the facility. They deployed sprinklers and helicopters to soak down the buildings and adjacent trees. During the day, thousands of birds from the forest took cover in the humidity that all the moisture created. At night, the remaining staff would sit back and watch the wildfire on the hillside put on a show that looked as if dancing dragons were breathing fire on the landscape.

Although the crews were successfully holding off the fires from spreading to the lodge, the battle was quickly being lost on several other fronts. The Tokumm and Verendrye fires continued to grow in

Figure 4-2 The 2003 fires in Kootenay and other places in western Canada and the United States taxed firefighting resources to and beyond limits. In some places, triaging was the order of the day. (Niddrie, Parks Canada)

size, and then lightning and hot weather brought life to old and new fires in neighboring Yoho National Park at Emerald Lake, Little Yoho Lake, and Takakkaw Falls. To complicate matters even further, the initial attack on one of them had to be delayed because of an unusually large number of campers in the area who disregarded Parks Canada's backcountry restrictions.

The Kootenay team finally got a bit of relief on August 6 with the arrival of a giant Sikorsky Skycrane, which has about eight times the loading capacity of the next largest chopper on-site. By this time, though, it could do little to contain the Tokumm and Verendrye fires, which had spread to more than 2,471 and 7,413 acres (1,000 and 3,000 hectares), respectively.

"At one point, I thought to myself, 'When will this ever end?' " recalled Kubian. "We were putting in eighteen hours a day and pushing all of our resources to the limit. And each time the five-day weather forecast would come in it would call for more hot, dry weather. We just couldn't get a break."

They never did get the break they were hoping for. On August 9, the Verendrye fire took a spectacular run toward Banff.

"We had worked and worked to contain it," said Kubian. "We put an unbelievable amount of water on that fire. And here was this big orange smile chugging up the valley towards the pass towards the Banff side. We estimated that at one point it was moving 2 kilometers per hour. It was an incredible sight."

The day of reckoning came in the third week of August when Rob Walker returned from a regular morning flight. He was convinced that a plan that Weir had hatched to back-burn at Vermillion Pass was the only thing that could stop the fire from moving into Banff and possibly forcing the evacuation of tens of thousands of people who were living there or visiting. If there was cause to reconsider, it was because of the way in which these fires were behaving. Severe wildfires are inherently unpredictable, but these fires were redefining just how difficult it is to read the mind of wildfire when it is so hot and dry and when there is so much fuel on the ground.

"This was not a normal fire," Walker recalled, echoing what Darby Allen would say about the The Beast in Fort McMurray thirteen years later. "It had a mind of its own. It defied everything that one learns about wildfire behavior. I had expected that the deciduous vegetation along the slide paths would slow it down because deciduous trees hold more moisture and burn more slowly than the conifers. But those trees just vaporized in the fire's path. It was like a dragon breathing fire on dry grass."

At 5 p.m. on August 18, a meeting was called for all the senior Parks Canada managers who had been involved in some way or another. Jillian Roulet, the superintendent of Banff, Gaby Fortin, the director-general for western Canada, Ed Abbott, the chief park warden for

Lake Louise, and Terry McGuire, the man in charge of highways and assets in western parks, as well as Boivin, Walker, Kubian, and Weir, attended.

They were in exactly the same situation that Otway and Smith had been in Jasper a few weeks earlier. Everyone realized then that they would be dammed if they didn't do anything and damned if the back-burn that Weir had proposed to light at Vermilion Pass got away on them. The stakes in this case were much higher. In the end, no time was wasted giving the team the go-ahead. Bulldozers, track hoes, portable retardant mixing bases, heavy lift helicopters, and an agricultural sprinkler system that Weir had brought in from Saskatchewan were used to build and hold this line in immature lodgepole pine and steep mountain topography.

Walker remembers well what happened next.

Pat Langan was given the job of overseeing the removal of all the trees along a 98-foot-wide (30-meter-wide) line on both sides of the road. Once that was done, recently arrived environment employees from the Saskatchewan government tied together 1.2 miles (2 kilometers) of heavy-duty hose. This line of sprinklers would be used to soak the vegetation. Langan was convinced the guard would do the job once they sprayed some of the hard-to-get areas with chemical retardants.

Others, however, admit there were times when they were holding their breath and crossing their fingers, wondering if a back-burn such as the one they were about to light was going to stop a fire that was moving like a freight train toward them.

Computer models that help formulate these kinds of maneuvers suggest that ignition should take place only when the winds are blowing 9.3 miles (15 kilometers) an hour or slower. The plan also required a number of helicopters to be on hand in case the fire got away on them.

Right about that time, though, the fire situation in Mount Revelstoke National Park was heightening to emergency levels, and the prescribed burn that got away from Pengelly's "Leftovers" overtook a power line that provided electricity to the Banff townsite. Power was out. As a result, the decision was made by Heathcott, the wildfire coordinator in Parks Canada's Calgary office, to send all Kootenay's heavy helicopters and three of its five medium-sized ones to deal with the new emergencies.

Without the air power, the Verendrye and Tokumm fires continued to spread on all flanks. On August 19, Kubian, Weir, and Walker looked at one another and realized that it was time to initiate the back-burn. There was just one problem, however, and it was a big one. The winds up at the pass were gusting beyond the 9.3 mile (15 kilometer) an hour limit, up to 16.7 miles (27 kilometers) an hour at times, so the chances of their back-burn getting away on the crews were significantly higher.

"I'll never forget what happened next," said Walker. "It was like a tailgate party. Michel Boivin was on hand, and we came over and gave him the bad news. We told him that we were better off risking failure than letting this thing come to us. You could tell he was nervous."

"For a second there, I could see that he was bug-eyed," said Weir.

"It was very windy and our fire was creating a lot of smoke." Boivin recalled. "Helicopters were flying everywhere and radios were crackling. The tension was palpable. I knew that if things went wrong that day, then it would have been perceived as us, not the wildfire, that set Banff on fire. It was a very stressful few hours."

The day of reckoning came when the Verendrye fire took another spectacular run toward Vermilion Pass. The plume of smoke it produced was so enormous that people in Lake Louise thought the fire was right on top of them.

"It was one of those sights that you'll never forget," said Kubian. "I was up in one helicopter with Jeff Weir and Rob was in another. From up there, the fire looked like a freight train going up the valley. We knew that in a matter of hours it was going to challenge our fireguard."

Ahead of the fire that day, huge pieces of charred branches and lichen rained down on the fire crews at Vermilion Pass, but when the so-called freight train hit the fireguard, the giant leading plume of smoke stood up on itself and came to a halt as the fire ran out of fuel to burn. The gutsy strategy did exactly what the cheering firefighters had hoped it would do.

～

The 2003 fire season didn't end there. Fires in British Columbia later that summer forced the evacuation of 45,000 people. The Cedar fire that burned a record 280,000 acres in October and November destroyed nearly three thousand homes and buildings. States of emergency were declared.

Most everyone was beginning to realize that no one was prepared for the carbon bomb that was waiting to be ignited by lightning, an arsonist, or careless people living, working, or recreating in the northern forests. They also sensed that the 2003 fire season was forcefully signaling the new wildfire paradigm that was emerging.

Following the Big Blowup of 2003, inquiries were called and debriefings were conducted. One of the most comprehensive looked into the firestorm that engulfed much of the interior of British Columbia. Former Manitoba premier Gary Filmon, the man who headed up that inquiry, suggested that this fire season offered up a "once-in-a-lifetime opportunity to implement risk reduction policies and legislation while the devastation of Firestorm 2003 is fresh in the public's mind and the costs and consequences of various choices are well understood."⁹

Decision makers, however, didn't listen, at least not to the degree they were being asked and told to. Big fires, for which firefighters weren't prepared, followed in Slave Lake in 2011, all across the United States and Canada in 2015, and in Fort McMurray in 2016. Of the ten years with the largest amount of acreage burned in the United States, eight have occurred since the 2003 fire season, nine if you go back to the 2000 fire season.

No one quite appreciated it at the time, but the legacy of these megafires and future fires would live on for years to come in the quality of river water that flows from the burned forests, in the air people breathe, and in the effects the fires have on wildlife and human safety. Increasingly, megafires would ignite those so-called carbon bombs that would continue to drive wildfires to burn even bigger, hotter, and faster and in more dangerous ways.

Chapter 5

Water on Fire

Sullen were we in the sweet air, that is gladdened by the Sun,
carrying lazy smoke within our hearts; now lie we
sullen here in the black mire.
— Dante Alighieri, *The Divine Comedy*

If you are a wildfire fighter or scientist, you know the story of the Hayman fire that burned 138,000 acres (56,000 hectares) of forest in 2002. The fire started on June 2 and burned out of control in and around the counties of Douglas, Jefferson, Park, and Teller for the next six weeks. For a short time, a squall of white ash transformed the city of Denver into an early Christmas scene, albeit one that was filled with acrid smoke instead of fresh mountain air and snow. In a single day, the fire made a 19-mile run. It was an unusually severe fire for a low-elevation ponderosa-dominated forest landscape. Like the Horse River fire that burned fourteen years later in northern Alberta, this fire burned so hot that it created its own weather. Governor Bill Owens famously stated at the time that "it looks as if all of Colorado is burning."[1] It was not. But that, and rumors suggesting the fires were "bearing down" on the city of Denver, did stop many tourists from coming to the state.[2]

If you're a forest firefighter, you know that Terry Lynn Barton, a US Forest Service worker, confessed that in an overwrought moment of despair, she drove up to Lake George in the front range of the Rockies, lit a match to letters from her estranged husband, and tossed them into a campfire pit before the fire somehow got away on her. She spent five years in jail after her lawyer negotiated a plea bargain for her.

Given the damage that was done by the fire and lingering doubts about Barton's story, many people thought the sentence was too lenient.

Six lives were lost in the Hayman fire. Five of them were Oregon firefighters who died in a traffic accident. Six hundred structures, including 133 residences, were destroyed. Some 5,340 people were forced to evacuate; 14,000 were told to be ready to leave on a moment's notice.

The fire had a devastating effect on the state's economy. Pike National Forest, home to Canada lynx, the flammulated owl, and dozens of other species of concern, was shut down for most of the busiest part of the tourist season. Ranchers lost feed, equipment, and fencing. Small businesses suffered. That was expected. By most accounts, the lynx, owls, and other animals recovered. So did the ranchers and the small businesses. What was unexpected was the impact the fire had on water, the water in which fish and other aquatic forms of life live and the water people drink.

Water is something to fight fire with, but as the Hayman fire showed, the hydrologic relationship between watersheds and wildfire is much more complex, with each affecting the other in ways we need to study more carefully. The state of Colorado, and the city of Denver in particular, paid a very high price learning this lesson. Hundreds of cities in the more northerly boreal regions of the continent may soon pay the price as well.

Here's what happened in the years that followed the Hayman fire. Fire removed many of the trees from parts of the mountain landscape. The soils in those denuded landscapes baked in dry, hot drought conditions that followed. Some spring-fed streams stopped flowing. Chemical compounds that were vaporized by the fire got driven into the soil. As they condensed, they formed an impervious layer just below the surface. *Hydrophobic* is the word that geologists use to describe such soils.

Without trees, vegetation, and a stable soil structure to absorb the heavy rains that eventually followed in the denuded Rocky Mountain landscape, tons of ash, debris, heavy metals, and nutrients were flushed through the watershed. Washed-out highways were the least of the problems. The after-effects of the fire also led to the precipitous decline of the blue-ribbon South Platte River trout fishery, which was the best of any river in the United States within a one-hour drive from a major city. Worst of all was that the affected watershed provides drinking water to 75 percent of the state's residents. Hundreds of tons of sediment filled lakes and reservoirs. Intakes got clogged. Water quality suffered, not just for a few days, but for several years.

To find a solution, more than sixty scientists from various disciplines were brought in. Crews dredged out tens of thousands of tons of sediment. More than 175,000 trees were planted. Still, the drinking water quality problems persisted.

Michael Stevens, a US Geological Survey hydrologist who monitored water quality in the years that followed the Hayman fire, notes that this kind of thing has happened before, most notably in 1996 when a once-in-a-hundred-to-a-thousand-year thunderstorm resulted in a record amount of rain falling on the denuded landscape that burned two months after the Buffalo Creek fire near Denver. US Geological Survey colleagues Deborah Martin and John Moody tracked the flow of organic debris, sediment, and chemicals all the way to the city of Denver's drinking water reservoir.

This kind of erosion is not unique to the geological landscape of Colorado. It occurs in the granitic regions of Idaho and other places. The scale and longevity of what happened following Hayman nonetheless surprised Stevens.

Two years after the fire, 2.2 inches of rain fell on the area. It took just forty-five minutes for the flow of water in West Creek to rise from 62 cubic feet per second to 2,170 cubic feet per second.

"It's pretty shocking just how much sediment and debris can be yielded in an event such as that following a fire," said Stevens. "It required some pretty heroic efforts by people working for the city of Denver to prevent it from overwhelming their water treatment operations."

The Hayman fire may have been an outlier in the severe ways it burned, but it was a wake-up call that put phone numbers of under-appreciated forest hydrologists and engineers across the continent at

7/12/06

Figure 5-1 The Hayman fire of 2002 in Colorado resulted in serious flooding that threatened trout, wildlife, and the drinking water of 75 percent of the state's residents. The stick that is being held here in this photo shows how high water levels rose in just 45 minutes. (Michael Stevens USGS)

the fingertips of municipal and agency officials. Two-thirds of the municipalities in the United States and most of those in Canada get their drinking water from forested areas. Many of these watersheds are already feeling the strain of drought, industrial pollution, and climate change. The increase in severe wildfires will pose a big challenge in the future.

More than thirty of Colorado's largest wildfires have occurred since 1996. The Waldo Canyon fire of 2012 was the most expensive. It resulted in more than $250 million in insurance claims, $16 million in suppression costs, and a still-running total in mitigation treatments designed to prevent flooding and maintain water quality. The Rim fire that burned parts of Yosemite National Park the following year created similar challenges, impacting as it did the Tuolumne River watershed that supplies water to San Francisco and other communities in San Mateo, Santa Clara, and Alameda Counties.

As the climate warms the boreal and montane forests to the north, similar challenges will follow, just as they did in Fort McMurray.

~

Uldis Silins was, at one time, one of those underappreciated forest hydrologists. Not anymore. He was in his office at the University of Alberta in Canada when he got a call in early May 2016, shortly after the Fort McMurray wildfire ignited in the forest 3.7 miles (6 kilometers) south of town. The call was from Dr. Ronald Reid, the drinking water quality regulator with the Alberta government. That initial conversation led to a series of one-on-one conference calls with various people in government to assess the immediate risks and determine what could be done to prevent what happened in Colorado in 1996, 2002, and in 2012 and in California in 2013.

"I had forty-four emails in my inbox that day," Silins recalled. "A series of first-order and second-order assessments and actions were scoped out. Over the next several days, meetings and conference calls laddered this information into a broader group of government organizations dealing with immediate assessment and planning issues for this fire."

Monica Emelko was one of the first people Silins called. It was Mother's Day. The American-born, University of Waterloo engineer was at Florida's Disney World with her children. Still rebounding from a five-year bout with cancer, Emelko hesitated only for a moment before she accepted the invitation to come to Fort McMurray.

Emelko and Silins are Canada's version of Marc Edwards, the American environmental engineer who has spent a good part of his career exposing the breakdown of America's aging waterworks in cities such as Washington, DC, and Flint, Michigan. Unlike Edwards, who investigates contaminants like lead that are already in the system, Emelko and Silins specialize in preventing contaminants from getting in.

Like Denver, San Francisco, and most modern North American cities, Fort McMurray has a state-of-the-art water treatment plant with the ability to deal with chemicals and harmful pathogens. The inevitable overload of dissolved carbon and sediment coming from a big fire burning just a few hundred feet upstream of the intake pipes, however, has the potential to interfere with the disinfection process, just like plugging the drain of a dishwasher. When that happens, water quality can change rapidly, to the point at which it becomes extremely dangerous. Carbon reacts with chlorine and produces undesirable chemical by-products, including known and suspected carcinogens. No one working at the treatment plant had the expertise to deal with a public health threat such as that.

Silins and Emelko flew up to Fort McMurray. They collected water samples upstream of the plant, surveyed the burn area by helicopter, and then met with senior water treatment operator Guy Jette and his crew to discuss the challenges they were already facing and the ones they would likely confront down the road when it finally rained.

Jette was his own media story. He was there from the very beginning when fire and smoke surrounded the water treatment facility shortly after the entire town was evacuated. He and nine others stayed behind, working twenty-hour shifts to make sure water would get to the firefighters in town. They slept on the floor and ate days' old lunches that had been left behind in the refrigerator. When smoke disabled part of the computer monitoring system, they reverted to guesswork, looking out the control room window to see where the fires were burning in the city and where the limited supply of water they could pump was needed most.

Increasing the water supply through four newly installed filters, as Jette needed to do at one critical point, would have required him to conduct time-consuming bacteria tests. With no time to spare as the fire continued to rage, he made a call that gave him the go-ahead to pump. The result was a boil-water order for residents who returned in June.

Residents eventually got the clean water they needed, but not without having to pay a steep price. In 2015, Fort McMurray spent about $1 million on chemicals to treat its water. In 2016, the city had to spend about $500,000 more. Because there is still so much dissolved carbon and sediment entering the river from the fire-scarred zones, the city may have to pay as much as $2 million in 2017.

~

The science of wildfire hydrology has been around for some time. P. J. Gerla and J. M. Galloway described how the 1988 wildfire in

Yellowstone National Park dramatically increased nitrates, phosphorus, and dissolved solids in Jones Creek.[3] Because the effects of wildfire in most cases were not long lasting or were poorly documented, most government agencies wouldn't consider funding research into this field of expertise.

When the Buffalo Creek and Hayman fires came along, that kind of thinking began to change, not just for cities such as Fort McMurray with state-of-the-art treatment systems, but also for cities like Victoria in British Columbia that don't have filtration systems because the quality of the raw water used there is so high. The water supplies of cities like Victoria would be particularly vulnerable if a wildfire were to flush ash, sediment, and dissolved carbon into their watersheds.

Silins's involvement in this field had a serendipitous beginning. Between 2000 and 2003, he was scoping out watershed studies at sites in the Rocky Mountain House region of west central Alberta. Each time he rooted himself in a place that satisfied his criteria, however, an oil and gas operation would come in and force him out, not because they didn't want him there, but because their presence negatively affected what he had hoped to do.

In August 2003, Silins got a call from Bob Anderson of the Alberta Forest Service asking him to come down to Crowsnest Pass. Anderson wanted to see if Silins would do a watershed study on the Lost Creek fire that was burning out of control and forcing the evacuation of 2,000 people in the Rocky Mountains in southern Alberta.

"The fire was still out of control when I got there in August," said Silins. "We had a number of field meetings before I got up in a helicopter to have a look. In October, I was back selecting watershed sites that would be best suited for our hydrometric and water quality gauges, and for our climate stations. It really evolved from that point on. I ended up bringing a small mobile home to sleep in because there was no room in the government bunkhouse."

Silins was telling me about his work when I caught up with him at the wildfire study site he had set up in the Castle Crown Wilderness. The Fort McMurray forest was still on fire at the time.

Castle Crown is a part of the Rockies where loggers and grizzly bears have clashed, where environmentalists have been arrested for trying to stop logging, and where ATV drivers greatly outnumber hikers.

Heavily disturbed as it is, it is a mountain setting that still takes the breath away with its beauty.

Silins suggested that we drive up toward Mt. Coulthard on ATVs to get a better look at what he, Emelko, and their team of eleven scientists were up to. The route took us through an enduring scene of devastation that occurred in 2003 when the Lost Creek fire burned for nearly a month before consuming more than 54,000 acres (21,853 hectares) of forest in the headwaters of the Oldman River basin. In most of the forest we passed through, the trunks of trees that burned were still standing. In other places, they had fallen over, pushed down by powerful mountain winds or by rotting roots.

"The fire burned so hot in some places that it incinerated the seeds of the pine trees," Silins said as we stopped to look at one mountainside that had yet to recover in any appreciable way. "Instead of pine coming back, we got spruce that grew up from seeds had been blown in by the wind."

With his weathered face and handlebar moustache, Silins looks a little like Sam Elliot, who plays the cowboy in the cult film *The Big Lebowski*. Instead of a Stetson and spurs, however, Silins wears glasses and a baseball cap. He used a cane to steady himself when we stopped and walked along Lyons Creek, a fast-flowing trout stream that was burned over in 2003. When I asked about the cane and his noticeable limp, Silins told me matter-of-factly that it was because of multiple sclerosis. "Surprisingly, it is much better now than it was when I was younger," he said as he picked his way across the slippery rocks in knee-deep water.

Silins's original goal was to measure water quality and water quantity in this forest stream area that burned, in others that flowed through areas that had been salvaged by loggers, and in streambeds where there was no fire. It eventually morphed into a bigger study that examined how the fire affected vegetation, aquatic life, and water quality downstream of the forest. Virtually every rung on the food chain was monitored.

"See those rocks there on the creek bottom?" he asked as we walked along the banks of Lyons Creek. "What do you see?"

I picked up one of the rocks. It was slippery and almost completely coated in green algae.

When we stopped at another creek that flowed through a part of the forest that didn't burn, Silins offered an explanation. The rock that I picked up from that second creek bed was polished and free of vegetation.

"These are generally very nutrient-poor streams here in the mountains," Silins said. "Once you introduce nitrogen and phosphorus into the water, as wildfires do, you get algae and other plants growing very fast. Insects and macroinvertebrates feed on those plants. The size and diversity of these populations increase. Trout and other fish that feed on them grow bigger and faster. We've documented all of this thoroughly."

Outside of the boreal, subalpine, and montane regions such as those in the front ranges of the Rockies in Colorado, water quality generally recovers quickly after a wildfire. In the forests that Silins is studying, though, the changes in water quality have persisted much longer, even longer than Stevens and his colleagues documented. Thirteen years and counting, he and his colleagues were still seeing spikes in water quality that are beyond the range of normal.

According to Silins, the sedimentary nature of the rocks that are found in the foothills of the northern Rockies largely account for these spikes. Many of these rocks have been ground down to fine sediment by advancing and receding glaciers. These sediments act as vectors for heavy metals and contaminants that get flushed into a stream or river.

~

The following day, Monica Emelko joined us on a ride up to another part of the study area. Once again, it was hot, sunny, and windy. Emelko was jubilant at the prospects of getting to do a little hiking and to breathe some mountain air.

"A year ago, I wouldn't have had the stamina to spend a day out here doing this," she said. "Now, I'm beginning to feel normal again."

Unlike Silins, who is a forest hydrologist, Emelko approaches this field of study with a background in environmental engineering. It's a small world. She attended MIT at the same time I was there as a Knight Science Journalism fellow. From there she went on to the University of California, Los Angeles before ending up in Canada to do a doctorate followed by a professorship at the University of Waterloo in Ontario. She is married to Mike Stone, another scientist who works

Figure 5-2 Thirteen years and counting after the 2003 Lost Creek fire, scientist Uldis Silins (shown here) and his colleagues were still seeing spikes in water quality that are beyond the range of normal. (Edward Struzik)

on this project. He would have been there that day had the city of Calgary not called him in to help with some water quality issues that had emerged in the Glenmore Reservoir.

"Most of the municipalities in Canada and the United States get their drinking water from forested areas," Emelko told me after we walked across another fast-flowing stream to get to one of the water stations. "What we're seeing here and in Fort McMurray is going to be happening elsewhere, especially as the climate warms and as more severe fires burn.

"Megafires like this one at Lost Creek are the ones that decision makers should worry about," she said. "The more megafires that burn, the more money downstream communities such Fort McMurray will have to invest to improve their water treatment capabilities."

～

In the summer of 1982, I was driving up the Alaska Highway to do some hiking in Kluane and Denali national parks when a police roadblock stopped me and other cars near the northern British Columbia town of Fireside. A massive fire had recently burned through the area, so we needed to wait for a patrol car to ensure our safety. Up until that point, the Fireside fire was the second largest in British Columbia's history. I had never seen anything quite like what our convoy slowly passed through. In some places, the trees had been completely reduced to carbon. Female bears with cubs were walking along the road worried less about the approach of slow-moving cars and trucks than having to flee into a smoldering mess of charcoal. It looked like the aftermath of a nuclear winter that Sagan and others talked about in the 1980s.

Wildfires in the boreal region rarely turn a forest into ash. In most cases, there is enough pulp still standing for logging companies to come in and economically salvage what remains. For communities in the Lost Creek area that had already been hit hard by mine closures and other economic setbacks, it was a way to make the best of a bad situation.

Salvage logging is seen by some as good for the environment because it disturbs the soil and breaks up the hydrophobic soils that wildfires create. Thirsty seedlings end up getting more water and grow faster. The faster the trees and vegetation recover, the less chance there is for erosion and flooding to occur.

Research done by US Forest Service scientist Joseph Wagenbrenner suggests that it is not as simple as that. Over a ten-year period, Wagenbrenner and his colleagues looked at burns in Montana, Colorado, and Washington that had been left unlogged and compared them with burned-over forests that had been left to nature. Their findings suggest that burned-over forests recover faster if they are not salvaged than if they are.

Uldis Silins and Monica Emelko discovered something similar in the Lost Creek study site. In the areas that were salvaged, some chemical parameters were slow to recover to normal. Phosphorus was one of the most notable. Even after thirteen years, levels of phosphorus remained abnormally high. It was the first time anyone had seen the biological effects of a wildfire last that long.[4]

What baffled Silins and Emelko for a time is that the stream water temperature did not change, as one would expect would happen when more sunlight is allowed to come through. This finding is good news because the colder the water is, the less likely it is for phosphorus and other nutrients to promote vegetation growth, starve the water of oxygen, and kill trout and other fish. For the longest time, Silins wasn't sure why, but he eventually discovered that frigid groundwater that was percolating out of the mountainsides was keeping the streams cool. If and when that groundwater stops percolating, these mountain streams will be in serious trouble.

～

The day after I left the Lost Creek Study site, I was in a small bush plane piloted by Ric Hauer, a limnologist at the University of Montana in Missoula. The flight had really nothing to do with my research on wildfire and watersheds, or so I thought at the outset. (I learned later that Hauer's early research was foundational to the work that Silins was doing in the Oldman River watershed.)

At the behest of Harvey Locke, cofounder of the Yellowstone to Yukon (Y2Y) conservation initiative, I was there to hear what Hauer had to say about Y2Y's efforts to have Glacier and Waterton Lakes national parks in Montana and Alberta expanded to include a big chunk of the unprotected Flathead River watershed to the west.

Y2Y is near and dear to my heart. In 1998, I had written a magazine article on the initiative of reweaving the patchwork of protected areas from Yellowstone to the Yukon shortly after Locke and a small group of like-minded conservationists, scientists, and economists had come up with the big idea. Their goal was to create an interconnected wilderness corridor that would allow grizzly bears, wolves, cougars, lynx, wolverine, and other animals to move from one area to another.

From the airport in Missoula, we headed north in the single-engine plane to the Spotted Bear River along the Chinese Wall, which forms the Continental Divide. In the Bob Marshall Wilderness and in Glacier National Park to the north, we passed over fly fishermen who were casting into deep pools of stream water in forests that had been allowed to burn in recent decades. By the time we got to the Canadian border a few miles southwest of Castle Crown in the Flathead National Forest, a fog bank forced us to turn back.

Hauer began his research studying bull trout and stream ecology in this part of the world in the 1980s. He believes there is no other place like it on the continent. "It is a mixing zone for a wide variety of plants, fish, and animal species that converge from the north and south and from the east and west," he explained. The heart of it is the Flathead River, which flows out of Canada into Montana.

Hauer and Locke were part of large team of researchers from the University of Montana in Missoula, the US Geological Survey, and the University of Lethbridge in Canada that assessed the biological importance of gravel-bed river floodplains that flow out of the Rockies. In the journal *Science Advances*, they concluded that these are some of the most important ecological habitats in North America.[5]

"If you consider the Flathead River, flowing from British Columbia into the US and along the western edge of Waterton-Glacier International Peace Park, you might assume that the river is only water flowing in the channel," said Hauer. "But, it is much more than that. The river flows over and through a floodplain system, which from valley wall to valley wall supports an extraordinary diversity of life. The river is so much bigger than it appears to be at first glance."

That conclusion arose from many years of fieldwork in the Rockies on both sides of the border. The scientists found that 70 percent of the region's birds use the forested floodplains. Half the region's plants are found there. Grizzly bears, wolves, caribou, elk, and deer depend on these ecosystems.

That's when I realized how wildfire figures into the picture that Hauer was laying out for me. As these conflagrations continue to burn bigger, hotter, and more often in the subalpine, montane, and boreal forests of Canada and the United States, watersheds will continue to be degraded, as has already happened to many because of climate change, industrial pollution, and other human disturbances. Mitigation can perhaps save trout and other aquatic forms of life, but it will be very expensive. The only way grizzly bears, wolves, wolverines, and other predators are going to survive in a world in which wildfire is accelerating is for them to be able to move through safe wilderness corridors to get from one degraded forested watershed to another that is healthier. As time allows those degraded watersheds to recover, the animals will be able to return, if necessary.

The battle for many species may eventually be lost in the front ranges of the Rockies of Colorado where fire and climate change continue to degrade and dry up mountains streams at an alarming pace. The trout fishery on the South Platte is still not what it was before Hayman burned. Farther north, however, in places such as the Flathead, the Oldman, the Bow, Athabasca, and Peace River watersheds, there is still a lot of mountain snow and ice and plenty of ice-cold groundwater, shady trees, and water-filtering wetlands to make the northern forest ecosystem resilient to the fires that will inevitably come. Refugia such as these places provide some environmental stability for species that dwell in and around them.

Where these fire refugia are, how they form, and the reasons for their resilience aren't altogether clear, but knowing more about them, according to many scientists—including Meg Krawchuk, Sandra Haire, Jonathon Coop, and others who are trying to map and better understand them—may help land managers make better decisions about establishing protected areas, wildlife corridors, and prescribed burning strategies.[6]

The challenge for decision makers is to start connecting the dots between the curse of wildfires burning bigger, hotter, faster, and more often at a time when industry and people are encroaching on wildlands at an unprecedented pace and the blessings of healthy watersheds that nurture fish and wildlife and provide the majority of people in Canada and the United States with the drinking water they need.

Silins, the once unappreciated forest hydrologist, had no need of being reminded of the challenge when I last talked to him in March 2017. He had just returned from Fort McMurray to find an email from officials in Tennessee asking for some advice on how to deal with the water quality issues that the Gatlinburg fire in Great Smoky Mountains had created when the forest there began burning in late November 2016.

Chapter 6

The Big Smoke

He at the serpent gazed, and it at him;
One through the wound, the other through the mouth
Smoked violently, and the smoke comingled.
— Dante Alighieri, *The Divine Comedy*

In the fall of 1996, I traveled to the Chernobyl nuclear site in Ukraine with Dr. Clare Moisey, a Canadian doctor who was associated with a nonprofit organization called the Chernobyl's Children Project. After the unnerving, unofficial visit to the Pripyat village site, which was a ghost town by then, Moisey decided to detour to the outlying areas of the so-called exclusion zone, where hundreds of mostly elderly people were beginning to illegally resettle. They had gotten tired of living in the drab, concrete apartment towers they were relocated to in Kiev following the disaster. "I would rather die of radiation poisoning than spend my last year rotting in that place," said one widower we visited. We heard the same from others.

Moisey and his colleagues were fearless in their efforts to get to the heart of the radiation problem. Most of the children he and other doctors treated, however, were suffering more from malnutrition and psychological trauma than they were from radiation sickness. Moisey, though, was certain there was more to the radiation story than what he was seeing in children. Every 10 miles or so on the drive through the exclusion zone, he got out of the car, walked into the forest, and took out a Geiger counter to measure the level of ionizing radiation. In each case, the radiation levels far exceeded levels deemed to be safe for people subjected to long-term exposure.

It was cloudy, cold, and gloomy driving through a postapocalyptic landscape like this one. There were no cars on the road, no people in most of the farmhouses we passed, and no animals such as we could see, although many animals such as wolves, boars, and badgers had begun to migrate into this former agricultural heartland.

Moisey's amateur investigation came to an abrupt halt when we stopped to see what the radiation levels were in a forest that had burned a few years earlier. As we were about to get out of the car, two police cruisers pulled up and, without asking any more than a couple of questions about our reasons for being there, escorted us to the local station. Fluent in Ukrainian, Moisey was the one the police chief interrogated while I sat in another room. When Moisey came out about ninety minutes later, I was in a cold sweat. Poker-faced, Moisey didn't say a word until we drove off. It was then I learned that the police chief wasn't at all that concerned about our presence in the exclusion zone. He was more interested in having Moisey examine his young daughter. He was convinced that she was suffering from radiation sickness.

Making the connection between radiation from Chernobyl and human health has been a subject pursued by thousands of doctors and scientists in the years since the nuclear reactor melted down. The connection between Chernobyl and wildfire, however, wasn't made in any serious way until 2015, when a team of scientists led by Nikolaos Evangeliou used computer models to demonstrate that 8 percent of the cesium released during the 1986 nuclear meltdown was likely redistributed by wildfires that burned in the exclusion zones in 2002, 2008, and 2010. In their report, published in *Ecological Monographs*, they warned that even larger wildfires could result in crops and cities in Europe being contaminated.[1]

In the summer of 2015, a larger wildfire made headlines around the world when it tore through the exclusion zone near Chernobyl.

A significant spike in radiation was detected near one of the villages Moisey and I visited.

"The worst scenario—and the most likely one—is that particles of plutonium and uranium will be re-suspended and ... there will be a slight increase in cancer in nearest areas," Cristopher Busby, the scientific secretary for the European Committee on Radiation Risks, was quoted as saying at the time.[2]

Because the effects of radiation take years and usually decades to manifest themselves, it will likely be some time before we know whether this worst-case scenario unfolds.

The idea that wildfire may liberate chemicals that are harmful to humans is well established. It's the reason frontline firefighters wear self-contained breathing apparatuses. But wildfire experts and public health officials are just beginning to appreciate that toxins that are liberated by fire can migrate to far-flung places where most people are completely unaware of the consequences. Some of the most dangerous elements are coming from forests that had been contaminated by mining and other industrial activity.

~

On the drive from Missoula to Kootenay National Park, where I planned to revisit that big fire that burned in 2003, I took the long route around Kalispell so that I could pass through Libby, a historic town that sits almost picture-perfectly in the middle of the Kootenai National Forest. My visit to Chernobyl was by then a faded memory.

There was, however, something wrong with the picture as I drove through Libby around dinnertime during the peak of the tourism season. There were few cars on the highways and none of the hustle and bustle I had seen a few days earlier when I had passed through Kalispell. Commerce seemed to be unusually lethargic on such a warm, sunny evening in a place that seemed to have it all: mountains, forests, trout-filled streams and lakes, and hundreds of hiking trails. People were as friendly as one would expect them to be. There was, however, one thing that reminded me of Chernobyl: an exclusion zone northeast of town with a fence marked by several "Keep Out" signs.

Libby's history is a typical Northwest story. In 1809, explorer David

Thompson was the first European to visit the region when he traveled south along the Kootenai River that flows into Montana from the Rocky Mountains in British Columbia. In addition to his goal of mapping the Columbia River basin, Thompson was scouting out trading opportunities with the Kootenai tribes that lived on the west side of the Continental Divide. An influx of trappers and traders who followed constructed a number of small trading posts in the area.

Prospectors took over in the 1860s with the establishment of a number of gold mines along Fisher River, Sherry Creek, Cherry Creek, and Libby Creek, which was named after "Libby" Allen, the daughter of one of those prospectors. At one point, six hundred men and women were searching for gold in the gravel beds. Some did well; most did not. Among the losers was a group of Chinese workers who tried their luck at panning in played-out mining sites along a set of cataracts and waterfall near Libby. That is where Kootenai Indians would camp and sometimes hear long-dead ancestors whispering at night. This sacred place came to be known as China Rapids.

The existing town of Libby was established in the early 1890s when the Northern Pacific Railroad negotiated rights-of-way through the region. The town grew quickly after that with the establishment of a lumber mill, schoolhouse, newspaper, and hotel by 1892 and a Methodist Church that followed five years later. When 56 million acres of forest and mountains were set aside in 1901 so that the Kootenai National Forest could be established five years later, many of the settlers were opposed to the plan. The aim may have been "the greatest good for the greatest number over the longest time," as Gifford Pinchot, the first chief of the US Forest Service once declared in summing up the reason for national forests, but locals saw it as an attempt to stop agricultural, mining, and timber developments.

Rapid progress in mining and the development of the timber industry continued nevertheless, even after the town nearly burned down in 1910 when powerful, hurricane-force winds gave new life to a number of small fires in Idaho and northwestern Montana. The wall of flames and smoke was 50 miles wide in some places. As the fire headed toward Libby, more than two hundred people created a fire line in hope of keeping the wildfire at bay. Libby survived. The fires burned a big area just south of town and another to the northeast. The charred ruins of that historic fire can still be seen along one of the trails I hiked near the Sex Peak Lookout in Kootenai, the naming of which is left to the imagination.

According to Jim Harmon, a retired journalist who grew up in Libby hearing countless stories of that fire from his parents and his grandparents, every forest fire that followed—and there have been many in the Kootenai National Forest since 1910, including forty-nine in August 2015—was compared in some way to the Big Burn of 1910.

The wildfire that worries everyone in Libby these days is one that hasn't happened yet. When "Operable Unit 3," as the site of this future fire is being called, burns in a 47,000-acre (73 square mile) forest area centered 7 miles northeast of town, it could unleash a firestorm like no other. The region is thick with coniferous trees that have reached the age of maturity.

Many firefighters have already given notice that they have no intention of being on the ground when that happens. In the summer of 2016, Senator Jon Tester of Montana described the potential for a fire in Operable Unit 3 an unprecedented public health threat and appealed to the US Forest Service to do all it could to protect the people of Libby.

Everyone in the US Forest Service, the Environmental Protection Agency (EPA), and the National Institute for Occupational Safety and Health who has their eyes on this future fire agrees, but many acknowledge that managing the conflagration will be extremely complex. In addition to the heat, smoke, ash, and burning embers that will inevitably be released in this steep and rugged landscape, this fire will spew out needle-like, cancer-causing asbestos fibers, an unwanted, unintended by-product from asbestos mines that operated in that area from around 1923 to 1990.

The long background to this story offers a sobering message to people living and working in and around industrialized forest landscapes that are vulnerable to wildfire. This one begins innocently enough in 1881 when a prospector drilled 40 feet down in the forest northeast of Libby and found vermiculite instead of gold. Vermiculate is a glossy mineral that can absorb three times its weight in water. The mineral stayed there until local prospector and hotel owner Edward Alley revisited the site in 1919. When he exposed the mineral to heat, he discovered that it puffed up and popped, but did not burn. Sensing a commercial opportunity, he created Zonolite, a company that sold the vermiculite for insulation and plaster formulas and for treating garden soil. No one at the time was aware that the mineral was laced with asbestos fibers.

Asbestos comes from the Greek word "sasbestos," meaning "inextinguishable." It was used to wrap embalmed pharaohs and for wicks that lit the eternal flames of vestal virgins. Throughout the Middle Ages, it was used to insulate military coats of armor. By the time the first industrial asbestos mine was opened in Quebec (Thetford Mines) in 1879, asbestos was widely being used to insulate pipes, ovens, kilns, and other high-energy burners.

The recognition that asbestos was a potential killer came early on when the Roman naturalist Pliny the Elder (AD 23– AD August 25, 79) called asbestos the "disease of slaves." He came up with the name after observing slave miners using the membranes of goat or lamb bladder as mouth filters to prevent respiratory problems associated with the excavations.

After the first medically documented case of the lung-scarring disease was published in 1899, evidence that asbestos is a killer mounted in very many ways and tragic manners. Like the case against tobacco, which took decades to resolve, the case against asbestos was constantly being undermined, however, even when the US Navy listed it as a hazardous substance in 1922, around the time the first commercial mine began operating in Libby. When researchers found an 81 percent increase in lung cancer among mice exposed to asbestos in the 1940s, industry officials claimed the findings to be "inconclusive." They did the same in 1949 when Dr. Wilhelm Heuper, the first chief of the environmental cancer section of the National Cancer Institute, linked asbestos to asbestosis in workers involved in the manufacturing process of insulation and packing materials. Asbestosis is a chronic lung disease that some people get when they inhale asbestos fibers. The scarring of the lungs can lead to labored breathing and premature death.

W. R. Grace and Co. bought Zonolite in 1963 for $10 million and ramped up production even when x-ray tests performed by a local doctor a year later showed a "great deal of lung abnormalities" among the miners.[3] At one point, the company was producing 200,000 million tons of vermiculite a year, 80 percent of the world's total supply.

Figure 6-1 Established in 1919, the Libby Mine site was added to the National Priorities List of Superfund sites eighty years later. Terry Spear (left) and Tony Ward discovered asbestos needles imbedded in the trunks of trees outside of the Superfund site where residents traditionally harvest for firewood. (Julie Hart)

The Montana State Board of Health didn't help in 1967 when it responded to a union-backed asbestosis-related lawsuit with a report that suggested that dust counts at the mine site were within the state's threshold in 96 percent of the samples taken. Only after it became painfully evident that miners and processors were either prematurely dying or suffering serious respiratory problems were the links to the asbestos mine made in a serious and ultimately legal way.

In 1999, the EPA responded to citizen and local government concerns and to investigative reports by Andrew Schneider of the *Seattle Post-Intelligencer* with a plan to assess the extent and nature of the contamination. Two years later, when W. R. Grace was in bankruptcy protection and facing thousands of lawsuits, the EPA declared the situation "an imminent and substantial endangerment." The Libby asbestos site was added to the National Priorities List of Superfund sites.

"Instead of coming in, looking around, and spending a few months cleaning things up, they ended staying," said Mike Giesey, president of the board of directors for the Center for Asbestos Related Disease (CARD) in Libby. "And it looks like they're going to be here for a very long time because the situation just keeps getting more and more complicated."

CARD was established in 2003, right around the time the US Geological Survey released a study showing that the asbestos in Libby's vermiculite is a unique mixture of at least five chemically similar fibers. This form of asbestos has a tendency to fracture, forming long, needle-like fibers that stab the lungs. As the fibers scar the lining of the lungs, the lining hardens over time, making it difficult for people to breathe on their own. Workers involved in processing Libby vermiculite also demonstrated an increased risk for the development of mesothelioma, an extremely aggressive form of cancer that often goes undetected until it is at an advanced stage.

CARD is devoted to health care, outreach, and research to benefit all people affected by exposure to Libby amphibole asbestos. When Affordable Care Act funding was made available, CARD was also providing treatment for people who are uninsured.

The situation, however, is complicated.

Not everyone is affected the same way, according to Giesey, and that presents a problem for CARD doctors, nurses, and health technicians when they screen people and try to educate them. "The diagnoses tend to be very alarming," he said. "For some people, it's a death sentence, the date of which they don't know will come. It often takes decades before the symptoms show up. Not all people suffer the same symptoms."

The EPA was initially so busy trying to decontaminate homes, businesses, playgrounds, and schools that were contaminated with Libby asbestos that it didn't have the time or the inclination to look for fibers farther afield. That oversight began to change in 2004, however, when Tony Ward of the School of Public and Community Health Sciences at the University of Missoula in Montana and Julie Hart and Terry Spear at Montana Tech began a project to assess whether logging could be safely conducted in forested areas near the old vermiculite mine.

None of them expected to discover what they found. After analyzing soil and tree bark samples collected in close proximity to the mine site beforehand, they discovered that asbestos fibers were imbedded in the bark of the trees. "That was a game changer," said Ward. "From that point on, our research went in another direction. We decided to go back the next year to see if this was occurring in areas outside of the mine site, within the town of Libby, and in railroad corridors outside of Libby. The results of those investigations demonstrated that it was."

The potential for these fibers to be liberated by wood harvesting, woodstove burning, and wildfire was tested on-site by Ward and his colleagues, in fire chambers by the EPA, and in small experimental burns conducted by the US Forest Service at the mine site. A test burn showed that a fire would expose firefighters to asbestos at well above the risk target set by the EPA.

The findings, the discovery of asbestos in Libby, and the corresponding effects on health were alarming enough to compel the EPA to declare a public health emergency in 2009. It was the first time in its history that the agency had gone that far. The reasons were clear. Because asbestos is resistant to fire, the almost indestructible fibers attach to the ash of the wood that is burned. Homeowners who used contaminated wood to heat their homes could easily have reintroduced the asbestos into the houses while removing the ash from their stoves.

Ward's latest project in Libby was in summer of 2015, but many questions still remain. The question that begs to be answered, he said, is whether residential wood burning or a wildfire has already undone—or will some day undo—all that the EPA has done to clean up the town. He also wonders whether similar legacies are present in other mine sites in the forested parts of the world.

By the spring of 2017, the EPA had spent more than $370 million on the Libby cleanup. It had investigated more than 7,500 properties and completed cleanups at 2,447 properties. Christina Progress, supervisor of the Superfund site, told me that it is easily the most complex cleanup she has been involved in throughout her career. Each month, she said, seems to bring new surprises, more challenges, and insights that on another project she would normally not have to consider. The biggest surprise came when her team started to assess what might happen if a wildfire swept through the contaminated forest.

One of the more sobering insights came in an email to Progress from Nikia Hernandez of the US Forest Service in July 2016. At the time, Hernandez had twenty-three years of experience fighting more than a hundred wildfires. In that email, he summed up what scores of scientists have learned about fire behavior: that it can create its own weather and carry ash and other contaminants long distances before it falls to the ground. By way of example, he described how ash from the 5,000-acre Klatawa fire that burned 7 miles southwest of Libby in August 2015 forced the evacuation of some people in Libby. The ash ended up on cars in town and on Hernandez's car, which was 10 miles away from the edge of the fire. When it burns, the Operable Unit 3 fire would be closer than that.

"My point here is just to make sure everyone understands that wildland fires have enough energy in them to loft and transport particulates of very small sizes, ash, and even larger pieces of debris," he wrote to Progress. "How far all these things are transported is dependent on many factors such as size and shape of the particle/debris, size and height of the convection column, topography, and transport winds to name a few."[4]

Hernandez also noted something else that most everyone in wildfire science understands. Despite the great strides that have been made in predicting fire behavior, some big wildfires are inherently unpredictable in the way they move and behave.

That lesson was driven home in 2015 when the Bear Creek fire burned on the Spotted Bear Ranger District of the Flathead National Forest in August 2015. The fire ultimately burned 70,000 acres and traveled far beyond the expected perimeter to the east. The models predicted that the fire would have a less than 0.2% probability of doing that. It easily beat those odds in a single run.

When Operable Unit 3 burns is a question no one can answer, but eventually it will burn. According to research by Philip Dennison and his colleagues at the University of Utah in Salt Lake City, the odds of a large wildfire occurring in the West have been steadily increasing each year since 1984. As temperatures continue to rise, he said, bigger fires are going to happen more frequently.[5]

Residents of Libby know that. So do the EPA and the US Forest Service. When the EPA asked residents what concerned them the most, the most common response was what would happen if there were a wildfire that burned the contaminated forest. "I know that my kids work for the forest service and have the option to sign a waiver to fight forest fires on that property," said one interviewee. "I don't know if there is enough information or not. There is a fear it will catch fire and then there will be asbestos smoke blanketing the community." Others feared for teenagers who might end up riding into the forest to party. At least one person doubted whether the problem could ever be resolved.

To allay public concerns and to make sure that a fire in Operable Unit 3 doesn't spread, the EPA and the US Forest Service allocated $2.1 million in the summer of 2016 to station two helicopters, bulldozers, firefighting equipment, and attack crews in Libby. Only four of ten positions were filled when the call initially went out in 2016. Some firefighters wanted no part in suppressing a fire that could add to the risks they already face.

Progress believes that a larger specially trained team of firefighters could be called upon if the fire in Operable Unit 3 showed any sign of getting out of control. But she also acknowledged that the steep and rugged terrain will make it a challenge for on-the-ground firefighters whose movements would be slowed by the respirators they would have to wear to avoid inhaling the asbestos-filled smoke.

Respirators are a problem for firefighters on the front lines. Many who fought the Fort McMurray fire ended up with respiratory problems. The mask can plug, or safety glasses can fog up. More often than not, firefighters dispense with their respirators after a while. Jamie Coutts, the fire chief who fought wildfires in Slave Lake and Fort McMurray, concedes that he has a better than average chance of getting cancer. "It is what it is," he said. "That's the life of a firefighter."

No one knows for certain whether the scenario that Hernandez laid out for Progress will unfold in a way that will affect public health in Libby. "We don't have the answers to that question because there are so many variables to consider," said Progress. "There are people working on that. But for the time being, the best way to protect public health is to stop the fire from spreading."

What interested me even more is the question that Ward is asking about the potential for similar situations to unfold in forests elsewhere. Are there other abandoned mines in forests such as the one near Libby that might liberate toxins that are threat to human health? The abandoned asbestos mine at Clinton Creek in the Yukon came to mind.

"It's a question we're starting to ask ourselves," said Progress.

In the early 1980s, I was living in the town of Yellowknife in the Northwest Territories of Canada, a town with a rich history of gold mining.

During the time I was there, a Libby-like story was unfolding in a similar way. The issue on the shores of Great Slave Lake, however, was arsenic trioxide, which is even more deadly than asbestos.

Arsenic is sometimes found in gold-bearing rocks such as those mined in the Yellowknife area by two major mines that had been operating in the region since the 1930s and 1940s. When the gold-bearing rock is crushed and roasted, arsenic is liberated. It is white, odorless, and tasteless, and a single spoonful of arsenic trioxide may be all that is needed to kill an adult. That's why it became known as the "poison of kings" and the "king of poisons." Nero used arsenic to poison his stepbrother, Tiberius Britannicus, so that he could assume Tiberius's position as Roman emperor. During the Middle Ages, members of the Borgia family of Italy routinely put arsenic in wine to do away with bishops and cardinals in elaborate plans to take over their properties.

Once again it was Pliny the Elder who saw it as another "disease of slaves" involved in the mining of metals such as gold and copper. If it could kill people, he assumed, it could be used to control insect pests. If it could kill people and pests, medical researchers later figured, it could be used to treat diseases such as syphilis and cancer. Strangest of all human uses of arsenic was the consumption of arsenic wafers that nineteenth-century women of means purchased to lighten their skin.

Few of us living in Yellowknife at the time were aware that a First Nations toddler from the community of Ndilo a few miles outside of Yellowknife died of acute arsenic poisoning in April 1951 when the Giant Gold mine was spewing out 22,000 pounds of arsenic per day. The town had no indoor plumbing or water delivery system at the time. The child apparently died after drinking meltwater laced with arsenic trioxide. When it became evident that livestock and pets in the Yellowknife region were also dying and that adult men and women were suffering from skin problems that were likely linked to arsenic, pollution control measures were put in place, and the company began storing arsenic trioxide underground. Because there was no effective way of treating arsenic trioxide, treatment was not an option.

Despite the control measures, arsenic continued to be emitted at a rate of 7,250 pounds per day. Concerns about swimming in or drinking water from lakes in which tailings were dumped persisted. People wanted answers in the 1960s, but they didn't get them in timely fashion from an epidemiological study that suggested a possible link between arsenic exposure and elevated cancer rates in the Yellowknife region;[6] instead, the results were kept secret for six years. Three uncontrolled releases of arsenic into Great Slave Lake resulted in another two studies in 1977, one of which was conducted by the University of Toronto's Institute for Environmental Studies on behalf of the National Indian Brotherhood of Canada.[7] Although that study found high levels of arsenic in mill workers and in the hair of aboriginal children, a Canadian Public Health Association task force downplayed the risks to the public. That same year, documents attesting to government concerns about the underground storage of arsenic came into play.

By the time I arrived in Yellowknife, the mine was still spewing arsenic into the air, albeit at a small fraction of what was being emitted in the 1950s. Some of us knew that it was going somewhere. But because the Con and Giant gold mines were important economic institutions in the city, there was not a lot of enthusiasm among government officials to find out where the arsenic trioxide was going and where it had gone in the past.

Then, a series of tragic events that eventually led to a violent strike and gross mismanagement at the mine drew much of the attention away from the pollution story.

The day of reckoning came in 1999 when Royal Oak, owner of the gold mine for nine turbulent years, filed for bankruptcy protection. The rights to the mine were sold to another company, but the $1 billion pollution liability was left for the Canadian government to assume. Approximately 261 tons (237,000 tonnes) of arsenic trioxide were being stored underground in permafrost-chilled chambers linked to groundwater channels leading to Great Slave Lake, which is home to a commercial whitefish fishery and some of the biggest lake trout in the world. Ways were needed to secure the underground arsenic in place and clean up the arsenic on the mine site.

Heather Jamieson, an environmental geochemist who specializes in arsenic and mine site contamination, began research in the area in 1999. As her investigations progressed over the coming years, she and her students at Queen's University were surprised to see how the arsenic trioxide, most of which was released in the 1950s, persisted in the soil and in lake sediments. They found concentrations of total arsenic in the top few inches of soil to be as high as 7,700 parts per million on the mine property. Typical background concentrations for arsenic in Canadian soil is about 12 parts per million.[8]

Jamieson had a hunch that some arsenic migrated beyond the mine site boundaries, but she had no idea how much. The contract she signed initially prohibited her from searching for arsenic contamination in areas farther afield.

Efforts to look beyond the mine began in 2014 after the Yellowknife Dene (First Nations), the city of Yellowknife, and local environmental groups put pressure on the government to do so. Kevin O'Reilly was among them; that was before he was elected to the represent the city of Yellowknife in the Northwest Territories legislature. In an interview, he suggested what I and others had always thought: that some government officials had been willfully ignorant of what was going on outside the mine site. "Up until then, the government and the cleanup team had such a big problem on their hands, it seemed like they just didn't want to look farther and find more problems," he said.

Jamieson and her team found arsenic trioxide in the soil and in the sediment of lakes several miles away from the mine site. The only good news was that sand that had been brought in to line the shallow waters of the swimming lake muted the presence of arsenic in the offshore shallow sediments.

Further evidence that arsenic trioxide may have traveled far beyond the borders of the mine site and the city came serendipitously from another study that University of Ottawa scientist Jules Blais was conducting in the Yellowknife area at the same time.[9] Blais and his students were examining core samples of lake sediments to trace the environmental record back hundreds of years. In those cores were the shells of tiny crustaceans that formed part of the lake's food chain. Like tree rings that hold a record climate over long periods of time, these samples held a record of the pollution.

The one thing they did not expect to find was high levels of arsenic that likely killed off the crustacean population during the period when Giant and other gold mines were in operation. "It was like coming to the scene of a terrible accident," Blais told me in the summer of 2016. "You realize that there was a problem, but only after the damage was done."

Blais said there is a halo of arsenic that can be detected in lakes up to 9.3 to 12.4 miles (15 to 20 kilometers) away from the Giant mine. That halo covers a boreal forest area of 309 to 348 square miles (800 to 900 square kilometers). Preliminary analysis suggests that arsenic concentrations in the lakes are exceeding levels that are required to protect aquatic life.[10]

Relatively few studies have been done to determine how arsenic may be taken up by plants and trees in a contaminated mine site like that near Yellowknife. We do know that trees absorb arsenic because an arsenic-based compound was judiciously used on citrus trees in Florida to promote the early growth of fruit in the years before and after the turn of the twentieth century. Arsenic-laced insecticides were also sprayed on trees to control insects. In one case documented in 1915, as much as 2.93 percent of arsenic trioxide was found in an insecticide that was in common use at the time.

For decades, the government of British Columbia used an arsenic-based insecticide on lodgepole pines to the slow the spread of the mountain pine beetle. A study conducted in 2008 and 2009 found arsenic in the cores of the tree trunks and in the surrounding soil. In three cases, arsenic concentrations in soils exceeded health and safety guidelines, resulting in a recommendation that people be advised not to pick berries in the affected areas.[11]

We also know that arsenic is likely passed on to woodpeckers that feed on those insects burrowing in the contaminated bark of pine trees. Studies suggest that this method of transmission may be affecting the long-term health of these and other birds in the boreal forest.[12]

What we don't know is what would happen to this arsenic once a fire liberates it. "It may not represent any kind of serious problem in the Yellowknife area," said Blais. "But the fact is that we don't know because no one has researched the possibility of that scenario occurring."

Jamieson said she also doesn't know. "The issue never came up except for one time when we first went up to look at the site. We took all the precautions necessary because we didn't know what was there. I remember wondering what would happen if there was a fire and what would happen if toxic arsine gas was formed and firefighters were exposed to it," she recalled.

Arsine is a colorless, flammable, nonirritating toxic gas with a mild garlic odor. In low doses, it causes nausea, confusion, headaches, muscle cramps, and shortness of breath. Breathed in higher doses, it can lead to convulsions, paralysis, loss of consciousness, and respiratory problems that can result in death. That's why it was investigated as a possible chemical weapon during World War II.

The Giant mine may be unique in the magnitude of the challenges it presents, but there are a great many abandoned and orphaned mines in Canada and the United States. The US Bureau of Land Management reports that as many as 10 percent of the 100,000 to 500,000 small to medium-sized abandoned hard rock mines are considered to be a health and safety hazard. Up to 2 percent present an environmental risk.[13] In Canada, there are 10,000 abandoned sites, many of which are still being assessed, and many of which are located in the boreal forest regions.[14]

~

When I lived and worked in the Northwest Territories, I was assigned a number of times to paddle along pristine rivers flowing through the boreal forest and tundra. My companions and I would routinely spend the last evening smoking an expensive cigar while drinking cognac and warming ourselves around a campfire. For me, it had more to do with ritual than any sensual pleasure. Cigars and cognac are supposed to be the perfect pairing. The aftertaste never did much for me, and the ritual finally stopped in 1995 when I spent three weeks paddling down the Coppermine, a big river that flows through the west central Arctic forests and tundra before spilling violently into the Arctic Ocean.

It had been a long, hot summer and a truly exceptional one for wildfires in northern Canada. Between early May and mid-July, a record number of firefighters across the country had been dispatched to try to deal with the situation. The Northwest Territories, which fought only those fires that threatened communities, was having one of its biggest fire years ever. We could tell by the pall of smoke that migrated north and blocked out the sun nearly every day of the trip. When the orange ball revealed itself occasionally, it did so as the kind of eerie glow that one sees on smoggy days in big cities.

The smoke, which came from afar, was so thick at times that it reddened my eyes, bloodied my nostrils, and left an acrid taste in my

Figure 6-2 The 2014 fires that burned near Yellowknife and throughout the southwestern part of the Northwest Territories were among the most severe in recorded history. (Government of the Northwest Territories)

mouth. The cigars we smoked around a tiny campfire that last night tasted like a wet ashtray. It was clear to me then that breathing in smoke from a wildfire, a campfire, and a cigar, all at the same time, was neither healthy nor pleasurable.

Most everyone now knows about the harmful chemicals in tobacco smoke. In addition to tar and nicotine, there is benzene, which causes several cancers; cadmium, a carcinogen that damages the brain, kidney, and liver; chromium, which causes lung cancer; lead, a heavy metal that damages the nerves in the brain; and mercury, a neurotoxin that can affect human health in a variety of ways. The entire list includes six hundred ingredients. When burned they create more than seven thousand chemicals, many of which are poisonous.

Smoke from wildfires contains most of the chemicals found in tobacco, but figuring out exactly how human health is affected by smoke has eluded science and health officials for some time. Fay Johnston, a physician and environmental epidemiologist at the Menzies Research

Institute in Tasmania, and Sarah Henderson, an environmental epidemiologist at the British Columbia Center for Disease Control, headed up a team that tried doing so when it was apparent that the wildfire problem was worsening.

The team included experts in the field of global fire modeling who were able to tap into satellite data that could track wildfire around the globe. The information they provided was broken down into grid cells. The researchers were able to work out where the fires were burning, how much smoke was being emitted, where that smoke was going, and how long it stayed in the atmosphere. They were then able to combine that data with information about the number of people that live in the affected areas along with the underlying health and population death rates. Putting all that together, they estimated that smoke from wildfires is globally responsible for 260,000 to 600,000 deaths a year.[15]

That is, at best, an educated guess. Linking wildfire smoke to adverse health effects is difficult because smoke lingers for only a few days in most cases. It is also unethical for researchers to conduct experiments that expose people to anything that is likely to harm them.

What we do know, apart from the number of deaths we think are attributable to wildfire smoke, is disturbing. People exposed to smoke often have a hard time breathing because of very fine particles of black carbon that get into and irritate the lungs. In some cases, the result is a huge spike in the hospitalization of people such as the sick and elderly, who are especially vulnerable. You don't have to be close to a wildfire to suffer. Public health experts at Johns Hopkins University and other institutions linked smoke from 250 wildfires that were burning in the province of Quebec in July 2002 to a 50 percent increase in the rate of hospitalization of people sixty-five years or older living in the eastern United States where the smoke traveled. Like Johnston and Henderson's team, the Johns Hopkins researchers based their findings on satellite data that tracked the plume of smoke and health records of 5.9 million elderly people living in eighty-one counties in eleven states.[16] The findings are in line with more than sixty epidemiological studies linking wildfire and human health.[17]

As Michael Fromm found out in his studies of smoke that rises high into the stratosphere, the migration of these plumes is a lot more common than we used to think. In June 2015, NASA's Earth Observatory posted satellite images of smoke from fires in the Northwest Territories and around the oil sands plants in northern Alberta darkening the skies over much of Saskatchewan, Alberta, Manitoba, North Dakota, South Dakota, Minnesota, and Iowa. On the day the satellite images were posted, there were 168 uncontrolled fires and 273 controlled fires burning in Canada.[18]

In most cases, concentrations of ozone and carbon monoxide emissions produced by a wildfire may be high enough to affect the health of firefighters on the ground but rarely enough to affect people living in or near a forested area. When ozone and carbon monoxide are transported hundreds and sometimes thousands of miles to cities that already have high levels of pollution, however, it can get to be a problem.

That is what happened in Houston in the summer of 2004 when smoke from fires in Alaska, the Yukon, and western Canada migrated south to Texas. The ozone concentrations in the air over Houston—which were already high—rose by 50 to 100 percent from preexisting levels. The quality of the air was so bad in Harris County, which at the time ranked third in the country in toxic emissions, that it was almost off the charts.[19]

Oxygenated organics such as formaldehyde and acetaldehydes, both of which are carcinogenic, are found in smoke as well. Hotter fires tend to result in more free radicals being released into the atmosphere. Free radicals are likely having an effect on human health, but no one knows with any degree of certainty how much they will be affected.

Then there's mercury, the ingredient in smoke that is perhaps the most dangerous because it has the longest-term environmental impact. Much of the mercury in the environment comes from decades of coal burning and other industrial emissions that eventually settled into the soil and were absorbed by plants and trees. When a wildfire sweeps through, it liberates mercury in the same way that it liberates arsenic and other chemicals. Those plumes of smoke from wildfires in Quebec that hospitalized so many people in the northeastern part of the United States in the summer of 2002 contained a significant amount of mercury.

Even though soil-bound mercury volatilizes during fires, it doesn't elevate atmospheric mercury to such a great extent that it's a health concern. But this mercury can, over time, fall back to Earth's surface, where it builds up in the food chain. In northern Minnesota, where Voyageurs National Park is located in a southern boreal forest and wetland landscape, some pike were found to have concentrations ten times higher than what is safe for people to consume. The mercury in the aquatic environment was passed on to loons and bald eaglets that consumed the fish.

On the surface, it appears that ongoing efforts to reduce mercury concentrations in pike, loons, bald eaglets, grebes, and other creatures might be undermined as forest fire activity increases in the future and liberates more mercury.[20] In 2006, Canadian scientist Dave Schindler and his colleagues linked a fivefold increase in mercury in brown trout that dwelled in Moab Lake in Jasper National Park to a fire that burned three-quarters of the trees along the shoreline.[21]

Linking wildfire to elevated levels of mercury is not as simple as that, however, according to Mark Brigham, a US Geological Survey scientist who was involved in a study of mercury in the nation's lakes and streams, where more than 80 percent of the freshwater fish have elevated concentrations of mercury. For example, he and his colleagues studied a small lake in Voyageurs National Park that had been directly affected by a wildfire. They found no significant change in mercury or methylmercury levels in the lake water or in young yellow perch that inhabit the lake. But they did find evidence to suggest that mercury was liberated from the soils in the watershed.

The hotter the fire is, according to Brigham, the more the soil burns and the more mercury there is that goes up into the air before settling in another place. This process may be good for a local watershed because it removes the mercury from the soil in the region, but it isn't good for the ecosystem in which the atmospheric mercury ends up. The Arctic is a case in point. A substantial amount of mercury is carried into the Arctic by air and water currents from human sources at lower latitudes. The result has been a tenfold increase in mercury levels in the past 150 years in top predators such as the polar bear. Although polar bears and marine birds can excrete mercury in their hair and feathers, toothed whales such as narwhal and beluga are less able to get rid of the toxin.[22] That's a concern for the Inuit, who rely on marine mammals for food.

Then again, it depends on the ecosystem. Bacteria can transform inorganic mercury in an aquatic system into methylmercury, the kind that bioaccumulates, as long as there is plenty of oxygen to energize the bacteria. If not, the inorganic mercury remains relatively stable. The bottom line is that there are too many ecosystem variables in play to suggest that wildfires will lead to an increase in methylmercury into the aquatic food chain in a specific area. The methylmercury, however, will end up somewhere.

As much as four-fifths of the world's peatlands are located in the high-latitude boreal forest and tundra regions at high latitudes. Peat absorbs more mercury than any other soil because the mercury is buried as more peat accumulates over the top of it.[23] In 2006, scientists Merritt Turetsky, Mike Flannigan, and others laid out a grim scenario. They used a twenty-year record of wildfires to estimate how much mercury stored in boreal peatlands of western Canada might be released into the atmosphere as fires continue to burn in the region. They calculated that the projected increase in the incidence of fire could result in a fifteenfold increase in mercury emissions to the atmosphere. Whichever way one looks at that, the regional implications for mercury accumulation are profound. All the mercury that has settled in and has harmlessly been stored in permafrost peat could some day be liberated by megafires that are now extending their reach to the tundra and the Arctic coast. Some of that mercury will settle back into the tundra. Some of it will end up in lakes and wetlands, where it may morph into methylmercury and climb up the food chain.[24]

～

In 2015, a group of scientists and public health experts from Canada and Australia attempted to summarize the current state of knowledge about wildfire smoke and the risks it presents to public health. Although they found that a great deal of research had been conducted on the topic in recent years, they concluded that there was still a considerable amount of uncertainty.

"Most health studies on exposure to wildfire smoke tend to be focused on particulate matter," said coauthor Mike Flannigan. "Very little is known about how the other constituents affect health when people are exposed to very high concentrations over a very short period of time or lower concentration over a period of weeks or days. Until we have answers, it is going to be difficult for public health officials to inform the public about the risks."[25]

What's becoming increasingly clear is that the health effects associated with wildfire smoke are costing states, provinces, and territories more than they pay to suppress fires. That's what happened in 2008 when fire in the Poquoson Lakes National Wildlife Refuge in North Carolina burned 45,000 acres of forest and peatland over a two-hundred-day period. The amount it cost to treat people who suffered from respiratory and cardiac problems far surpassed the amount that it cost the state to put out the fire.[26]

Many firefighters have accepted the possibility that they may not live as long as they would were they in another profession. "It is what it is," said Jamie Coutts, the fire chief who fought two notorious wildfires, one in his hometown of Slave Lake and the other in Fort McMurray. "The chances of me dying of cancer are probably a lot higher than they are for most people. I was diagnosed with asthma and later with lung sarcoidosis. I can't say for sure that smoke was the cause, but I suspect that it was."

What isn't clear enough is how lakes, wetlands, and cities in which people live are affected by smoke that may be transported from tens, hundreds, and possibly thousands of miles away. Some of those chemicals will enter the food chain. Some will be breathed in by unsuspecting people. What is clear, however, is that when the smoke is heavy, everything and everyone are at risk.

Chapter 7

Drought, Disease, Insects, and Wildfire

Not green the foliage, but of color dusky; not smooth the
branches, but gnarled and warped.
— Dante Alighieri, *The Divine Comedy*

I n the late summer of 2008, Ted Hogg and Mike Michaelian, scientists with the Canadian Forest Service, drove to the Fort Mc-
Murray area to follow up on an aerial photo survey conducted
the previous year by their colleagues. That 2007 survey had showed
extensive browning of the white spruce forests in the region and a
notable absence of leaves on the aspen trees. Initially, Hogg thought
that the spruce browning might have been caused directly by drought,
which has been drying out the region since the turn of this century.
As Hogg soon discovered, however, it was the spruce budworm that
did the damage to the spruce and forest tent caterpillars that severely
defoliated the aspen.

Hogg and his colleagues have seen this kind of infestation and tree
mortality many times before in the northern forests of Waterton and
Glacier national parks on the Alberta/Montana border where white
bark pine and limber pine are on a rapid path to extinction: in the Red
Deer River valley of central Alberta, where white spruce numbers are

being decimated; in the urban forests of Edmonton, Alberta, where birch trees are disappearing; pretty much everywhere balsam fir are found; and in British Columbia, Alberta, Montana, Oregon, Colorado, Idaho, California, and many other places in the West where tens of millions of lodgepole pine are being destroyed by bark beetles.

No one knows just how much the die-off of trees in northern Alberta contributed to the momentum of the massive 2016 Horse River fire, but the deadfall was extensive. It may not have been evident on the tree and vegetation maps that firefighters used to help suppress that inferno. The maps that were being used were more than fifteen years old, and the data used to produce them came from the forestry industry, not from a fire agency that needed to see where the diseased and dead trees were located, where recent burns lay, and where young stands of relatively fire-resistant deciduous trees might be found to act as firebreaks. Fire managers flew in to have a quick look to verify what was on the maps, but the effort produced superficial results.

The relationship between drought, disease, insect infestation, and wildfire is as intimate and complicated as the interplay between weather, oxygen, and fuels in the fire triangle. And in the interplay that takes place in the fire triangle, only one of the elements needs to be removed to control a fire.

In a wildfire quadrangle that includes drought, disease, insects, and wildfire, humans can try to control insects and disease, almost always with limited success. Even then, serious damage can still be done to the forest, especially when climate change is factored into the equation. That is why the challenges of wildfire have become so daunting.

Drought alone can kill a tree and alter the structure of a forest. As the soil dries during long periods of intense heat, the fine roots of trees tend to increase to exploit what little moisture there is left. If the soil continues to dry out, these roots begin to die off. In some cases, the plumbing that transports water from the roots to the leaves through the xylem loses its elasticity and breaks down. When it does finally rain, the weakened tree is unable to take up enough moisture and nutrients to keep it alive.

In the northern forests, deciduous trees such as aspen, poplar, and birch are often the first to suffer a dieback during a prolonged drought. Conifers, which have a fatty, waxy substance covering the needles, tend to do better.[1] Some conifers rely on a plant hormone that more effectively closes the stomata, the tiny openings in leaves and needles that allow a tree to take in carbon dioxide and release oxygen and water. Closing down the stomata reduces the amount of water the tree loses through transpiration. Conifers also have an internal plumbing system that holds up better when severe dehydration puts damaging pressure on the xylem.

Mature conifers, however, will suffer if the drought is an extended one. In the 1950s, a protracted drought in the Jemez Mountains in New Mexico resulted in a 2-mile upslope regression of the ponderosa pine–dominated forest, according to Craig Allen, a research ecologist who has been studying landscape changes in the region since the 1980s. That drought, he noted, was part of a typical climatic cycle that had little or nothing to do with human-driven climate change. A sixteenth-century drought that lasted longer, he adds, was so catastrophic that it drove the Pueblo Indians out of the same mountains.

More often than not, disease and insects come with drought. When they do, the devastation can play out spectacularly, as it has done in Washington, Idaho, Montana, and British Columbia, where both the mountain pine beetle and the Dothistroma needle blight have been at play, and in California, where 120 million trees—62 million in 2016—have died as a result of bark beetles and a brutal drought that parched the landscape from 2010 until the rains finally came early in 2017.

Former US Agriculture Secretary Tom Vilsack may have overreached by describing the carnage as "40 million opportunities for fire."[2] Even if the dead trees don't elevate the chance of wildfire igniting, they are, as many wildfire specialists believe, likely to affect ignition and fire behavior potential, complicating efforts to respond effectively and adding risk to people living, recreating, and working in the forests.

Hogg has been studying the relationship between climate change, drought, insects, and wildfire since he joined the Canadian Forest Service in 1992. Early in his career, he predicted that trembling aspen, the most dominant deciduous tree in the boreal forest, would suffer periodic diebacks and a reduction in distribution and productivity if the climate continued to warm and exacerbate drought conditions, as was being predicted back then.[3]

For a time, Hogg assumed that the aspen dieback he and others were seeing in northern Alberta starting in the mid-1990s was a quintessentially Canadian phenomenon. That was until he crossed paths with James Worrall, a plant pathologist with the US Forest Service in Colorado, at a meeting of the Western International Forest Disease Work Conference. Worrall was seeing a similar dieback of aspen in the southern Rockies, and it appeared to be related to the drought that had been drying out the forests of Colorado.

Their detective work continued when Craig Allen weighed in with insights he had gathered since he had started studying landscape changes in the American Southwest in the late 1980s. Like the American West and western Canada, the Southwest had been in the midst of a drought that was subjecting the region to wildfire and a catastrophic die-off of trees.

If even hotter droughts continue to prime the forests for more intense and frequent wildfire, as Allen suspects they will, given the climate change scenarios, the pinion pine and ponderosa pine forests of New Mexico and the American Southwest will continue to move upslope until they run out of room. At lower elevations, the forest will morph into shrub and grasslands as well as small island forests dominated by different tree species.

Like Hogg, Allen suspected that what he was seeing regionally might be happening elsewhere, but he didn't want to fall into the trap of projecting regional events onto a global pattern. So, at two international meetings—in 2007 and 2008—he mustered the expertise of a number of scientists in the international forestry community to see whether this drought-related trend in forest environments was globally related to climate change. He and scientists such as Hogg, who was involved in the report that was published, concluded that no forest type is invulnerable to future droughts, even in environments like northern Alberta that have a lot more water on the landscape.

"If what we're seeing is the start of a major ecosystem shift in our northern forests, it is going to be a very big story," Hogg told me.

~

Since World War II, meteorologists have been attaching human names to hurricanes and tropical storms because the previous practice of assigning them latitudinal and longitudinal designations was difficult to remember and hard to communicate. The tradition continues for that reason, except that the names are no longer exclusively female. The hurricane season of 2016, which was the most violent and costly since 2012, introduced us to Hurricanes Alex, Earl, Gaston, Hermine, Matthew, Nicole, and Otto and tropical storms with names such as Bonnie, Colin, and Danielle.

Large wildfires also get their due. Fires are named after the town, region, or watershed (Yarnell, Virginia Hills, Lost Creek); diabolical creatures like The Beast or Black Dragon, emotional responses like the "holy shit fire," or days of the week as the Australians often do: Red Tuesday (1898), Ash Wednesday (1983), Black Thursday (1851), Black Saturday (2009), Black Sunday (1955). In many cases, the naming rights go to the initial attack crew. Some do it with a sense of humor. The Burnt Bread fire in Northern Cascades National Park paid homage to nearby Sourdough Mountain.

Although droughts often do more economic damage than even the most powerful hurricanes or wildfires, they don't get the same kind of respect outside of Texas and California, where drought has forced officials in places such as San Antonio and Orange County to turn sewage into drinking water. A notable exception is a drought that parched much of North America between 1999 and 2005.

"Ada," as some unofficially called that drought, was responsible for one of the worst modern-day natural disasters. For those who were living in the West at the peak of that drought in 2000–2001, thirty-two massive dust storms swept across the prairies of western Canada and the Great Plains of the United States. Tens of thousands of waterfowl were unable to find suitable wetlands in which to nest because most of the shallow lakes dried up.[4]

Adding to the woes of farmers and rural dwellers were swarms of grasshoppers that chewed up withering crops and, in some cases, the paint on houses. In one Saskatchewan district, there were as many as one hundred grasshoppers per square yard of land.[5]

"They came in biblical proportions," recalled Alberta rancher Colleen Biggs, who raises grass-fed, antibiotic-free cattle with her husband, Dylan, in the Hanna region of central Alberta. "We lost 6,000 acres of grass to grasshoppers in six days. They ate everything green that was not 10 feet above ground. It was enough to curl the hair in your nose. We ended up shipping our cattle north because we ran out of grass to feed them."[6]

Water was so scarce in some places in 2001 that farmers in the St. Mary's irrigation district on the Montana/Alberta border were literally put on rations. On average, they were allocated only 60 percent of the water they traditionally get.[7]

It wasn't just the Great Plains of the United States and the prairies of Canada that suffered. Ada dried up virtually every part of the continent. Atlantic Canada had its third driest summer ever.[8] According to the National Oceanic and Atmospheric Administration, 36 percent of the contiguous United States was experiencing a moderate to extreme drought that summer. Wildfires like those in Kelowna, Kootenay, Jasper, Banff, Waterton, and Glacier national parks and the Salmon-Challis National Forest in Idaho burned at five times the average rate.

In the lead-up to the 2,500 wildfires that swept across British Columbia in 2003, the province's southern interior was in the midst of its worst drought in a century. From 2000 to 2002, only two of twelve seasons were wetter than normal. Only one season was colder than normal. By the time the summer of 2003 arrived, southern British Columbia had gone through its driest three-year period on record. According to an Environment Canada report, the Fraser River peaked near the first of July and was at one of the lowest stages since record keeping began nearly a century earlier. Hungry bears roamed the suburbs, hordes of beetles bored into pine trees, salmon suffocated in lethally warm streams, worried utilities imported energy, and water-desperate ranchers culled herds.[9]

Just when everyone thought that it was as bad as it could get, a high-pressure system planted itself over the coast of the province, preventing cool wet weather over the ocean from moving east. The town of Kamloops didn't get a drop of rain in the forty-four days that led up to the fires that swept through the region.

Then, when the fires ignited, the forest literally exploded in flames.

As well adapted to fire as these forests are, the recovery that followed did not occur as quickly as foresters had expected based on what they had seen in Yellowstone in 1988 and in other places. Instead, the prolonged and persistent drought starved the seedlings of the water they needed to take root and grow. The same thing is happening pretty much everywhere in the northern forests.

~

In addition to making forests more vulnerable to wildfire, drought weakens trees and leaves them susceptible to the second major ecosystem shifts we are likely to see shaping forests over the next several decades. Insects and disease are programmed to exploit this vulnerability.

The exceptionally warm winters, early springs, and hotter summers that followed the wildfires of 2003 are a reminder that the drought in the West never really ended. With a few excepting years, the drought continued well into 2016, helping to drive wildfire to burn bigger, faster, hotter, and more often. In 2015, much of western North America and Alaska experienced some of the biggest fire seasons in recent memory.

The drought also gave added momentum to spruce bark beetle population expansion, already on a steady march through Alaska, the Yukon, and much of western North America. As it headed east into Alberta and south into the United States at the same time, the mountain pine beetle destroyed billions of dollars' worth of timber, fundamentally altered wildlife habitat, realigned forest structure and stand dynamics, and compromised water quality in rivers and lakes.

The bark beetle is not the only pest or pathogen threatening forests. Dothistroma needle blight is a fungal disease that turns needles brown and results in early needle drop. Needle loss slows tree growth, and severe infection several years in a row can result in tree death. Dothistroma needle blight has been killing pines throughout many parts of North America. In Montana and other parts of the West, the white pine blister rust is another deadly intruder that has laid waste to five-needle pine forests.

The mountain pine beetle, however, is the leader of the pack of insects that are devastating North America's coniferous forest. Its recent surge into the boreal forest of Alberta may turn it into a runaway train of destruction that will not run out of track any time soon. No longer satisfied with chewing on lodgepole pine, the beetle has added jack pine, a close cousin, to the menu.

Jack pine is found almost everywhere in the northern forests of

Canada and part of the United States. Its range extends east from the Mackenzie River in the Northwest Territories to Cape Breton Island and Nova Scotia. It is found in Maine, New Hampshire, Vermont, northern New York, Michigan, extreme northwestern Indiana, and northeastern Illinois as well as northwest through Wisconsin and Minnesota to Manitoba, Saskatchewan, central Alberta, and extreme northeastern British Colombia. Jack pine has been planted outside its native range in the central states and in Alaska.[10] In short, it is everywhere, waiting for mountain pine beetles and drought to help it burn.

I got to see the mountain beetle at work several years ago when Parks Canada fire and vegetation specialist Dave Smith brought me along on a beetle-counting survey in Jasper National Park. With us was Gary Roke, an insect pathology technician with the Canadian Forest Service. First on our stop was a century-old pine that had been seriously worked over by pileated woodpeckers that had come in to feed on the beetle-infested tree. Smith peeled away some bark to show me what happens in the first year of the infestation. He did it with a disarming sense of humor.

"There's mama and there's buddy what's his name here in the vertical chamber," he said as Roke looked on smiling. "Here are the pupae that would grow into adults by now if it hadn't been so cold this summer.

"And look at this gal," he said as he followed a path of what he thought was a female adult burrowing her way up high under the bark of the tree. "A male never followed her, and well, you know," he said as he struggled to find the right words.

"She dies an old maid," Roke interjected.

Females that mate lay their eggs in vertical galleys or tunnels. When they hatch, the grub-like larvae spend the winter feeding under the bark. After they pupate in spring, they quickly grow into adults by July or August. If the wind and weather cooperate, they fly to another stand of trees that are old and thick enough to lay their eggs in.

Mountain pine beetles are native to the Canadian Rockies, and outbreaks are nothing new. In Kootenay National Park, where wildfire burned 12 percent of the park in 2003, there have been two major outbreaks since the beginning of the twentieth century. The first one, which began in 1930, lasted for fifteen years. In a 25,600-acre stand of forest along the Kootenay River, the beetles killed 80 percent of the lodgepole pine.[11]

Historically, the mountain pine beetle has been a balancing force in northern forests, attacking old, less resilient trees to make way for young, healthier forests. But a combination of decades of forest fire suppression and exceptionally warm winters has tipped the scale heavily in the beetle's favor.

In 2010, Dave Smith was content just to count beetle-infested trees in Jasper because there were so few in the park. He counted four hundred beetle-infested trees that year. Not long after, he and his colleagues gave up because there were too many to record individually. In 2014, the insects were found feeding on an area that covered 298 acres of forest. By the summer of 2016, the area colonized was 53,000 acres.

So far, there doesn't appear to be an answer to the problem. Governments on both sides of the border have tried to slow the march of the beetle by spraying forests with insecticides, planting pheromone traps, cutting down stands of trees that have been affected, and cutting down healthy trees to create buffer zones. Smith and his colleagues were hoping that a series of prescribed burns in the fall of 2016 would slow the infestation down. Mother Nature, however, closed the door on that strategy. Too much rain fell for Parks Canada to proceed.

Smith fears the worst if a fire comes roaring down the beetle-infested forest along the Yellowhead Highway from Mount Robson Provincial Park in British Columbia toward the Jasper townsite. That's one reason Parks Canada has embarked on a fairly aggressive prescribed burn program in Jasper and other mountain national parks. Thinning out the forest in this way, however, depends on weather cooperating at the right time of year. Mountains are a meteorologist's nightmare because they force air to rise and sink through valleys. The result is gravity waves, wind gusts, canyon flows, cool air pooling, updrafts, downdrafts, cross flows, and the Venturi effect that comes when a rapidly moving air mass tries to squeeze through a narrow mountain pass. It's akin to the violent rapids that one sees when a wide, fast-moving river has to descend and squeeze through a narrow gulch.

"The mountain pine beetle has created a new type of fuel on the ground, and this new fuel is forcing us to rewrite the book on how

Figure 7-1 In 2010, there were almost no pine beetles in Jasper National Park. By 2016, they had spread to an area covering 53,000 acres. (Edward Struzik)

we will fight wildfires in the future," said Smith. "Once the fire season starts in this part of the world, I have a hard time sleeping at night."

Like Smith, many wildfire experts believe that the destruction the mountain pine beetle has brought to the forest of the Northwest will seriously complicate the challenge of wildfire. But a study done by Garrett Meigs suggests that that has not happened, at least not yet. He and his colleagues came to that conclusion by mapping the locations of insect outbreaks and wildfires throughout Oregon and Washington from 1970 on. Based on the data they collected, they suggest that the chances of fire burning in beetle-infested forests are neither lower nor higher than in forests that have not been damaged. They then did the same comparison on forests damaged by the western spruce budworm, with even more surprising results. The chances of wildfire in this case actually appear to be slightly lower.[12]

Martin Simard, Monica Turner, and their colleagues at the University of Wisconsin–Madison had previously come to a similar conclusion using another form of modeling when they assessed the severity of six wildfires that burned in pine beetle–stricken forests in the Northern Rockies in 2011. Like Meigs, they found no positive relationship between fire severity and the beetle-infested forests. If anything, there was "a dampening rather than an amplification of fire behavior and intensity."[13]

When many people took this conclusion to mean that the beetle infestations have no effect on wildfire and that no special management action is needed, Marty Alexander was horrified. The first thing that came to mind was that the assumptions did not consider how a forest infected with mountain pine beetles challenges the ability of fire managers to suppress wildfire with ground crews. "When you have so many dead trees still standing or lying on the ground, it complicates the fire suppression strategy in various ways," he said. "It makes the identification of escape routes difficult, if not impossible to find. The downed debris and trees slow the movement of firefighters. Those dead trees that are still standing can fall down and injure firefighters."

In an effort to dig more deeply into the subject, Alexander teamed up with Wesley Page and Michael Jenkins at Utah State University in Logan. In the paper they published, they concluded that the simulation that Martin and Turner conducted did not jive with what some firefighters and fire specialists were seeing in the real world.[14]

A fire that stood out in their investigation was one that tore through a heavily infested part of Idaho's Salmon-Challis National Forest in 2011. Its spread rate was 3.3 times higher than the predicted maximum. It was one of the reasons a bulldozer and transport driver got trapped. No one saw it coming as fast as it did.

Another fire that got their attention was an experimental burning that Brian Stocks conducted in the mid- to late 1970s in forests in north central Ontario damaged by the spruce budworm. Stocks and his colleagues, including Alexander, carried out that project two years after Stocks had been temporarily shut down over the so-called nuclear winter fire media showdown. This ensuing experimental fire displayed extensive crowning, high spread rates, and prolific short-range spotting, even under relatively mild burning conditions.

Alexander concedes that once the majority of the needles have dropped from the crowns and the pine trees have entered the gray stage of mountain pine beetle attack, the potential for active crown fires decreases dramatically. Until more experimental studies are done in the field to prove otherwise, however, he is convinced that the spread rate of fire will double or triple in recently attacked forests that are still in the red needle stage.

Looking at this bigger picture, Turner sees a real possibility that the tremendous resilience that she documented in Yellowstone's forest ecosystem following the famous fires of 1988 may be weakened by climate change, insects, disease, drought, and other disturbances. She suspects that the recovery we will see in the future will likely be much different. That said, she would not go as far as to say that all bets are off now because we know a lot about the mechanisms involved in wildfire recovery. "The problem is that we don't know how, when, where changes might be seen on the landscape," she said.

If there's a takeaway message, it's that neither the insects nor the disease that comes with them are going to go away as the climate continues to warm and droughts become hotter and last longer. Fire will burn bigger, hotter, faster, and, in some places, with increasing frequency. When and if that happens, according to Marc-André Parisien, a research scientist with the Canadian Forest Service, the trees and vegetation that rise up afterward may result in an ecosystem that little resembles anything that was there for hundreds if not thousands of years.

In his Edmonton office, Parisien showed me what he meant with pictures of a boreal landscape in the Nyarling River area of Wood Buffalo National Park. Wood Buffalo is the second largest national park in the world. It is a nesting refuge for the world's last remaining population of migrating whooping cranes and a place where a unique population of wolves prey on the largest free-roaming bison herd on Earth. It is a land of deltas, wetlands, and a boreal forest that seemingly goes on forever.

There have always been big fires in this part of the world. The one that burned the landscape in the picture Parisien showed me burned in 2004 and again in 2014, when the Northwest Territories experienced one of its biggest fire seasons since the 1950s.

Two years after the second fire, the scene in the picture looked to me to be one of utter devastation. There are no aspen popping up and no sign of pine that were once there. Even if the winds blow some pine or spruce seeds in, they are unlikely to germinate because the fire vaporized most of the organic matter in the soil. "This was a pine forest for centuries. It may be decades or even centuries before it's a pine forest again," said Parisien.

Ellen Whitman agrees. She is a PhD student working on the Nyarling River site. Parisien and Mike Flannigan are her supervisors. "The photos Marc showed you were taken during a summer of drought," she said. "It looked a lot bleaker back then than it does now. There is some vegetation growing there, but it certainly isn't pine seedlings."

Two things happened that have made pine forest regeneration unlikely, she said. "To have a truly successful regeneration, you need to have a good seed crop. For that to happen, the pine trees have to be ten to twenty years old depending on stand characteristics; some say they have to be much older. In this case, the trees were just ten years old when they burned.

"Even if there was a good seed crop, they would need some sheltering sites and water, maybe shade from time to time to grow. The fire in 2014 was so severe that it completely removed what was left of the organic soil layer. Seeds are trying to grow on sand that doesn't hold much moisture. Some vegetation is coming back, but there is almost no sign of trees. They wouldn't have been able to produce a seed crop that is necessary for the forest to grow back the way it was before the first fire in 2004."

During her fieldwork in Wood Buffalo, Whitman found a forest site that has one of the shortest fire intervals on record. Those two fires burned in the late 1990s and first decade of this century, far enough back in time for the trees to regenerate if they could. Whitman found the site by following bison trails. The bison were evidently attracted to the site because of the grass that has grown up in the postfire landscape. Although there are scattered, stunted aspen trees in this reburn, the dense pine forest that burned in 1998 has completely disappeared.

Parisien sees these short-interval fires happening everywhere in the boreal forest. When the fires around the Cree community in Eastmain in northern Quebec burned approximately 1.4 million acres (583,000 hectares) in 2013, he said, they should have been slowed by stands of

Figure 7-2 Increasingly, fires are burning so severely that they leave nothing in the ground to allow spruce and pine to recover. Drought and dry, hot weather that sometimes follow don't allow those seedlings that might take root to grow. (Ellen Whitman)

young deciduous trees that had risen up from a fire that had burned the area in 2008. In the photo that Parisien took three years later, however, there are no signs of seedlings anywhere.

"That young forest should have slowed that fire in 2013," said Parisien. "But like Fort McMurray in 2016, this fire burned in temperatures that were near record highs, when the fuel on the ground was dry, and when the winds were blowing hard. Mother Nature does what she wants to do in conditions like that. Nothing is going to stop her."

Parisien said it is ill-advised to make any kind of generalization about what the future will bring to the boreal forest because there are just too many unknowns and variables to factor into a definitive forecast. "One thing I will say is that much of it won't look anything like it is now," he explained.

Andrew Larson, an associate professor of forest ecology at the University of Montana, agrees. I spent some time with him in the Lolo

National Forest and Flathead Valley in Montana, where fire has been burning bigger, hotter, faster, and more often than ever before.

"It is difficult to predict what the forests here will look like in fifty or a hundred years because we have forests that are at high and low elevations and forests that are moister in the Northwest than they are elsewhere," he said.

"Tree species also have different mortality rates and different tolerance to drought and disease," he continued. "It may surprise people to know that smaller and younger trees typically have higher rates of mortality than larger, older trees of the same species. The twist to that story is that in extreme droughts, the oldest and largest trees are more likely to die first."

At Seeley Lake in the Flathead Valley, Larson took me to a stand of ancient fire-scarred western larch trees, including one 153-foot-tall tree that is more than one thousand years old.

This giant has survived at least forty burns. It began to grow at a time when there were 250 million people in the world, compared with the seven billion we have now. According to the signpost at the site, it takes about fifteen children holding hands to wrap themselves around this tree.

The western larch, I discovered that day, is incredibly resilient when it comes to surviving fire, disease, and even drought. These trees die off at a rate that is typically one-half to one-fourth those of Douglas fir and subalpine fir that grow in the same region.

When push came to shove in my asking Larson to look into his crystal ball and tell me what he thought these forests in Montana, Idaho, southeastern British Columbia, and southern Alberta would look like by the middle of the twenty-first century, he offered this prediction. "I expect that forests in dry, low elevation areas will suffer the most," he said. "These are forests that are dominated by ponderosa pine, and to a lesser extent by Douglas fir, grand fir, and western larch. Unnaturally intense wildfires that will come with climate change will likely be even more common than they are now, especially in areas where we have suppressed fires for decades. These dry forests will likely be experiencing drought-caused tree die-off by midcentury. It's going to look different. That's for sure."

Climate change may be the elephant in the room when it comes to future wildfires. What worries some scientists even more, however, is that the future droughts will almost certainly be hotter and will also last much longer.

Paleoecologists such as David Sauchyn at the University of Regina, Saskatchewan, are fairly certain of this outcome. Sauchyn bases his opinions on an analysis of tree rings that he and his colleagues have collected in the boreal forest in western Canada. In reconstructing a nine-hundred-year history of climate and weather patterns, they see droughts that have lasted for decades.

Jason E. Smerdon, a climate scientist at the Lamont-Doherty Earth Observatory, sees the same thing happening in the Southwest and the Great Plains of the United States. When he and colleagues Benjamin Cook and Toby Ault did a quantitative comparison between projections for the future with decades-long droughts that occurred in medieval times, they concluded that the medieval droughts of the past will seem like "quaint walks through the Garden of Eden" compared with what is going to happen by 2050.[15]

John Pomeroy is the Canada Research Chair in Water Resources and Climate Change at the University of Saskatchewan. Pomeroy was around to see the drought that parched much of the West from 1999 to 2005. When I spent a day hiking up to his research station in the southeast slopes of the Canadian Rockies, he told me that we are already into a drought phase that has only been periodically interrupted by extreme flooding, such as the flood in the city of Calgary in 2013 and the floods that followed fires in Alaska and Fort McMurray in 2016.

Since 1975, according to Pomeroy, the glacier-covered area in the South and North Saskatchewan River basins on the east side of the Rocky Mountains has declined by about 37 percent and 22 percent, respectively. Snowpack, which provides most of the water that flows downstream in spring and early summer, is also diminishing. Pomeroy's research station at Marmot Creek has been operating almost continuously in the Rockies since 1962. Since then, recorded daily low winter temperatures have increased by 9°F (5°C), reducing snowpack volumes at low elevations by half and streamflow in Marmot Creek by 25 percent.[16]

He predicts that the drying will continue in ways that will be so extreme that the oil sands will no longer have enough river water in northern Alberta to separate oil from bitumen.

"If we go through dry periods that are more severe than the droughts we've experienced so far, how do we deal with that, especially in the West where we are already water-starved in many places?" he asked. "Do we have enough water for irrigation, for our hydroelectricity, and for our cities? Can we deal with future wildfires which are going to burn bigger and more often, or do we have to start making very difficult choices?"

There are not many choices beyond reducing greenhouse gas emissions. Nothing, for example, can be done about drought. Using arsenic-laced insecticides and other chemicals to control insects and disease can negatively affect much-needed insects and birds as well as people who harvest berries and mushrooms. Prescribed burning comes with a price, potential risks, and a public that gets cranky when the air it breathes becomes acrid, but no amount of prescribed burning will solve the problem. Mechanical thinning might reduce the severity of wildfire, the sale of timber could offset the high cost of wildfire management options, and scientific research might offer other solutions.

So far, though, the political answer to dealing with wildfires burning bigger, hotter, faster, and more often is to take money away from the insect, disease, drought, and climate change forest scientists to make up for the rising cost of suppression. Forest management has suffered as a result. The ecosystem shifts that we are already seeing strong signs of in southern Canada and the northern United States will become as pronounced and catastrophic as they currently are in the forest and tundra of the sub-Arctic and Arctic regions.

Chapter 8

Fire on Ice

After the smoke and the prayers ascend to God, the angel
fills the censer with fire, from the altar, and throws it
to the Earth causing noises, thunderings, lightnings, and
an earthquake. . . . The first angel of seven sounded his
trumpet: "And hail and fire followed, mingled with blood,
and they were thrown to the earth" burning a third of the
Earth's flora, scorching all green grass.
— Book of Revelation

On June 19, 2015, a slow-moving low-pressure system with spectacular thunderstorms that produced little rain began making its way through the Alaskan interior. When the storms finally petered out about a week later, 61,000 bolts of lightning—15,000 in one remarkably electric day—had been unleashed on a boreal forest in the state's interior. No one had ever seen anything quite like it, not even in 2004, when 8,500 lightning strikes were recorded in one day.[1]

The 2015 storms in Alaska triggered 270 fires. Just over 5 million acres of forest burned. Seventy homes were lost. Mercifully, no one died. The only significant difference between the two major fire seasons was one of timing. The 2004 fires burned in July and August. The 2015 fires burned in June and July. Everything else followed a similar pattern. Lightning was the trigger for most of the fires. Heat and tinder-dry conditions fueled the flames. Most significantly, human-driven climate change was likely the reason for the extraordinary heat, the low humidity, and the violent thunderstorms.

Although we cannot assume that climate change is a significant factor in every wildfire scenario, these Alaska fire seasons showed clear indications of climate change influences. Scott Rupp, a wildfire ecologist at the University of Alaska Fairbanks and university director of the Interior Department's Alaska Climate Science Center, and twelve other scientists came to that conclusion after spending months poring over data that might theoretically link the probability of the wildfires of 2015 to anthropogenic climate change. Remove regional warming from the picture, they concluded, and the forests of Alaska would very likely not have burned as severely as they did.

If the rains hadn't come, according to Rupp, as much as 10 million acres might have burned. That would have made it the largest runaway wildfire season for a state, province, or territory in modern-day North American history. It would have rivaled the Black Dragon fire of 1988, which was the biggest fire documented in human history.

I met up with Scott Rupp in the summer of 2016 when it appeared that the wildfire season was going to be off to another early start. In February, a fire had started on the open tundra thanks to a live-fire training exercise by military personnel in the Donnelly Training Range. There was so little snow on the ground that the dry grass and sedges lit up like kindling when the ordinances exploded. Winds of 20 miles an hour spread the flames quickly.[2] Some of the other fires that ignited early that spring were ones that had burned the year before and had smoldered beneath the snow through the winter. The Soda Creek fire of 2015, which flared up again in May 2016, was one of those.

June and July rains preceded my Alaska sojourn with Rupp, making it impossible for him to take me to the Bonanza Creek Experimental Forest. The roads and trails were too muddy. Bonanza was established in 1963 in the Tanana Valley State Forest 12.4 miles (20 kilometers) southwest of Fairbanks. Since it was expanded in 1969 to include more than 12,000 acres, the research there has focused on improving the understanding of the long-term consequences of changing climate, wildfire, and other disturbances in the Alaskan boreal forest. With few other options, we drove instead to the Agee Creek fire site that burned in 2015. That is where the Alyeska pipeline carries oil from Prudhoe Bay to Valdez, Alaska.

Once we got there, Rupp couldn't resist saying the same thing I had said to myself when I saw how wildfire had almost overrun the oil sands region earlier that summer: "The intersection of two worlds passing each other," he said. "An oil pipeline carrying fossil fuels that are warming the climate and a wildfire that is being fueled by fossil fuels making fire burn more frequently."

Alaska has endured being called Icebergia, Polaria, and Walrussia since it was purchased for a song from Czarist Russia in 1867. Like many other Arctic places, its inhabitants have unique words that only they use to describe what it's like living there. Ice yowling is the screech one hears in the dead of winter when ice contracts on lakes and creates cracks that are miles long. Firn is compacted snow that will eventually turn into glacier ice. A pingok, pingo, or mud volcano is a dome-shaped mound that rises up from the hydrostatic pressure that comes with permafrost. Ice fog is as one might imagine: fog with ice crystals floating in it. As cold as it can be in winter, the land of the midnight summer sun burns like no other place on the continent.

As big as fires burn in Alaska, no one down south notices until a fire season like the one that took place in 2015 comes along. In many ways, it was a year like no other, according to Rick Thoman, a meteorologist who saw something like it, but nothing quite as severe as it turned out to be, coming in March when he issued his annual forecast for the upcoming fire season. The smoke, he recalls, was as a thick as a London fog and was so noxious at times that he considered the otherwise unthinkable thought of leaving his beloved state and moving south.

The media did notice. For perhaps the first time, climate change in the Arctic, which was typically being linked to the decline of polar bears, the annual recession of sea ice, the hasty retreat of glaciers, the thawing of permafrost, and the sliding of coastal communities into the sea, was suddenly being measured by wildfire impact. The buzz was as much about caribou surviving in a world where both trees and tundra were being threatened as it was about polar bears unable to hunt for seals on the sea ice.

"It was not news to us in Alaska who have been living with fire and studying it for some time," said Rupp, who freely admits that in 2015 he routinely ran down to Thoman's office a floor below to look at satellite images that showed how big the fires were burning. "So when I was asked what was going on with these big fires, I told the media that it took forty years to burn 25 million acres in the state, and the next 25 million acres took less than twenty-five years to burn. What set the 2015 fire season and the last two decades apart from the historical record is the growing number and frequency of large fire years we are having in Alaska."

Climate is playing a role in the way fires are burning, bigger, faster, and more often in northern forest and tundra regions and in the warmer temperatures that are throwing the once-predictable recovery process off kilter. It is especially true in the Arctic, where the climate is heating up twice as fast as it is anywhere else on Earth. In a world where snow, ice, and permafrost have dominated for so long, it has become increasingly apparent that the conifers of the boreal forest, the sedge meadows, and lichens of the tundra are not responding well to the changes in hydrology, soil acidity, permafrost thawing, and slumping that come when severe wildfires join forces with warmer, earlier springs and summers and extended droughts. The frozen landscapes that once favored millions of free-roaming caribou are morphing into shrubbier tundra and aspen-dominated forest that moose, bison, and invasive species such as deer favor.

~

Like many Alaskans, Rupp traveled "north to the future"—the state's motto—for the research opportunities and the freedom and adventure that Alaska's vast wilderness offers.

"When I first came to Fairbanks, I fell in with a group of people who had come here and figured out how not to leave," he told me. "You either loved it or hated it. I fell in love with it."

So did his soon-to-be wife, Kerry, a former Penn State alumnus like Rupp, who also came to Alaska to pursue a graduate degree. Penn State is so massive that they never crossed paths while they were studying there.

They now live off the grid in the boreal forest about 35 miles outside of Fairbanks where they raise 500-pound hogs, free-range chickens, and dairy goats. They make goat cheese and sell the cheese and eggs to local co-ops. In his spare time, which doesn't amount to much, Rupp runs his sled dogs along the Yukon Quest race trail that passes just a few miles away from their property.

"It wasn't easy embracing all the craziness that comes with living without electricity or plumbing, especially when it's minus 40 degrees and dark for most of the time in winter," he said. "At first we used kerosene and headlamps to get around in the dark. But that got old, especially when we had kids. They grew up thinking we were Cyclops. In 2008, I installed solar and battery power. Now we live a cushy life. But we still have to take our dirty clothes to a laundry."

Few people down south realize it, but summer temperatures in the interior of Alaska, the Yukon, and the Mackenzie River valleys can, on occasion, reach 95°F in June and July. Because the sun goes down for only a few hours at that time of year, the burning heat doesn't dissipate as quickly as it does elsewhere. The forest can dry quickly, even after a hard rain. Fire doesn't go to sleep at night as long as it does down south.

Living in the boreal forest, Rupp and his family have learned to live with the threat of wildfire in summer, as most everyone in the interior does. A year after they moved onto their boreal farm, the Boundary fire of 2004 got within 10 miles of their property. Then, in 2013, a fire ignited in a nearby bombing range. That fire burned hot and moved very quickly. Because of unexploded ordinances on the ground, firefighters could not deploy ground crews to fight it.

Rupp had no idea that there was a fire burning nearby until three air tankers flew overhead. He was on the roof hammering nails into an extension and was nearly knocked over by the roar of the planes flying so low directly above him.

As a scientist who spends most of his time behind a desk and computer trying to figure out patterns of wildfire frequency and plant succession, Rupp became obsessed watching the plume of smoke mushrooming over the mountain in the near distance. He'd never been as close to a big runaway fire such as this one. At one point, firefighters came in to set up some hoses and sprinklers on the property, which Rupp had fortunately made relatively fireproof by clearing trees around the house, barn, and other buildings. Kerry and their daughters left to stay with a friend. Rupp remained on the farm to take care of the goats and other animals.

"At one point, I could feel the heat of the fire on my skin," he recalled. "I couldn't see the mountain that was about a half mile away. The smoke was thick and ash was falling. The goats were beginning to freak out. Fortunately, the fire stopped at the river side, and then the rains came."

Rupp grew up in southeastern Pennsylvania, not far from the Amish communities. While studying at Penn State, he was inspired to pursue a career in wildfire science by a forest ecology course taught by a professor named Mark Abrams. "It was a great course," said Rupp. "Abrams was very good at explaining how forests such as those that are dominated by oak and pine in the East can morph into something completely different like red and sugar maple when wildfire is suppressed over a long period of time. It was all new to me back then and a relatively new field of study in wildfire science. I had thought that the forests I grew up around were the same forests that had always been there."

Rupp got hooked on this idea of forest and plant succession in post-fire environments. Alaska, a state with 18 percent of the country's trees and plenty of big fires, beckoned. So, on July 1, 1993, he headed to Fairbanks with all his worldly possessions to pursue a graduate degree at the University of Alaska in Fairbanks and to work with a group of scientists who were just beginning to see how forest succession was playing out on a landscape that was rapidly thawing and burning bigger and more often than it had done before.

⌒

Although the university in Fairbanks may not register high on the radar of most American students looking for a college degree, it has had no shortage of freedom-loving academics who have made a colorful, and sometimes emphatic, mark in wildfire science, Arctic ecology, and climate change, which some faculty members saw coming long before the rest of the world was paying attention.

Bill Pruitt, a mentor of mine, was one of them. He came to Alaska in 1953 after graduating from the University of Michigan. Like Rupp, he lived for a time in a log cabin without electricity or plumbing. Before joining the faculty, he spent months in the field, tracking the movement of caribou by dog team.

I thought Pruitt was a one-of-kind scientist until I read and heard about Les Viereck. Right around the time Pruitt was settling into the land of the midnight sun, Viereck and two friends from Dartmouth College in New Hampshire drove a Model A Ford up the Alaska Highway, which looked more like a winding switchback than the paved road it eventually became. He returned to Alaska several times to conduct research for a degree in plant ecology at the University of Colorado. Like Pruitt, he got hooked. In 1954, he climbed Mount McKinley, the highest peak in North America, and worked for a time as a national park ranger before joining the faculty at the University of Alaska in Fairbanks.

Viereck and Pruitt came together in a way that neither one of them could have envisioned at the time. When the Atomic Energy Commission came up with a plan to use nuclear bombs to excavate a harbor along the northwest coast of Alaska, not far from where a small group of Inupiat people lived, the University of Alaska in Fairbanks became the research contractor. As Alaskan historian Dan O'Neill documented in his book *The Firecracker Boys*, Pruitt, Viereck, Don Foote, and others quickly recognized the insanity of "Project Chariot." Faced with the realization that both the commission and the university were distorting and underestimating the environmental effect of detonating nuclear bombs buried below the surface of the coastline, they put their careers on the line by going public. Both Viereck and Pruitt were fired by the university for going public and for trying to put a stop to this plan.

Pruitt ended up at the University of Manitoba, where he became one of Canada's top boreal scientists and one of the first—if not the first—scientist to establish a link between wildfire and the growth of lichen that caribou depend upon. The lichen is a crusty, sponge-like form of vegetation that takes a half century or more to recover from fire. Viereck stayed behind to work for the Alaska Department of Fish and Game before becoming the principal plant ecologist at the US Forest Service's Institute of Northern Forestry Forest Science Laboratory. The lab, ironically, was based on the campus of the University of Alaska in Fairbanks, where Viereck was still scorned by the administration but greatly admired by the faculty.

Viereck was a tough act to follow in Alaska. He defined the roles that wildfire, flooding, and glaciers play in plant succession and how forests respond to these disturbances. But many of those who later joined the University of Alaska faculty in Fairbanks—Glenn Juday, Terry Chapin, Dan Mann, and David McGuire to name but a few—continued with some groundbreaking research.

In some ways, Juday was the polar opposite of Pruitt and Viereck. He had no intention of politicizing any of his research when he arrived in Alaska in 1977 as the first Alaska Ecological Reserves coordinator. Nor did he want to be seen as an advocate, for fear that decision makers might think he had an agenda.

Juday sensed that something odd was going on with the climate in Alaska almost from the moment he arrived, however. Wildfire burned a record amount of tundra on the Seward Peninsula that first summer in 1977. Temperatures the following year were the second warmest they had been since meteorologists started recording weather data in 1916. In the winter of 1981, mean monthly temperatures in January were 30°F above normal.

" 'All right,' I thought. These could just be coincidences, but it seemed like we were rolling dice and always getting a four or five coming up," he said. "At the time, global warming was a concept that I thought was a distant prospect, not something I would see in my time. But if this was climate change we were seeing, and I thought maybe it might be, I wanted to make sure we had the ability to measure it at the natural areas that we had set up in the state."

With the support of colleagues and the university, Juday organized a national meeting in April 1982 to consider how global climate change might affect a specific region such as Alaska. It was one of the first to be conducted in the United States. In the lead-up to the conference, Juday pulled together all the meteorological data he could get his hands on to see if a trend was emerging in the state.

"The Institute of Northern Forestry had just obtained a computer with a pen plotter, which is primitive compared with today's technology. But it helped a great deal," he said. "As I added the data we had available, the squiggly lines on the screen kept going up and up, suggesting that the climate really was warming even when natural variability such as that which comes from El Niño events were factored in. I wasn't certain of it at the time, but the data suggested that if greenhouse gases began to overwhelm the natural range of variability, Alaska would experience a stairstep increase in temperatures, the peaks of which would reach unprecedented heights."

The conference attracted a number of high-profile scientists, such as Charles Keeling of the Scripps Institute of Oceanography. Keeling was among the first US scientists to alert the world to the greenhouse effect that would come with runaway carbon dioxide emissions. William Kellogg, a climatologist with the National Centre of Atmospheric Research, was there as well. He and Claire Parkinson pioneered studies in the role that satellites could play in tracking climate change. At the conference, Kellogg once again predicted what he and Parkinson had written in a paper they had famously published in 1979; that if greenhouse gases continued to rise, "the Arctic Ocean will become ice-free with a relative modest warming, one that could occur very early in the next century."[3]

We know now that it all proved to be true.

When the conference ended, however, Juday's boss gave him a congratulatory pat on the back, but the university administrators and funding agencies suggested that he go back to do some "real work." With no other choice, he bore down selecting, assessing, and establishing more ecological reserves.

Opportunity, however, presented itself the next year when a US National Science Foundation external review panel came to the university to evaluate work that had been done in fire ecology in the black spruce ecosystem that dominates much of Alaska's interior forests.

Once again, Juday saw opportunity presenting itself in a coincidental event. While the panel was meeting in 1983, the Rosie Creek wildfire raced across the forest west of Fairbanks, burning a significant number of white spruce trees in the Bonanza Creek Experimental Forest near Fairbanks. Juday worked quickly with his colleagues to develop a research plan that they sent to local legislators who were meeting with the National Science Foundation. To their surprise, the state quickly came up with funding for scientists to study the effects of the fire. Impressed by what they saw and heard as well, the review panel recommended that they expand the research to include white spruce. Four years later, the National Science Foundation added the Bonanza Creek

Experimental Forest to its Long Term Ecological Research Network.

As surprising as it might seem, political interest in wildfire was not unusual in Alaska back then. The Bonanza Creek Experimental Forest was established on state land in 1963 because of the Shageluk East fire that had burned 644,389 acres five years earlier. Alaskans feared that fire could seriously undermine timber harvesting and big game hunting opportunities. Bonanza Creek was the perfect spot because research on soil and white spruce growth, yield, and seed production was already under way.

The momentum continued right up until 1988 when Yellowstone National Park burned big and when scientist Jim Hansen made his famous speech to Congress saying that he was 99 percent certain that record temperatures were not the result of natural variation. "It's time to stop waffling so much and say that the evidence is pretty strong that the greenhouse effect is here," Hansen famously told reporters after the meeting.[4]

The waffling, however, continued with the Reagan administration, which carefully picked and chose what kind of scientific research it would fund. Climate change was not high on the list. Funding for NASA's Goddard Institute for Space Studies in New York, where Hansen worked, was cut, and for a time, many of the prescribed burns that were intended to thin the country's forests were put on hold.

As political and public interest in climate change declined, Juday was left wondering whether he should give up and move on to something else. He explained, "For me personally, the decision came down to this: how would I feel if the biggest change to affect northern forests in the past several thousand years occurred, and I was too busy to notice? I decided that even if the time scale of change put the confirmation of global warming effects past my retirement, I would go ahead and focus on the potential effects of warming on boreal tree growth and forest health."

With the help of Gordon Jacoby and Rosanne D'Arrigo of the Lamont-Doherty Tree Ring Laboratory of Columbia University, Juday started cutting down spruce trees that were killed in the 1983 Rosie Creek fire, not to reconstruct past climates, but to determine how recent change might have affected these trees. Not unexpectedly, Les Viereck's research at this site had previously shown that plants and trees grow best on warm sites. That is what should happen under normal climatic conditions.

Juday fully expected to see this kind of growth imprinted in the tree rings. Instead, he found the opposite to be true. The growth of the white spruce declined in years of hot, dry weather and resumed normal growth when the weather cooled.

Fearing that he may have made a mistake or missed something, Juday enlisted Valerie Barber, a PhD student at the time, to see if she might be able to verify the findings by using carbon 13 in the wood to measure moisture stress. Her research and field research that was later conducted by Martin Wilmking, another doctoral student, clearly showed that it was drought and high temperatures that limited the growth of these trees. The spruce should have benefited from the heat, but they just didn't have enough water to take advantage of it. It was one of the early, hidden signs pointing to climate changes affecting plant ecology in Alaska.

In 2004, the Arctic Council, a high-level intergovernmental forum that addresses issues faced by Arctic governments and indigenous people of the Arctic, sponsored the Arctic Climate Impact Assessment, a major international collaborative study and synthesis of climate change and its effects across the circumpolar regions. Juday was part of a team of scientists given the task of pulling together information on forests, land management, and agriculture. By then, he had been observing changes in Alaskan climate, fire, and its effects on landscape for nearly thirty years.

"It was clear to us that a period of major, sustained temperature increases was under way in the North," he said. "In parts of the boreal forest with greater precipitation, such as eastern Canada, western Russia, and the Nordic countries, tree growth generally increased with increasing temperatures, but in the Russian Far East and central and western North American boreal region, temperature increases were often decreasing tree growth and increasing fire and insect outbreaks. I reported that in addition to white spruce, growth of some black spruce and Alaska birch populations responds negatively to warming."

Juday had expected that these rising temperatures, along with the spruce budworm and spruce bark beetle infestations that came with them, would have translated into more wildfire in Alaska, as was clearly happening in the rest of the world. But that didn't become obvious until a few years after the 2004 runaway fire season.

~

A record 6.7 million acres (2.7 million hectares) burned in Alaska in 2004. Another 3.7 million (1.5 million hectares) of forest burned in the neighboring Yukon Territory. Together they burned an area the size of Massachusetts and New Hampshire combined. Smoke from the fires could be detected all the way to the east coast of Canada and throughout many parts of the contiguous United States. Alaskans suffered for fifteen straight days when air quality in cities such as Fairbanks was deemed to be hazardous to health by EPA standards.

I remember the 2004 fire season well because my family and I had planned to do a canoe trip down the Wind River in the northern part of the Yukon Territory that summer. Because of the threat of fire, however, the Alaska Highway was temporarily shut down in a number of places, so it was a bit of a gamble to make the drive north. Still, we thought seriously about doing just that. Then my brother-in-law, a pilot, phoned from Whitehorse, where he and my sister live. He suggested that we call the trip off because, with all the smoke, there was no guarantee that a bush plane was going to be able to fly us into and out of the start and ending points along the river.

The 2004 fire may have been a record breaker that signaled a new era of fire in Alaska, the Yukon, and the Northwest Territories, which is also having its share of big fire seasons. But the fire that really caught the attention of the science community was a remote tundra fire that burned along the Anaktuvuk River on the North Slope of Alaska in 2007. It accounted for 40 percent of the area burned in the state that year.

Biologist Ben Abbott remembers it well. He and some colleagues were at the Toolik Field Station in northern Alaska playing a game of soccer on a gravel pad when he smelled smoke in the air. Initially, Abbott thought nothing of it because smoke from forest fires farther south in Alaska occasionally drifted into this part of the world. He and his colleagues quickly realized, however, that this smoke was coming from the North Slope of Alaska, where there are no trees.

Tundra fires are relatively rare in the Arctic. Phil Higuera, a

Figure 8-1 This photograph was taken July 14, 2007, three days after the Anaktuvuk tundra fire started. The fire accounted for 40 percent of the area that burned in Alaska that year. (Richard Reanier)

University of Missoula paleoecologist, said that the tundra around Anaktuvuk River hadn't burned in any significant way for five thousand years.

Higuera is not alone in suggesting that climate change will result in an increase in tundra fire severity and frequency. Not only will it liberate enormous amounts of carbon and methane that has been frozen in the peat, it will also alter mineral soil and nutrient supplies in ways that favor woody shrubs over moss, sedges, grass, and lichen.

The evidence for these changes in Alaska began with the pioneering research Chuck Racine did in the aftermath of the tundra fire that burned along the Seward Peninsula in 1977. In the years following the fire, Racine puzzled over the varying degrees of vegetation recovery. The severity of the burns in different places, it appeared, dictated how fast vegetation that had been present before the fire would grow. Woody shrubs, it appeared, were doing better than moss, lichen, and sedges in the more severely burned areas of the tundra.

Randi Jandt, one of the scientists who took over monitoring many of the tundra burn sites that Racine had scoped out before his retirement, said that the lichen and moss that once covered 20 percent of the tundra fire has not recovered. "What we do see is willows taking over," she said. She and others are seeing the same pattern of lichens and moss being replaced by willows wherever tundra fires burn. Tundra is being colonized by scrub brush, aided by wildfire.

Jandt came to in Alaska in 1986 to do a graduate degree at the university in Fairbanks. Climate change was not on her radar back then. Her initial interest was in moose densities and how they were affected by changes in habitat. In time, her interest in moose gave way to studying caribou, whose populations in Alaska, the Yukon, and Northwest Territories began to tailspin in the 1990s. This population decline would affect both native and nonnative people who relied on the animals for food.

Initially, overhunting was believed to be the problem. That idea, though, overlooked that pipelines, predators, disease, and climate were also at play. With Kyle Joly, Randy Myers, and Chuck Racine, Jandt began looking at caribou habitat in the central Arctic tundra areas that burned and didn't burn in 1972, 1977, and 1981. Comparing the two helped her and her colleagues connect the dots between climate, fire, caribou, and habitat.

"What we found was pretty incredible," said Jandt. "A quarter century after those fires, lichen cover on the tundra remained extremely low whether there were caribou there feeding or not. Fire, however, was not the only reason for the decline. We found that lichen cover also declined on the tundra areas that did not burn."

Jandt came to the conclusion that climate change had to be a big part of the explanation. In either case, she said, tundra fire and warmer temperatures will result in warmer soils and a longer growing season that do not favor lichens and other forms of tundra vegetation that caribou rely on.

In Alaska, the Yukon, and the Northwest Territories, that is bad news for native people, who see caribou in much the way southerners see cattle. Unable to afford the high cost of beef that has to be flown in, they, as well as nonnative people, hunt to put food on the table. (Given a choice, they would choose caribou over beef.) Some studies suggest that five caribou, which represent enough to provide the protein a family needs to get through a fall and winter, are equal to about $5,000 in grocery bills. In the Yukon-Koyukuk census area of north central Alaska, that amounts to more than a quarter per capita income.

Jandt and her colleagues are now talking about the threshold change that Glen Juday, Scott Rupp, Dave Mann, and others have already documented in the boreal forest of Alaska. The dramatic decline in the ratio of spruce trees to deciduous trees that began in earnest around 1990, they suggest, is moving forward quickly on a trajectory that will see those deciduous trees dominating by 2040.[5]

Jandt has no doubt that the boreal forest is morphing into something quite different than what it was when she first arrived in Alaska, but she wonders whether aspen and poplar are going to prevail in the long run because they do not do well in drought or permafrost conditions.

"The boreal forest we know now can only take so much change," she said. "Alaska is warming twice as fast as the rest of the world. Temperatures here have risen as much as 4.9 degrees from 1949 to 2012. Anchorage, which usually gets a month of subzero weather, got none in 2014. Between 1982 and 2010, the growing season began nineteen days earlier and ended eighteen days later. We have a lot more snow free days and a lot more lightning. With permafrost thawing and fire burning more often, there's only so much these forests can take."

~

Fox Lake is situated along the Klondike Highway in the Yukon. It is a very pretty spot, even if it's not quite the eye-popper like Kathleen Lake in Kluane National Park or Emerald Lake, an impossibly green body of water located near the town of Carcross. The image of Fox Lake is burned into my memory bank for two reasons. I caught my first big lake trout there in summer of 1978. I also saw how a wildfire scorched the hillsides twenty years later and temporarily turned it into an apocalyptic scene. What I remember most was the purple hue that colored the entire hillside in the years that followed, an illustration of how brilliantly the fireweed plant earned its name.

Jill Johnstone and her husband live at one end of Fox Lake in a house that has no plumbing or central heating. From one side, they have a view of the lake. From the other, they can gaze upon a wetland and stream that snakes through the boreal forest. Inside they have a grand piano and most of the luxuries and conveniences one has in an urban setting. They are not the only people living along the lake. A couple that live nearby make a living selling fireweed honey, wild mushrooms, and jams.

Johnstone is both a Canadian and an American citizen. She first got interested in the Arctic while studying at Middlebury College with Bill Howland, who was then the director of the Northern Studies Center. I just missed meeting Johnstone on Ellesmere Island, the northernmost island in the Arctic, when she was doing a master's of science thesis with Greg Henry, a tundra ecologist I know who has spent more than a quarter century trying to determine how tundra plants respond to climate change. I was on the island when she was there in 1993, but I was unable to hitch a helicopter ride to their field site.

Johnstone fell in love with this part of the Yukon when she was doing her PhD with Terry Chapin at the University of Alaska. Over a three-year period, she drove 9,300 miles, (15,000 kilometers) along a loop that took her east from Fairbanks to the Tok cutoff near the Canadian border, from the Tok cutoff to the white-knuckle drive along the Top of the World Highway, from the Top of the World Highway to the historic gold rush town of Dawson in the Yukon, and then down the Klondike Highway to Fox Lake and Whitehorse before returning north to Alaska.

A few weeks after I met up with Rupp, I spent several days with Johnstone driving this loop to see firsthand what she learned by stopping at various points along the way, recording the plants and trees that grew up after a wildfire. "It's like a card game," she said. "After a fire, there is a shuffling of the deck, and once the cards are dealt, the ecosystem has to play the cards it receives. In the boreal, where the ecosystem has very few tree and plant species compared to, say, the Amazon, there are only a certain number of ways that the game can be played out. Controlling forces such as soil acidity, precipitation, heat, permafrost, and north- and south-facing slopes helps determine which plants and trees are most successful. So does climate change, now more than ever before."

Johnstone picked me up at my sister's house in Whitehorse, and we began the drive north toward Kluane National Park. We didn't stop to see how the spruce bark beetle had ravaged the park's forests because the Parks Canada fire and vegetation specialist wasn't allowed to take us on a tour. (I had made the request six weeks beforehand.) The muzzling of Canadian scientists that occurred in the years when Stephen Harper's climate-change-denying Conservative government was in power still lingered in the first year of Prime Minister Justin Trudeau's administration.

Hearing Johnstone talk about her fieldwork on Ellesmere Island, the Yukon, Alaska, the Northwest Territories, and northern Saskatchewan and about her teaching, her supervising graduate students, and her living off the grid in the wilderness, I couldn't help but remark out loud about how much I admired her confidence and capabilities.

"Truth be told, if I was an animal, I'd be a lemming," she scoffed. "The lemming is the only animal I know of that can die of stress. I suffer a lot from anxiety."

As we headed into Alaska toward the Tok cutoff, we stopped at a spot where a small wildfire had burned more than two months earlier. The first thing you notice when you walk into a fresh burn is the charcoal that blackens your skin and clothes as you bushwhack through and brush up against fire-scarred branches. The next thing you notice is how quickly the landscape recovers. There was already so much fireweed and other plants sprouting up that Johnstone had doubts about whether what we were seeing was this year's burn. Looking closer at the dead trees, we could see where the woodpeckers had punched holes into the bark to get at the beetles. "If there are enough beetles, you can sometimes hear them feeding. It's that loud," she said.

Like most Alaskans—80 percent of them live in the boreal region— the residents of Tok have learned to live with fire. Almost everyone was evacuated in 1990 when a fire tripled in size in a couple of days, producing its own lightning, as the Fort McMurray fire did. At one critical point, the highway Johnstone and I were driving along was closed at the Canadian border. Despite the danger, about a dozen locals stayed behind in the local bar while firefighters bulldozed a firebreak around the edge of town. Had the winds not changed direction at the last minute, Tok would have likely been razed.

At times on the drive from the Tok cutoff to Chicken, Alaska, and the Top of the World Highway, it was difficult to see how fire can be such a monstrous force in this part of the world. The summer season is a short one, and when it rains, as it did during most of our trip, nothing

Figure 8-2 Wildfire scientist Jill Johnstone digs into the soil in a forest burn in Alaska. Controlling forces such as soil acidity, precipitation, heat, permafrost, and north- and south-facing slopes help determine which plants and trees are most successful in recovering from a fire. (Edward Struzik)

burns easily. I have often learned this same thing to my dismay on rainy canoe trips in the Arctic.

Then I was reminded of something Scott Rupp had told me a few weeks earlier. As wet as this summer had been that year, there was a three-day period in mid-July, after all the fire crews went south, when the temperatures in Alaska rose to the low 90s and high 80s. Over a three-day period, 45,000 strikes of lightning ignited one hundred fires. Had a cold front not moved in shortly after, he said, it might have resulted in another runaway fire season.

For scientists like Rupp, Jandt, Juday, and Johnstone, Alaska and the Arctic offer a unique opportunity to study climate change because the human population is too small and too scattered to produce noise on a local scale that can confound the data. The Anaktuvuk River on the North Slope of Alaska is one such place, as is the Seward Peninsula and the Bonanza Creek Experimental Forest. The 320-mile-long drive along the Klondike Highway from Dawson to Fox Lake provides several more baselines. Since the 1950s, six major wildfires have burned the landscape here in ways that are made obvious by signposts that the Yukon government smartly posted to educate people about fire.

We stopped at one of the fires that burned at Braeburn, a road stop that is famous for its giant $12 cinnamon buns and a picture on the wall of legendary actor Steve McQueen on a motorcycle he bought from the owner. I ate my first giant cinnamon bun here in 1978 shortly after catching that lake trout. Judging by the reception that Johnstone and I got that day, the owner was more interested in bus tours than walk-ins like us. The cinnamon buns seemed to have shrunk as well.

After a very quick lunch, Johnstone put the truck into four-wheel drive and drove me up a steep south-facing hillside that burned in 1998. It didn't occur to me until she pointed it out that the spruce trees that once dominated this landscape are no longer there. It's pretty much all aspen, as you might expect it to be in the decade after a fire. By now, spruce should have been taking over. After almost twenty years, however, that wasn't happening.

Johnstone had one of her students assess the tree rings of the white spruce that burned in the 1998 fire to find out why there was so little spruce regeneration. Some of the trees that burned turned out to be more than 200 years old. Most were in the range of 120 years, beneficiaries of fires that burned around 1880 or some time after. Like Glenn Juday did decades earlier at Bonanza Creek, the student discovered that by 1998, these mature spruce trees were already stressed by heat and drought. They were growing, but not very well during the hot, dry summer months.

With the cards that have been shuffled from the deck that came with the wildfire in 1998, Johnstone doesn't envision spruce playing a role in the Fox Lake environment in the future, at least not on the south-facing slopes where the heat is most pronounced. Spruce are present on the cooler north-facing slopes, but even there, they may have a tough time coping with the hotter, drier temperatures that come with climate change.

～

There are not one or two, but, rather, several wild cards in the deck that is being played out in Alaska and the northern forests and tundra of

Canada. The first two are drought and climate change. The third is the cold weather and the permafrost at the northern end of the boreal forest that make it difficult for anything but black spruce to push the tree line northward. Black spruce is without a doubt the most charismatic tree in the boreal forest, if one can say that about a tree. Stands of black spruce growing out of frozen soils are akin to a group of drunks, precariously leaning against one another in a bar. With the thawing and freezing permafrost, the trees have a hard time rooting themselves in a way that allows them to grow straight up. Trudging through a wet black spruce forest, I have a peculiar sense that the trees are leaning over to get a better look at me. That strange sense of being watched is most pronounced in the early fall, when the darkening afternoon sky is painted with sweeps of orange and Tyrian purple.

Shuffle the wild cards into the regular deck and you get a number of what-if scenarios. What if the frequency of fires increases in the northern boreal forest and the tundra as the temperatures continue to rise? What happens if fire destabilizes the permafrost as it has done many times along Arctic rivers and lakes? What happens if droughts persist and peatlands ecosystems begin burning in a big way?

Scary is an inappropriate word to use when describing scientific research, but there is no other way of describing what Merritt Turetsky, Mike Flannigan, Brian Stocks, and Mike Wotton concluded when they assessed what might happen if the peatlands of the boreal forest and Arctic tundra start to burn in a big way. Fires like those don't candle as they do in pine and spruce forest. Instead, they smolder, often for months or longer. If they burn deep enough down, they can continue to smolder beneath the snow through the winter.

There is twice as much carbon trapped in permafrost as there is in the atmosphere. As more of this carbon is released, temperatures are going to rise even faster. And as more of that black carbon falls onto the glaciers and sea ice that keep the northern regions cool, the melting will accelerate.

Following the 2015 fire season, Randi Jandt, Scott Rupp, and others got together to discuss the what-if scenarios.

"What if that 2.5 inches of rain hadn't come in July 2015 and fires kept raging through September, like they did in 2004?" wondered Jandt. "We'd be at some whole new level of fire.

"Sooner or later, this scenario is going to manifest itself as it did in Fort McMurray in 2016. Given the fact that we're warming twice as fast as the rest of the world, it's almost certain that we are going to have bigger fires burning hotter and more frequently. This is going to have an impact on everything from permafrost to caribou and people who live here. We have to start asking ourselves if we're ready for this. And if we're not, we need to start asking what we can do."

~

Several summers ago, I was camped on Axel Heiberg in an uninhabited region of the High Arctic, about 600 miles (1,000 kilometers) south of the North Pole and next door to Ellesmere Island, where Jill Johnstone conducted her research on tundra plants in the 1990s. With me was a small team of scientists who were searching for the fossil remains of animals that roamed the great plains of this polar desert many millions of years ago.

It was monotonous, if not grueling, work. Each morning, we got up and climbed a small mountain of dirt and rock above the tent camp we had set up in a narrow valley where two glacial streams converged. Hunched over, with eyes focused on the brown, frozen ground, we spent hours on end searching for anything—the enamel of a tooth, for example—that might look like it didn't belong there. To untrained eyes like mine, it was maddening, not only because I did not have a clear idea of what I was looking for, but also because I could not make that leap of faith to believe that there was anything of importance to be found.

Unlike parts of Ellesmere Island to the east or Banks Island to the west, where there are oases of life tucked between verdant, south-facing hillsides, there seemed little in the frozen history of this polar world. There is certainly nothing important enough to fill in the blanks of an ancient past or reveal anything about its future. All that lay beyond our small mountain was a broad, sedgeless plain that stopped at the foot of a giant ice cap on one side and a frozen fjord on the other.

But each time doubts like these clouded by thoughts, I turned to look at the tree stumps that were sticking out of the ground behind us. Frozen in an aerobic environment for the past 45 million years, these remnants of an ancient dawn redwood forest in the Arctic were being revealed by wind and erosion and by scientific pursuits such as ours. In and around these forests, herds of brontotheres—rhino-like creatures—roamed.

In the years that followed, I participated in similar expeditions on Devon Island, where these same animals ran rampant in High Arctic forests 23 million years ago; at Strathcona Fiord on Ellesmere, where we found 4.5-million-year-old fossils that conjured images of miniature beavers on the lookout for ancient black bears and badgers that lived in the region at the same time; and on Banks Island in the western Arctic, where 4-million-year-old spruce trees continue to erode out of the permafrost.

The Arctic, we have come to learn, has been warm enough to grow forests for most of the past 100 million years. No one really knows exactly why it was warm for so long. Earth's climate has responded in the past to natural forces—variations in Earth's eccentricity, axial tilt, and precession[6]—unlike our current situation in which greenhouse gas emissions are the main driver for the climate change. Volcanic ash, the formation of gyres, and methane seeping from permafrost and percolating from the ocean floor were other factors that likely controlled Earth's thermostat.

What we do know from fossil evidence found in ancient lakes and ocean floor beds, ice cores, and permafrost suggests that a trend to cooling began shortly after large mammals replaced the dinosaurs 65 million years ago. This gradual cooling, interspersed with episodes of increasing warmth, led to the gradual buildup of ice sheets in the Arctic. In the time of miniature beavers on Ellesmere, 4.5 million years ago, a catastrophic cycling of advancing and retreating glaciers in the Arctic began to take hold.

In relatively rapid-fire fashion, the cold wiped out the High Arctic forests, miniature beavers, black bears, and badgers. Even the woolly mammoths, American mastodons, saber-toothed cats, and giant sloths that took their place hundreds of thousands of years later were unable to weather the cycles of cooling and warming. These cycles glaciated 30 percent of Earth's surface at one end of the extreme and turned huge swaths of tundra into forests and shrublands on the other. What we are left with today in the Arctic are the survivors (specialists is a better word)—the polar bears, narwhals, bowheads, belugas, muskoxen, and caribou—that were able to evolve and adapt to this vicious climatic cycling and to the deep freeze that has characterized the Arctic's most recent past.

These are heady times for scientists, especially those tough enough to live off the grid, endure freezing temperatures, and put up with smoke-filled air in the summertime. With the rapid warming of the Arctic, we may well be on a trajectory that will result in more fires, less forest, dwindling tundra, and more animal extinctions and extirpations. Glenn Juday sensed that something big was happening back in 1977. Big things, it turns out, are happening all across the Arctic.

Chapter 9

Agent of Change

Into the eternal darkness, into fire and ice.
— Dante Alighieri, *The Divine Comedy*

In the summer of 1955, a floatplane flew a small group of American climbers to a lake near the edge of a massive icefield straddling the Continental Divide along the Yukon/Northwest Territories border in northern Canada. When the group saw the cluster of jagged peaks and sheer rock walls they were searching for, they were stunned. Emerging from the edges of the Brintnell/Bologna icefield was a 9,000-foot palisade of ice-polished granite that bore an uncanny resemblance to the craggy spires of Yosemite.

Having underestimated the challenge he and his team would confront that day, expedition leader Arnold Wexler turned to his partners and declared most of the icy peaks to be "unclimbable." Today, still largely untrodden because of its extreme remoteness, the "Cirque of the Unclimbables" is now part of Nahanni National Park, a United Nations World Heritage Site. It remains legendary in the world of rock climbing.

In late August 2015, I accompanied glaciologist Mike Demuth and a group of Canadian researchers monitoring the retreat of the icefields

surrounding the Cirques as well as the lichens and other forms of vegetation that have been rising up around them. It was my third visit since
the late winter of 2006, when Demuth had just begun to scope out the
area for a long-term climate change study. As extraordinary as the first
two expeditions were, this one was, in some ways, the most memorable.

On one evening, we were bewitched watching a violent thunderstorm mushroom upslope from the heavily forested Nahanni River
valley below before it swept across our alpine camp, with lightning
thudding against the ground not far from our tents. That was just days
before the beginning of September, when it's usually heavy, wet snow
that falls on the ground this high in the mountains. On another evening, we watched nervously as a grizzly bear sauntered up valley and
crossed the glacier toward us before veering off in the fading light.

The image that struck me most, however, was the one I didn't expect
to see when we first landed. Instead of pristine, crystalized layers of firn
that are typically left over from past winter seasons and periodic late-
summer snowfalls, we found an atrophying glacial surface darkened
by sand and dirt that had slid down from the adjacent mountainsides.
Further dulling the color of the icy surface was soot that had been
transported in from wildfires that have been burning bigger, hotter,
faster, and more often in this part of the world.

This glacier was dying, and we were reminded of that every day as
we trudged up its slope with crampons afoot. Raging rivulets of water
were streaming down along dozens of deeply carved channels in the
ice, forcing us to run and jump over them wherever we could. Every
once in a while, we would see the bones of boreal animals such as caribou, wolverine, and porcupine melting out of ice they had been trapped
and died in, presumably after slipping into a crevice or moulin many
years or decades earlier.

I was well aware at the time that the western Arctic is warming
twice as fast as the rest of the world. But the implications for wildfire
and the wholescale landscape and ecosystems changes that wildfire
promises to bring were driven home by my trips to Alaska in 2016 and
to the ones I have made to many other parts of the Arctic. This wild
synergy between fire and ice, I learned, is not only melting glaciers
and rapidly thawing permafrost, it is mowing down trees, degrading
forests and watersheds, and making refugees of many wildlife species

Figure 9-1 Soot from wildfires in the Arctic is darkening the surface of glaciers, like this one in the Canadian Arctic, as it absorbs the sun's heat and accelerates the melting that is already taking place. (Edward Struzik)

in as profound a way as the Buffalo Creek, Hayman, and Waldo fires have done in the front ranges of the Rocky Mountains in Colorado.

Wildfire is nothing new to the Arctic. As the University of Alaska's Glenn Juday and his colleagues learned when they first went north in the 1970s, fires routinely burn in the interior of Alaska, as they do in the Yukon, the Northwest Territories, and the boreal forest of Siberia and Scandinavia. But according to wildfire data gleaned from various fire agencies and from a report that was done by the nonprofit organization Climate Central, nothing in the seventy-year human record of fire in the Arctic compares to what has been happening since the turn of the twenty-first century.[1] In fact, a 2013 study done by Ryan Kelly, Philip Higuera, and others suggests that the severity of fires in Alaska is the highest it's been in the past 10,000 years.[2]

Arctic wildfires began to increase in size and severity in the 1990s. By the end of the first decade of the twenty-first century, large wildfires increased in size tenfold compared to those that burned in the 1950s and 1960s. The 2004 and 2005 wildfires burned more area than all that was burned from 1950 to 1964.

The wildfire season is starting earlier and lasting longer. Alaska's fire season is now 40 percent longer than it was in the 1950s. That has given fire an extra month to ignite and burn there and in Arctic and sub-Arctic regions to the east in the Yukon and Northwest Territories. The warming that has come with climate change has also extended the reach of lightning to the regions of the far north, where thunderstorms were once rare. The massive Anaktuvuk tundra fire that burned on the North Slope of Alaska in 2007 was a testament to that. It accounted for 40 percent of all the area that burned in the state that year.

American glaciologist Jason Box made a name for himself in 2012 when he and others linked the Arctic wildfires that were burning big during that record hot year to the dark soot that was falling on the Greenland ice cap, where it absorbed the sun's heat and accelerated the melting that was already taking place. The connection between wildfires and blackened glaciers was, in fact, made more than a decade earlier when scientists tracked a plume of smoke and ash from a pre-scribed burn that lit up 900 acres of mostly black spruce forest in the boreal forest interior of Alaska in July 1999. After scientists from the University of Alaska and colleagues in Japan traced soot from that fire to the Gulkana Glacier south of Fairbanks, they suggested that boreal fires could play a strong role in sea-ice melt and glacier retreat.[3]

They were right, even if it is impossible to say exactly how much wildfire is contributing to the retreat of glaciers. The regression of ice has been a worldwide phenomenon, with various other factors at play. What happened in the icefields near the Cirque of the Unclimbables reflects the bigger story. Between 1982 and 2008, the glacier-covered area contracted by about 30 percent, from 101 square miles to 71 square miles. Its retreat has accelerated since then at a pace that could result in it disappearing by the end of the twenty-first century.

As big an impact as wildfire is having on the hasty retreat of glaciers, its impact on permafrost, another form of ice, is beginning to really rattle climate change and ecosystems scientists. NASA is so focused on this relatively new and emerging development that it is spending a chunk of the $100 million it has for its Arctic Boreal Vulnerability Experiment (ABoVE) on ground-ice research.

Michelle Mack, a Northern Arizona University scientist who is leading one part of that study, concedes that thawing permafrost may not have the cache that blackening glaciers galloping in reverse has. But if you can appreciate that permafrost is the cement that holds up buildings, roads, and airport runways in the Arctic, that it is an integral part of the plumbing system that maintains wetlands, watersheds, and tundra ecosystems, and that it prevents massive amounts of carbon from further warming the climate and fueling more wildfires, the dull image of ground ice with peat frozen into it becomes much more colorful.

Mack was part of a team of scientists who flew into the Anuktuvuk tundra region a year after it burned in 2007. Part of the goal was to see how much carbon that fire released into the atmosphere. They found that as much as 2.2 million tons of soil carbon were liberated, equivalent to what the entire Arctic absorbs and stores each year. That is a lot by any standard, but not nearly as much as may have burned if the deeper frozen layers of peat weren't so moist and fire resistant. The fire resulted in some subsequent thawing of the permafrost, but not so much that it would result in transformative landscape changes.

What concerns Mack and her colleagues at ABoVE more is the prospect of more fires burning through those layers of moss, leaves, and other organic material in large swaths of the Arctic where the icy layers below the surface aren't as rock-hard cold or as deeply penetrating as they are on the North Slope and at higher latitudes throughout the Arctic.

The Yukon-Kuskokwim delta is one of those places. Located along the Bering Sea on the west coast of Alaska, the delta supports one of the largest and most diverse populations of breeding shorebirds in the western hemisphere. More than half a million shorebirds use the refuge. Among them are black turnstones, western sandpipers, and the entire global population of bristle-thighed curlew that land there for fall staging.

There are about 19.7 acres (8 million hectares) of tundra in the delta.[4] Seven percent of the delta is less than 100 feet above sea level. The soils here are so nutrient-rich and relatively warm that a man by the name of Tim Meyers has been growing organic food on the delta near Bethel since around 2008.

The list of things that scientist Gerald Frost is monitoring in the delta is so long that it would take a page or two to go through it. Frost is

Figure 9-2 Massive slumping that is taking place in many parts of Alaska where fires are burning and permafrost is rapidly thawing. (E. Miller)

leading an ABoVE-funded team of thirteen scientists and participants from the University of Alaska in Fairbanks, the US Fish and Wildlife Service, and other agencies. "We're just beginning to peel back the surface with the research we're doing in the delta," he said. "But I think it's safe to say that we are on the cusp of losing a lot of permafrost in this part of the world, and with the vegetation and hydrological changes that come with that, there will be winners as well as losers."

Wildfire, which is one form of energy that is thawing permafrost, is no stranger to this part of the world. The many fires that burned in 2015, however, were exceptional in the area they covered. More than 300,000 acres of mostly permafrost-laden uplands were affected. Some lakes and streams disappeared as the underlying ice melted. The regeneration that followed appears to be favoring shrubs in some places instead of tundra sedges and lichens.

As the permafrost thaws, hillsides slump and the elevation of what is already a frightfully low-lying part of Alaska sinks. It may not amount to much. But if you consider that sea levels are rising as storms in the region are picking up steam, it makes the future of the Yukon-Kuskokwim delta look like a watery one if the land continues to subside. In 2005, 2006, and 2011, storm surges sent floods of saltwater inland to lengths of 18.8 miles (30.3 kilometers), 17 miles (24.4 kilometers), and 20 miles (32.3 kilometers), respectively. The prospect of more warmish-water storm surges working in tandem with more wildfires and more permafrost thawing in the interior uplands doesn't bode well for freshwater ponds, permafrost, and nonsaline habitat as well as for many birds and animals that dwell in the region.

Not all the Arctic or near Arctic is being affected as dramatically as the Yukon-Kuskokwim delta. In the South Nahanni valley, the boreal forest is still relatively intact, free of bark beetles and budworms, with nothing to suggest that permafrost is thawing in a way that will throw the hydrology of the region off-kilter. Elevation and the cooling effect of the icefields and the mountains may be acting like a regional air conditioner. In the colder regions of the Arctic where permafrost extends to a depth of up to a mile, it's going to take centuries of heat and fire to unleash all the carbon that is stored there.

Seismic landscape changes occurring downstream of Nahanni in the Liard and Mackenzie River valleys of the Northwest Territories, however, offer hints of what may come slowly to some places in the Arctic and faster to others.

The most compelling evidence comes from Roger Brett, a forest health technician with the Canadian Forest Service. Brett has been helping resource managers in Nahanni and the government of the Northwest Territories keep track of what's been happening in the region since 1993. It's part of a broader forest-monitoring program that includes Jasper, Banff, Yoho, Kootenay, Glacier, Mt. Revelstoke, Waterton, Wood Buffalo, and Kluane national parks.

Each year, Brett conducts an aerial survey to see how the forests in those regions are faring. Even some of the more seasoned forest scientists and resource managers have been taken aback by the aerial photos he's shooting. In the Liard and Mackenzie valleys, 310 miles (500 kilometers) from the south to the north, huge stands of aspen are dying off. Jack pine are browning at Willowlake River in the Mackenzie River valley and around Buffalo River, a stream that flows through Wood Buffalo National Park to the southeast. Poplar trees southeast of Nahanni have severe sun scalding. Spruce budworm and the forest tent caterpillar are migrating north into regions where they have never been seen before. Somehow, the budworm has made its way north to the boreal forest around Inuvik, which is about 60 miles from the Arctic Ocean.

The one image that stands out is of the Mackenzie Bison Sanctuary southwest of Great Slave Lake. The sanctuary was created in 1963 to preserve one of the last remaining undiseased wood bison herds left in the world. In recent years, the sanctuary has been filling up with water almost as fast as the icefields in Nahanni are melting. Parts of it look like a dead zone. Tens of thousands of trees that cannot tolerate so much moisture have died. Large swaths of grassy and sedge meadows are now underwater. From 1986 to 2011, the area covered by water increased to levels that now cover almost 10 percent of the sanctuary. Falaise Lake, the biggest body of water in the sanctuary, has grown in area by 824 percent since 1986.[5]

In 2012, Jennifer Korosi and a team of scientists were asked to have a look and assess what's been happening. They were there for three field seasons, taking core samples from lakes and measuring tree-ring growth. "The short answer is that we do not know exactly what's behind this," she said. "But the tree ring and sediment coring that we did suggest that the hydrological changes that are taking place are unprecedented in the last 300 years. The area has flooded before but nothing close to the scale that is now occurring. This is backed up by the Dene elders who hunt and trap in the area."

The best guess is that several things are at play here. Summer temperatures in the southern part of the territory have risen from a mean of between 48°F and 54°F (9°C and 12°C) in the early twentieth century to 55°F and 59°F (13°C and 15°C) today. The result has been the kind of thawing that is occurring in the Yukon-Kuskokwim delta and many others parts of the Arctic. Recent wildfires in the region are likely accelerating that thawing and disrupting the hydrological forces that have kept this region dry. There is no other way to account for the sanctuary continuing to fill up with water when a drought has been drying up the region since 2013.

It is all bad news for Terry Armstrong, a biologist with the government of the Northwest Territories who is assigned the task of monitoring the health and movement of the bison population. The herd has been on a slow, steady decline since 1989. In 2012, an outbreak of anthrax that may have been triggered by intense precipitation and an ensuing drought killed half of the fifteen hundred animals that were remaining. Now the flooding of the forest and meadows they feed in has driven many of them out.

"Scientists talk a lot about how climate change will have an impact on the environment," he told me, "but I never imagined I would see things change so quickly. First we had the floods and then the anthrax outbreak. And then in 2014, we had a wildfire that burned almost half of the bison's territory. We went in to look for the animals in 2016 having no idea where they might be because we don't have tracking collars on them."

The bad news doesn't end just there. In many parts of the Arctic, there is more to peat than just organic carbon and ice. About 80 percent of the world's peatlands are located in the sub-Arctic and Arctic regions of the world. Peatlands, more than any form of soil, are very good at absorbing mercury that is transported in from volcanoes, wildfires, and far-flung industrial sources because each year brings with it another layer of dead leaves, mosses, and other decaying material that seals the mercury into the layer of permafrost. Fire can liberate some of this mercury. So can the flooding that follows. Some of the microbes that live in these aquatic environments convert the relatively stable mercury into toxic methylmercury that builds up in the food chain.

Scientist Dave Olefeldt and his colleagues have been conducting research in the regions south of the Mackenzie Bison Sanctuary, where fire has been burning big and more often. In the shallow lakes that have been created by wildfire and rapidly thawing permafrost thawing, he is finding 4.5 to 14.5 times more methylmercury concentrations than one would typically find in water draining from bogs before the thawing occurred.

"Fire is a big agent of change," said Olefeldt, who, with Alaskan and Russian scientists, recently produced maps identifying boreal regions that are most susceptible to dramatic permafrost thawing. He doesn't see the thawing as accelerating as fast as some other scientists, but he has no doubt that some landscapes and water chemistry are going to be altered in significant ways for some time to come.

"The organic matter that you find in permafrost thaws out like vegetables once they are out of the freezer," explained Olefeldt. "They start to decompose and release greenhouse gases. The most dramatic changes are likely to occur in places where permafrost thaw is accompanied by land surface collapse. This is what you often see after a fire."

The news, however, is not all bad.

Armstrong hopes that a big fire that burned in the sanctuary in 2014 and throughout much of the southern part of the Northwest Territories may reverse the decline of the bison population because bison are, like many animals, attracted to the grass and shoots that rise up quickly after wildfire. It's a similar story for the North Slope of Alaska, where moose may eventually take over what was once caribou habitat, and in the Yukon-Kuskokwim delta, where birds that favor upland shrubs will likely prosper. In these ways, wildfire is as much as blessing for some animals as it is a curse for others. Determining who the winners and losers will be, however, is a challenge that needs to be addressed before future resource and landscape management decisions are made.

Chapter 10

Resilience and Recovery

Be praised, my Lord, through Brother Fire,
through whom You brighten the night.
— Saint Francis of Assisi

I n the spring of 1999, I was with biologist Gord Stenhouse when
he captured a small grizzly bear on the east slopes of the Rocky
Mountains in Jasper National Park. G-16, as this bear came to
be known from that point on, was one of eighteen bears Stenhouse
caught in the first year of a long-term study designed to determine
the population and health of grizzly bears in a 2,066-square-mile
(5,352-square-kilometer) area along the east boundary of Jasper and
the Wilmore Wilderness.

The study was needed because grizzly bears at the time had been on
the decline in Alberta for a number of reasons. Oil and gas, logging,
industrial development, hunting, and poaching were all at play, but no
one knew to what extent.

For nearly three years, Stenhouse and his colleagues were able to
track this female with the help of a satellite collar that transmitted
her movements through the boreal forest and alpine regions of Jasper

several times a day. When a failing battery automatically triggered the collar's release in 2002, however, they never saw her again.

More than a decade later, I was with Stenhouse and biologist Terry Larsen searching for other grizzly bears they were hoping to find for the same study. This time, though, their work had dramatically expanded in scope and area covered because the population was not making a significant recovery, even after a ban on sports hunting. Once we reached the first of two mountain passes the pilot planned to fly through, a light rain, mixed at times with wet snow, began to fall. The prospects of success began to look grim. Thinking out loud, the pilot considered turning back. Then the skies cleared, as they often do in between mountain snow squalls, and we spotted a female and a cub moving quickly along a snowy alpine slope above the forest just ahead of us. Seeing that the female wasn't wearing one of his satellite tracking collars, Stenhouse signaled his desire to have her captured.

First, the pilot dropped Stenhouse and me off on a nearby mountaintop to lighten the load and remove the door on the passenger side of the helicopter. That gave the pilot the steadiness he needed in the air to give Larsen an unobstructed view to fire a tranquilizer dart into the female.

This was the fifth time I'd been out with Stenhouse since the first year of that study. Each time, I stood back, fascinated by the scene that unfolded from a distance.

On this day, the helicopter caught up with the two bears quickly. Larsen fired the dart. The bear slowed and within a few minutes lay belly down on the ground as the cub hovered over her.

When the helicopter brought Stenhouse and me back to the scene a few minutes later, Larsen was keeping a wary eye on the tranquilized bear, knowing that she could suddenly rise from her slumber. The cub had run off. To make sure there were no surprises, Larsen and Stenhouse moved in with a rifle, calling out softly to make sure the bear didn't startle and wake up. As a precaution, the pilot kept the engine running.

Satisfied that the bear was down and out, Stenhouse hooked her up to an oxygen tank he had brought along to ease her labored breathing. With only an hour to draw blood, extract a premolar to determine her age, secure some hair samples, and weigh and measure the length of the animal, time was tight and tensions were high as we waited for the veterinary team to be flown in from another nearby hilltop.

It didn't help when the cub, which was as big as its mother, returned to the site, dancing around the perimeter before disappearing once again into a stand of spruce trees.

"Keep an eye out," Stenhouse reminded us. "Mothers, we've learned from experience, can wake up suddenly when they hear or smell a cub that might be in distress. And cubs can do some pretty stupid things when they're separated from their mothers."

In the meantime, Larsen curled back the lip of the tranquilized animal to see if she had a tattoo stamped from a previous capture. She did. Records showed that the bear was G-16. She weighed only 230 pounds (104 kilograms) but looked to be in good health.

For the longest time, biologists had assumed that small bears, which are common in Jasper and the east slopes of the Rockies, are a product of natural selection. Given that winters are longer and harder here than they are on the west coast, it's tough for big bears to make a living when they are hibernating for five months of the year and feeding mainly on roots, rodents, berries, and, occasionally, sheep, deer, and elk. There are no salmon runs as there are on the west coast of British Columbia and Alaska. Natural selection in this case favors the little guys, just as it does on the Arctic tundra.

It's not that small bears are a lesser force to be reckoned with. Stenhouse once caught a grizzly the size of G-16, which had taken down a large quarter horse, before dragging and burying it in the forest for future consumption. He's seen a similarly small grizzly fending off a pack of wolves that was trying to move in on its kill.

Throughout the course of the study, Stenhouse occasionally saw bigger, fatter bears. I was there when he captured a 700-pound bruin that was so big that Stenhouse broke from the tradition of simply assigning letters and numbers to animals by calling him "Big Boy." The last time Stenhouse saw Big Boy, the bear was racing effortlessly down a mountainside with a bighorn sheep in its mouth. Stenhouse knows that Big Boy lived on because his DNA is imprinted on many of the bears Stenhouse has since caught and sampled for blood and hair.

Around the time Big Boy was captured, University of Alberta scientist Scott Nielsen began tracking and monitoring the fate of what

Figure 10-1 Like many other animals, grizzly bears do well in landscapes that have been burned by fire. Biologist Gordon Stenhouse, left, deals with G-16, a small bear he captured first in 1999 and then again more than a decade later. (Edward Struzik)

would eventually total 112 grizzly bears in Stenhouse's study area. In 2013, Nielsen, Stenhouse, and others came to the conclusion that age and sex help determine whether a bear is big and fat. But so does habitat. Smaller bears tend to be found in colder, less productive environments such as Jasper, where a half century of fire suppression has resulted in too many thick stands of trees and not enough roots and berries to sustain big, fat bears. Disturbed environments, which included those burned by fire or logged by timber companies, offered up more food, albeit at the expense of the bear being poached or killed by a car or truck.[1]

This finding was not altogether surprising to scientists who study grizzlies. Before the wildfires that famously burned so much of Yellowstone in the summer of 1988, biologists were monitoring the movement of thirty-eight bears in the park that had radio transmitters attached to them. Twenty-one of these bears had home ranges in areas that got torched. Thirteen of them moved back into the burn areas immediately after the fire front had passed through.

Three adult females with cubs stayed within a burn site while it was still smoldering. Some grizzly bears were seen feeding on carcasses of deer and elk killed in the fires. Others were seen grazing on newly emerged sedges and bluegrass, digging in logs and anthills for insects. As years progressed, there was no evidence to suggest that the fires had affected the bear's movements or choice of den sites in any negative way.[2]

In short, the bears benefited from those fires that horrified so many people at the time. The forest was not dying. It was giving birth to a new crop of roots, berries, and trees.

The list of living things that benefit from wildfire is extraordinarily long, as I learned early in my youth seeing fireweed growing on fire-scarred mountainsides in the Yukon. I began to appreciate it even more when I spent time with Elly Knight catching nighthawks in a burned-out forest north of Fort McMurray, talking to biologist Terry Armstrong about bison and fire in the Northwest Territories, and during that day in the field with Andrew Larson in Montana.

Larson has a lot of remarkable stories to tell from his field trips into the Bob Marshall Wilderness of Montana, where fire is allowed to burn in many areas, some that have never been logged. He and his research team hike in with a mule train packing their food and gear and float out on rafts at the end of the season.

A story Larson likes to tell is one that got him more news coverage than he's had for any other study. This one in Yosemite ended almost disastrously in September 2013 when the Rim wildfire burned 70 percent of the trees in a study site that he and his colleagues had just set up. Surveying the damage that was done a year later, Larson couldn't help but notice the plethora of morel mushrooms that were shooting up. "I am not an expert in mushrooms, but I love eating them," he told me. "My family is from the Northwest, and it was a tradition for us to go out and pick mushrooms on weekends. Still is when we have family get-togethers."

Mushroom lovers have long known that morels rise up from wild-fire. It's become big business for some because a pound of wild morels

Figure 10-2 Andrew Larson's research team floats out of the Bob Marshall Wilderness with fire burning in the distance behind them. Most wildfires are allowed to burn in this wilderness as long as they do not threaten people and infrastructure. (Andrew Larson)

can sell for as much as $50. In the boreal forest of Russia where fires burn bigger than any place on Earth, it is a national pastime. In the Yukon, it's no longer the gold rush that prevails, but the "shroom rush" that has taken over following big fire seasons. The government of the Northwest Territories saw so much economic potential arising from the 2014 wildfires that it commissioned a study to determine whether mushroom harvesting could play a future role in its depressed economy.

When Larson surveyed the scientific literature to learn about mushrooms and wildfire, he was surprised to find that only three studies had ever been done to quantify how the mushrooms respond to fires. Sensing an opportunity, he and his colleagues embarked on a study that eventually demonstrated that people could harvest morels in Yosemite for their personal purposes in the aftermath of a fire. Commercial harvesting of morels, they suggested, might require some long-term monitoring.

Increasingly, soil scientists, hydrologists, entomologists, botanists, and biologists have come to appreciate the role that wildfire plays in maintaining biodiversity. Most insect species, which are key to biodiversity in any forest, eventually bounce back nicely from a fire, according to David Langor, a scientist with the Canadian Forest Service.

Pyrophilous, or fire-loving beetles from the *Melanophila* genus, actually thrive on fire. These beetles have infrared sensors and supersensitive antennae that help them detect fires that are burning 40 miles away. These stump-humpers, as firefighters irreverently call them, enter burned stands even while the fire is still burning around them. The females lay eggs under the bark of burned trees that no longer have a chemical defense mechanism to fend off a feeding frenzy.

In field experiments, scientists Langor, John Spence, and Tyler Cobb tried to quantify how fire, salvage logging that often follows, and the spraying of herbicides in silviculture operations affect white-spotted sawyer beetle populations. These beetles are not pyrophilous, but they do exploit lightly burned timber. The results were striking but not surprising to scientists like Langor who are striving to find ways of improving management practices through emulation of natural disturbance patterns such as wildfire to promote biodiversity.[3] Beetles fared best when burned forests were not salvaged, logged, or sprayed.

"We tend to overlook the importance of dead wood in other ways as well," said Langor. "Not only does it promote biodiversity of thousands of insect species, and relatives such as spiders and mites, it also promotes the growth of fungi, lichens, mosses, and nematodes. In one small study in aspen in northeastern Alberta, we found about 2,000 species of insects and relatives living in just a few dead trees. The community of saproxylic beetles is enormously diverse and poorly understood."

Although there is plenty of deadwood in most harvested forests these days, the quality of the dead wood that is often left behind is of poor quality because of the harvesting that leaves the trunks debarked, broken up, and exposed to the drying effects of sunlight.

Used wisely, prescribed burns have helped endangered and threatened species recover. Officials in Aransas National Park on the Gulf Coast, for example, routinely burn to enhance habitat for the last two hundred migrating whooping cranes that fly from Texas to their nesting grounds in the boreal forest wetlands of Wood Buffalo National Park.

Banff has been burning to pave the way for the 2017 reintroduction of wood bison that used to dwell in the park. Elk Island National Park and Yellowstone burn to prevent elk and bison from eating themselves out of house and home.

Scientists once thought that wildfire in California, Washington, and Oregon would expedite the demise of the spotted owl, but research by biologist Monica Bond and her colleagues demonstrate that this isn't necessarily the case.[4]

It is, however, not as simple as that, according to field work conducted by Gavin Jones, a University of Wisconsin–Madison scientist. He has been studying the connection between wildfire and the California spotted owl. Spotted owl populations appear to hold their own when forests are thinned or are periodically burned with prescribed fires. But they don't fare well in big fires, such as the 99,000-acre King fire that burned through the El Dorado National Forest in 2014. That fire, he says, destroyed as many as forty-five spotted owl nests. There are no signs of the owls coming back, as they did in small prescribed burns on the other side of the park.

The most compelling evidence comes from Brian Linkhart, a Colorado College scientist who has been monitoring the fate of flammulated owls in the Manitou Experimental Forest on the front ranges of Colorado Rockies since 1981. Like the spotted owl, the flammulated owl does best in old-growth forest ecosystems. Linkhart has recorded a lot of fascinating things, including the first ever documentation of polygyny in the species in 2006. In this case, a single male was providing food for females and owlets at two nests that were 1,673 feet (510 meters) apart inside the boundary of the 2002 Hayman fire. The best

Figure 10-3 Many owls, such as this flammulated owl that scientist Brian Linkhart holds, fare best in old-growth forests where fire burns moderately. (Paul Bannick)

explanation, according to Linkhart, is that the Hayman fire was so severe that it drove most territorial male owls from there to take refuge in surrounding unburned forests, including the Manitou. This shifted the sex ratio of owls that remained in the islands of surviving forest in the Hayman in favor of females, which do not actively defend territories. It also resulted in an overall increase in the density of owls in the Manitou for eight to ten years, which is the approximate average life span of the owls.

Although that might sound like a positive development, Linkhart suggests that it is more indicative of the Manitou representing the best real estate in a market that is shrinking because of wildfires burning bigger, more severely, and more often, after many decades without any fire. "This is an owl that had adapted to low-intensity fires that historically burned relatively often in a ponderosa pine forest," he said. "The fact that we are shifting toward high-intensity fires such as the Hayman and Waldo may not bode well for their future or for other birds and animals that have adapted to this kind of ecosystem."

Prescribed burning may seem like the best way to reduce the threat of megafires in spotted and flammulated owl country, but it is complicated, as biologists and wildfire managers everywhere will tell you. Invariably, there are other factors to consider.

For example, the much larger barred owl started moving westward in the early twentieth century thanks to new forest habitat that emerged with the cessation of Native American burning and the systematic suppression of wildfires. The first barred owl was spotted in British Columbia in 1959. Within two decades, it expanded its range to Washington, Oregon, and California. Barred owls are now such a big threat to the smaller spotted and flammulated owls that the US Fish and Wildlife Service began shooting them in 2014 as a way of saving spotted owls. In 2015 and 2016 alone, Oregon Fish and Wildlife officials removed more than four hundred barred owls from the landscape.[5]

~

In the cold dark days of January in 2011, I spent a little over a week with Jasper National Park employees Mike Dillion and Greg Horne, retracing explorer David Thompson's historic winter journey over Athabasca Pass in the Canadian Rockies into the Columbia River Valley in 1811. The trip was a sobering introduction to what the boreal forest is like in winter when there can be 20 feet of snow piled up on a mountain pass, when it is dark for sixteen hours a day, and when it is so cold that exposed skin freezes in less than a minute.

Initially, there was not a lot to compare what we faced and what Thompson had endured. While Horne and I fattened ourselves up on wine and pizza the night before the trip, Thompson's men each devoured the 8 pounds of bison and moose meat they had been eating daily for almost a month. When the three of us set off on January 5 in temperatures of just below the freezing mark, Thompson and his men were already weeks on the trail, braving temperatures that had fallen to −15°F (26°C) or below.

As balmy as the first day of our backcountry trip was, the comfortable weather ended on the second night with a late evening blizzard that set off an avalanche behind our camp. Temperatures dropped to the minus 40s in hours. The only signs of life we saw or heard in the days that followed were a few American dippers skimming across what little open water there was, the tracks of wolves in the snow, and a boreal owl that screeched incessantly after the sun had set behind the mountains one night. Everything else, it seemed, had either flown south or was hibernating.

The boreal forest is a remarkably simple ecosystem, so silent in the dead of winter that one wonders if there are any animals there at all. Jason Fisher, a biologist I've spent time with in the field, studied wolverines in Jasper and Wilmore for more than seven years and never personally saw the animal in that time, yet the remote cameras he set up in the boreal forest were chock full of pictures of wolverines, wolves, grizzly bears, moose, sheep, and other animals that were attracted to the scents he pasted on nearby trees.

Seeing, of course, is believing, but most veteran boreal scientists will tell you that they can count on one hand the number of times they've seen a mountain lion. Lynx and fisher sightings are almost as rare. You are likely to hear more owls than you see, unless you have a live mouse that you can toss out onto the snow. I've seen biologist Gord Court catch or photograph all thirteen owls in the boreal forest of Alberta using this method.

There are 85 mammals that live in the boreal forest, compared with the 427 that dwell in the Amazon. The boreal region has 130 species of freshwater fish; the Amazon has more than 3,000. The Amazon has more than 12,000 species of trees. No more than 20 tree species are found in the boreal forest.

Among these trees, seven or eight types—white and black spruce, larch, lodgepole pine and jack pine, balsam fir, aspen, birch, and poplar—dominate. The northern forest mosaic differs from east to west, from north to south, and in places where soil, permafrost, and heat favor one species over another. I often marvel at how the boreal forest looks and smells the same whether you're in northern Minnesota or in Alberta; the iconic drunken black spruce stands of the northern boreal forest being a notable exception.

I was once again struck by these similarities when ornithologist Jeff Wells took me on a hike through one of the last remaining stands of boreal forest in Maine. The white sand on the forest floor and the stands of white spruce, pine, and poplar looked so much like the boreal forest along Lake Athabasca in northeastern Alberta and Saskatchewan that I took a photo to compare with those I had at home.

Wells at the time was the science and policy director for the Boreal Songbird Initiative and a scientific advisor to the International Boreal Conservation Campaign, which is dedicated to protecting globally important ecosystems and to restoring old-growth forests and wilderness in North America. He had previously worked as a conservation ornithologist at Cornell University's Laboratory of Ornithology in Ithaca, New York. From 1996 to 2003, he was with the National Audubon Society, first as bird conservation director for the New York State office and then as the national director of bird conservation. The boreal forest, he insists, is not as simple an ecosystem as one might think.

"Birds are the hidden part of the rich biodiversity one finds in a boreal ecosystem," he told me that day. "About half of the seven hundred species of birds that you find in the United States and Canada rely on the boreal for their survival. More than three hundred species regularly breed in places such as this. During the spring migration, up to three billion birds migrate north up to their breeding grounds in the boreal forest. In a good year, you might get five billion adults and offspring migrating back in fall."

To add color to his narrative, Wells asked me to listen and look as he identified the call or sight of blackbirds, vireos, yellow rump warblers, a ruby crown kinglet, and other birds that were nearby. Like a magician, he revealed a woodpecker and a few others species that I would not have otherwise noticed. "Nighthawks pass through in mid-August," he said some time later as he pointed to a flock of robins flying overhead.

Along a tributary of the Kennebec River that is famous for trout fishing, we spotted the fresh tracks of a moose. Without giving me the heads-up, Wells hooted like a barred owl, flushing out some flickers and other woodpeckers. "Better to see the enemy rather than be eaten by the enemy," he said, explaining why small birds expose themselves when they hear the call of an owl.

While he worked at Cornell, Wells was one of five people chosen to go to Arkansas and search for the ivory-billed woodpecker after initial reports in February 2004 suggested that the extinct bird had been rediscovered. The reports of the sighting made headlines all over the world.

"None of us saw or heard the bird while we there in 2005," he said. "Some individuals have since reported that they have seen or heard one. I'd like to think they are right, but I tend to think that it went extinct in the 1940s."

The ivory-billed woodpecker was nicknamed "Lord God Bird" or "Elvis in Feathers" because, like the king of rock and roll, people continue to spot the bird long after it has been declared extinct.

Wells doesn't hesitate to point out that the ivory-billed woodpecker's extinction is directly attributable to the clearcutting of the Deep South's old-growth forest, which reduced the chance of fire-scarred timber producing the boring insects the woodpeckers feed on.

"During that trip, I wondered what would it be like to be around and know that a bird or animal was on its way out as many people at the time knew," said Wells. "In many ways, it's personal for me because my wife and I grew up in Maine. In the time we've lived, more than 80 percent of the population of evening grosbeaks in the state's forests have disappeared, warblers and bay-breasted warblers have declined by 60 percent. There has been at least a 95 percent decline in rusty blackbirds.

"We used to have caribou in Maine, so many of them in fact that hunters from Boston and other big cities took rail car–loads back with them," he continued. "There isn't a single caribou to be found in Maine today. There have been attempts to reintroduce them. They failed."

Like biologists who have been tracking the recent demise of boreal caribou across Canada and Idaho, everyone saw the demise of caribou coming in Maine as well as in neighboring New Brunswick and Nova Scotia long before the last one was shot. On July 28, 1911, a Bangor newspaper declared: "Nothwithstanding the annual slaughter of deer and moose in the Maine woods it is probably true that both of those species of animals are increasing here. But the caribou, which 15 years ago were numerous all over the northern part of the state, have gone. It is doubtful there is a single one on this side of the Canadian border today."[6]

Caribou are not going to come back to Maine for a variety of reasons. Although 80 percent of state is heavily forested, only a fraction contains the prime boreal habitat that caribou rely on. Much of it was logged or pastured during the course of the past two centuries. In many places, the hardwoods have taken over.

What are left of the boreal forest are mostly mature trees that are less resilient to disease, insects, drought, and the hurricane-force storms that sometimes pummel the region. Wildfires that are required to allow the boreal forest to regenerate, to grow lichen for caribou and to become more resilient to disease, drought, and insects are being suppressed, as I learned while I was in Maine with Wells in the fall of 2016. When lightning lit up the boreal forest on Mount Abraham in June, ground crews and water-bucket-equipped helicopters were sent in to aggressively fight the fire. The option of letting the fire burn itself out was not seriously considered.

Wells doesn't envision the prospects for prescribed burning in northern Maine because 70 percent of the forests are privately owned. Lighting up a state-owned forest, he said, would also require extraordinary political willpower. The cofounder of Burt's Bees, he noted, donated 87,000 acres of boreal-like forest in northern Maine so that it could be set aside as a national monument. President Barack Obama did that in the summer of 2016, but opponents are hoping that President Donald Trump will overturn the decision. They see the new Katahdin Woods and Waters Monument as a roadblock to the recovery of the state's once-prosperous forest industry.

With climate change and drought driving fire to burn bigger, hotter, faster, and more frequently and setting the stage for disease, insects, and invasive species to move in, not a lot of people are optimistic about the boreal transitions zones and the island forests that are found in the Sweetgrass Hills of Montana, the Cypress Hills of southeastern

Alberta and Saskatchewan, and Turtle Mountain in Manitoba. The forests aren't likely to move north on the tundra, as some believe, because the permafrost and extreme cold will likely favor shrubs over trees and lichens.

Lee Frelich is the director of the University of Minnesota Center for Forest Ecology. He has been studying the impact of climate change, wildfire, disease, and invasive species in the boreal forest of the Boundary Waters Canoe Area Wilderness since the 1980s. I knew that he was hard core and committed to his research when he told me that he decided on a career in forest ecology when he was just twelve years old after reading books such as John Curtis's *The Vegetation of Wisconsin*.

Frelich and his students have hundreds of plots in the Boundary Waters area that they have been visiting for years, looking for patterns of growth and mortality. He has a detailed record of wildfire, windstorms, runaway deer populations, and invasive species, such as eight species of European worms that have a profound impact on the structure of the forest. As many homeowners know, deer love to feed on cedar saplings. European worms, I did not know, alter the nutrient structure of soil. With climate change, these invasive species have migrated as far north into the boreal forest as James Bay in northern Ontario and Quebec.

"We're just beginning to see the impacts of climate change in our boreal forest, and what we're seeing does not bode well for the future," said Frelich. "If I were to make a bet, I would bet that we are going to see a lot less boreal and lot more bur oak savannah. This century we might even lose all of the boreal and a third of all the plant and animals species we see in our state. As the climate continues to warm, we will see massive changes as biomes move northward."

The temptation, of course, is to throw up our hands and let events take their course. That is what happened when the grasslands of the Great Plains of the United States and the prairies of Canada were turned into corn and wheat fields. The best guess is that we have maybe 1 percent of the vegetation that dominated that ecosystem before settlers started to till the soil and put a stop to North American natives lighting fires. There are no more free-roaming prairie bison and very few prairie dogs, burrowing owls, greater prairie chicken, loggerhead shrike, mountain plover, piping plover, and sage thrasher. The American burying beetle has seen its best days. So have a number of fish that dwelled in prairie streams.

At a time when climate is driving wildfire to burn bigger, hotter, faster, and more often, it will be an enormous political challenge to let some wildlands burn and to purposely burn some wildlands so that grizzly bears, nighthawks, and many other birds, animals, and insects have a future in these northern forests that remain relatively intact. There may be no going back to the boreal forest that once dominated northern Maine, northern Minnesota, and Michigan, but there is still a lot of forest to work with on the continent. Canada's boreal forest alone covers approximately 2.2 million square miles (5.6 million square kilometers). Almost half of it contains areas of more than 193 square miles (500 square kilometers) that are not fragmented by roads and other infrastructure.

Wildfire might not be the only means by which biodiversity can be preserved in these places. It can, however, be more of a blessing than a curse if ways can be found to better manage and understand it.

Conclusion

The secret of getting things done is to act!
— Dante Alighieri, *The Divine Comedy*

The path to paradise begins in hell.
— Dante Alighieri, *The Divine Comedy*

Chris Maisch grew up in Cleveland when the city was suffering from crushing economic and environmental problems. He was there in 1969 when the Cuyahoga River was so polluted with oil and hydrocarbons that it caught fire, inspiring editors at *Time* to put a picture of a similar but more serious river fire on its weekly cover. The Cuyahoga became a symbol of the environmental degradation that was occurring in lakes and rivers right across the continent. The environmental movement that followed led to establishment of the Clean Water Act in 1972, the Acid Rain Program in 1990, the Great Lakes Compact of 2008, and a number of other legislative and publicly funded initiatives in Canada and the United States. The ongoing efforts to protect North America's watersheds have not been perfect and continue to be a work in progress, but they have helped avert a number of environmental and human disasters.

Maisch is Alaska's state forester and director responsible for overall leadership of both the forest and the wildfire management programs. Nowadays, he is at the forefront of another form of environmental degradation that is taking place in North America. Wildfire, which was and still is the key to rejuvenating large swaths of northern forest landscapes, is burning, bigger, hotter, faster, and more often than ever, compromising the air that people breathe, the water they drink and fish in, some of the birds and animals they hunt, the national parks and forests they visit, and the trees they rely on for timber. Wildfire is no longer a California spectacle. Increasingly, wildfires like the ones in Fort McMurray in 2016, Willow, Alaska, in 2015, and Slave Lake in 2011 are threatening people, industry, woodlots, homes, forest structures, and watersheds in the northern forests of the United States and Canada.

"Two days ago, we went out to a fire site to see how the vegetation there was recovering," Maisch told me as we chatted in a local coffee roaster café on a rainy day in August 2016. "One of the lakes at the site was gone. It was amazing because it was a very big lake. It was not caused by eutrophication. That takes several years to kill a lake. We speculate that it was because of thawing permafrost."

Maisch may not have been as concerned if it were just that one lake, but he and scientists working in Alaska are seeing things like that happen to water bodies all over the state. They're also seeing aspen taking over and eliminating coniferous forests, leaf miners attacking aspen, and shrubs taking over lichen and sedge meadows on the tundra.

"Factor in what the spruce bark beetle has done in the Kenai Peninsula and you begin to appreciate the scale of what is happening in addition to the escalation of wildfire events," said Maisch.

The challenges for Maisch and his colleagues are the same ones that forest managers and wildland firefighters across the continent are confronting. Almost everywhere, but especially in the west and the northwest part of the continent, the rising cost of suppressing fires is taking money away from forest management programs that support fisheries, tourism, timber harvesting, and wildlife conservation. To deal with the new wildfire paradigm, legislative and innovative program initiatives like the ones that were launched to protect the continent's lakes, rivers, and streams since the 1960s are needed. Setting aside more land for conservation and forest management and better educating people about the perils of wildfire and how to protect their homes and property would also help. So would new building codes.

It won't be easy. As we gradually became very good at fighting fires, we created an unnaturally large amount of mature forests that made them increasingly vulnerable to insects, disease, and wildfire. (Alaska is an exception, but drought and climate change have heightened those threats.) By the time decision makers figured out that the North American native strategy of lighting fires to rejuvenate forests was a way of promoting good fires instead of severe and sometimes catastrophic ones, the tables began to slowly turn back in favor of the old way of doing things.

There are a number of reasons for this swing.

Like his colleagues down south, Maisch is dealing with more and more people living, working, and recreating in the forested wildlands. That puts him in between a rock and hard place. On the one hand, the state of Alaska is selling off land, which encourages even more people to build houses and cabins in the forest. On the other hand, the state expects him and his colleagues to make sure that these people are safe when fire threatens. The same protection is expected for the more than one hundred remote Alaska native villages that have little or no fire protection, and for pipelines, army and air force bases, and defense structures. Caribou habitat is also on the list.

"When the Agee Creek fire burned in 2015 right next to the Alyeska oil pipeline, we had nothing to put on it because most of the firefighting resources had gone south where they were needed more because they were also dealing with a record wildfire season," he said. "We had no smokejumpers available. Resources were tapped. The pipeline wasn't going to blow up because there's coolant that runs through it, but the electronics and sensors that go with the pipeline were vulnerable."

Being proactive so as to protect people and buildings has become a challenge in some places. When Alaska firefighters were deployed in 2009 to ignite a back-burn to save three small subdivisions in the forest 45 miles southwest of Fairbanks, the homeowners sued. None of them lost their homes. Rather, they wanted to be compensated because the burn compromised the aesthetic appeal of their lakeside properties.

Some of the people who move into the forests are responsible for the most destructive fires. It happens in Alaska and pretty much everywhere people live, work, and recreate in forest environments. In California, it was an arsonist who caused the 2014 King fire, one of the worst in the state's history. In Alaska, the Sockeye fire that destroyed fifty homes and more than one hundred structures and cost $8 million to suppress was allegedly ignited by a couple burning debris on their property near Willow, without clearing the area or having water on hand on that hot, dry day. In May 2017, a jury found the couple not guilty; during the trial, the defense attorney argued that the state failed to prove "beyond a reasonable doubt" that the couple were guilty. That jury decision left both the state and victims to contemplate the possibility of seeking civil damages.[1]

Maisch allows that his beard went from red to gray during the record-breaking 2004 wildfire season and that the hair on his head went from thick to thin in 2015. As challenging and unique as those fire seasons were, it was the Fort McMurray fire of 2016 that really opened his eyes, and the eyes of many forest managers and wildfire experts, to what might be expected in the future.

"Fort McMurray was a bellwether for us," he said. "We kept calling with offers to help. But they declined. We couldn't figure out what was going on when all those people were evacuated at the last minute. Alberta is the gold standard when it comes to dealing with fire. If they were behind on this, we thought, then we're all in trouble."

It's not that no one is talking about the changing wildfire patterns in the northern and alpine forests of the continent. In 2005, Canadian experts came up with a wildlands fire strategy for the Canadian Council of Forest Ministers. It was written by a veritable "who's who" list of wildfire experts, including coleaders Kelvin Hirsch from the Canadian Forest Service and Peter Fuglem from British Columbia's Ministry of Forests and Range. No one in government embraced their recommendations for more fire, more science, more education, and better funded FireSmart–type programs in any meaningful way. When the report was updated a few years later, decision makers continued to ignore it. The same thing has happened in the United States for many of the same political reasons. As fires kept burning bigger, hotter, and more often and as the so-called urban/wildland interface kept growing, the

Figure C-1 Thirteen years after the fires forced the evacuation of Kelowna, the Bear Creek fire burned in a forested subdivision northwest of the city. Many homes still had cedar-shake shingles on their roofs and highly combustible ornamental cedars abutting their wood houses. (Edward Struzik)

investment in fire science, forest management, forest thinning, prescribed burning, and conservation lagged.

The people at FireSafe Montana, a private, nonprofit organization that addresses various issues related to wildfire, may have best expressed the exasperation of firefighters, forest managers, wildfire scientists, conservationists, and insurance companies when they launched the organization's "Enough Is Enough" campaign to get decision makers to listen. In a series of commissioned articles by wildfire research ecologist Stephen Arno, wildfire historian Stephen Pyne, former director of the US Forest Service's Fire and Aviation Division Jerry Williams, president of the International Association of Wildland Fire Tom Zimmerman, and others, the overriding message made abundantly clear was that we are not prepared to deal with the many wildland fire challenges that are unfolding.

Zimmerman summed it up succinctly when he stated that "business as usual is not going to be successful."

There have been success stories. The "right to burn" laws in the southeastern United States shield resources managers to a reasonable degree from lawsuits related to prescribed fires and back-burns.

FireSmart, Firewise, and other similar preventative and education programs have made some important strides in making forest towns and homes more resilient to the threat of fire. More than 80 percent of the homes that survived the Fort McMurray fire were deemed to be relatively FireSmart, according to Alan Westhaver, an investigator commissioned by the Institute for Catastrophic Loss Reduction. While the town was still smoldering, Westhaver was given permission to go in and determine why some homes survived with little or no damage while others were destroyed. He concluded that wind-driven embers, not direct flames or radiant heat from the forest fires, were the primary cause of ignition.[2]

Recognizing that fire is rapidly becoming a year-round threat, decision makers have extended the firefighting season pretty much everywhere. Allowing so-called natural fires to burn themselves out as long as they don't threaten people, properties, and assets is a good policy if one can define what is natural in a time when climate change is altering the flow of jet streams and when the timing and intensity of El Niño and other weather-wrenching events in the Pacific Ocean are increasing in the Arctic Ocean.

The national coordination and international sharing of firefighting resources has also gone a long way to limiting the threats to humans and the damage that is done in exceptional fire seasons such as the one that western North America went through in 2015.

Increasingly, conservationists and biologists are recognizing the important role that fire plays in maintaining biodiversity among insects, vegetation, and birds and animals such as nighthawks, woodpeckers, grizzly bears, moose, elk, and bison that need fire to keep their habitat healthy.

In this new emerging wildfire paradigm, however, firefighting resources are getting tapped out, as they were in 2003 and 2015 when triaging became the order of the day. In addition, there continues to be friction between what conservation biologists are striving to do in the forest and what wildfire managers and resource harvesters want to do to reduce the risk of severe and catastrophic wildfires.

Front and center in this push-and-pull scenario are caribou in western Canada and Alaska; the spotted and flammulated owls of Montana, Colorado, Idaho, Oregon, Washington, and California; the Columbia spotted frog in Idaho; and various other amphibians that are already stressed by drought and disease. Species will inevitably disappear, as caribou did in the boreal forest of Maine when it was heavily logged, farmed, and burned over by a series of severe fires. Two efforts to bring them back failed because the forest structure no longer supports them.

Figuring out who the winners and losers might be and what might be done about it requires much more research. Forest fires, we know, are increasing mercury levels in wetlands. As certain bacteria transform inorganic mercury into toxic methylmercury, the methylmercury rises up the food chain, making fish in many water bodies too toxic for people to consume with any degree of regularity, if at all. Biologists such as Julienne Morissette of Ducks Unlimited, however, say that, with the exception of mercury contamination, there is still a lot to learn about how wildfire affects the habitat of ducks and geese. Boreal Songbird Initiative scientist Jeff Wells acknowledges that fire is good for nighthawks, woodpeckers, and many other birds. But he says that the fate of the five billion birds that nest in the boreal forest of Canada and the United States is alarmingly unclear when you factor in wildfire with the disturbances and pollution that industrial development brings to a wildland ecosystem.

Meg Krawchuk, Sandra Haire, Jonathon Coop, and their colleagues know that there are fire refugia in the forest that are resilient to wildfire and that they provide some environmental stability for species that dwell in and around them. Where these refugia are, how they form, and the reasons for their resilience aren't altogether clear, but knowing more about them may help land managers make better decisions about establishing protected areas, wildlife corridors, and prescribed burning strategies.

David Pilliod, a supervisory research ecologist with the US Geological Survey in Idaho, echoes the views of many in summing up the research that he and his colleagues have done on wildfire and amphibians. As he said, "In the last fifteen years we have made some advances in scientific understanding of amphibian responses to wildfire, pre-scribed fire, and the various fuel reduction practices. But the subtleties of fire and fuel management practices create a dizzying amount of physical and ecological complexity, of which we have barely begun to scratch the surface of understanding."

As the need grows for more research, both Canada and the United States continue to take money away from fire science, forest manage-ment, and conservation initiatives to pay for the rising cost of fire. Fort McMurray was a testament to that. Coming off a record fire season in 2015, the Alberta government reduced the fire prevention and manage-ment budget by $14.6 million the next year.

Canada now spends as much as $1 billion each year fighting fires, five times the amount it spent in the 1990s. The Canadian Forest Service has been bounced around between fourteen government departments since it was established in 1899. In the early 1970s, it employed 2,400 people. In 2017, there were no more than 700 employees working there. Its fire research budget amounts to a paltry $1.3 million, compared with the $52 million the US Forest Service spends annually on research.[3]

The US Forest Service may have much more money to work. An ex-tra $407 million for wildfire was included as part of a bipartisan budget agreement to fund the government through to October 2017. Money, however, is a systematic problem because, unlike its Canadian coun-terpart, the US Forest Service is mandated to fight fires. In 1995, the budget for fighting fire made up 16 percent of the US Forest Service's budget. It rose to the 50 percent level in 2015 and could reach close to 70 percent by 2025. If Congress does nothing to address this disparity beyond adding funds annually on an ad hoc basis, programs that are dedicated to protecting watersheds, cultural resources, and education programs will take a $700 million hit. Those estimates were made be-fore 2017, when President Donald Trump was proposing to cut the US Department of Interior budget by 12 percent.

Mike Flannigan likens devastating wildfires such as Fort McMur-ray in 2016, Slave Lake in 2011, and Kelowna, Glacier National Park, the Salmon-Challis National Forest, and other areas in 2003 to bloody noses. At some point, though, he says that the blows are going to be lethal and that someone in a decision-making role is going to have to take note that "business as usual is not going to be successful," as Tom Zimmerman has noted.

That is what happened during the Australian summer of February 2009 when the state of Victoria suffered through the country's most devastating wildfire. On a day that came to be known as Black Saturday, 173 people died and a million acres of forest burned.

The parallels between Black Saturday and the Fort McMurray fire of 2016, the Slave Lake fires of 2011, and the 2003 fires in the western United States and Canada are there for decision makers to contemplate. The regions were suffering through a severe drought. Temperatures were approaching record highs. Humidity was at rock-bottom lows. Winds drove the fires faster than anyone had anticipated. The fires behaved like The Beast that Fort McMurray fire chief Darby Allen talked about when he warned people that the fire that entered his city "will look for them [people and buildings] and it will take them."

Australians had suffered through catastrophic fires in the past. The Black Friday fire of 1939 killed 71 people, and the Ash Wednesday fires of 1983 killed 75 people. By the time Black Saturday loomed large over the area, the government had a plan in place. Residents could either leave early, or they could stay and defend. The government got the first part right. The second part was flawed because many people were not prepared to deal with the fires when they came.

Black Saturday burned a hole in the souls of those who deal with fire in Australia just as the Fort McMurray fire has done in Canada, as the Yarnell fire in Arizona did when it resulted in the death of nineteen hotshots,[4] and as the Gatlinburg fire continues to do. In the search for answers, an Australian government inquiry recommended abandoning the stay or leave policy and suggested instead a "Code Red" plan.

In the end, the Code Red plan was adopted, but the Leave Early or Stay and Defend policy was maintained. Well in advance of a fire like the one that burned on Black Saturday, people are now given notice well ahead of time when it is time to leave. Those who stay are reminded of what they need to do to keep safe.

Many places in Canada and the United States fall far short of that plan, as the last-minute evacuation of Fort McMurray demonstrated. That no one died as a result of the wildfire had more to do with luck, wind conditions, demographics, and the heroic efforts of frontline responders than it did with an evacuation plan that fell far short of what was required. The fire made three runs into the city before the order to evacuate everyone was made.

As terrible as it may seem to suggest, the fate of sled dogs in Alaska gets more consideration than most people in North America receive when it comes to preparing for a wildfire event. That was made clear in the summer of 2015, when the Sockeye fire threatened the community of Willow.

There are almost as many dogs as there are people living in the community of 2,100 people. A week before the fire started, the mushers held a meeting to discuss what everyone needed to do if a fire threated their kennels. They talked about communicating through social media, mobilizing trucks and trailers, identifying safe places the dogs would be taken to, food that needed to be brought along, and who might be able to offer help if someone needed it. The idea was inspired in part by a musher-backed bylaw that requires an evacuation plan for anyone who wants to apply for or renew a kennel license. In the end, many kennels and buildings were damaged, but not a single dog was lost.

The Leave Early or Stay and Defend policy has divided the wildfire community in North America. Jack Cohen is the US Forest Service scientist who conducted groundbreaking studies that inspired the creation of Firewise, FireSmart, and similar programs. He has said on more than one occasion that the main danger to property in a wildland fire is not from the fire front, but from the embers that smolder after the fire passes. If a home and property are made resilient to fire, he says, there is no need to stay.

Bob Mutch has had a thirty-eight-year career in wildland fire research and management in the US Forest Service. He very much supports the Leave Early or Stay and Defend policy that is in places such as Montana as long as homes are made fire-safe and people are educated about what to do when a fire threatens.

He agrees, however, with Canadian colleague Marty Alexander, who wonders about the psychological ability of some homeowners (seniors in particular) to deal with a severe fire coming at them in a rural environment. Even experienced firefighters, like the nineteen hotshots who died in the 2013 Yarnell Hill fire, make mistakes, Alexander points out.

"I never gave that much thought until the Mustang fire threatened my cabin in Montana in 2012," said Mutch when I pointed that out. "That was an awesome wind-driven fire. I had nearly sixty years of experience with wildfires by that time, but this was something to behold. I had done everything I could do to protect my buildings, and I had three safe places I knew I could get to. Still, I wondered at one point whether it was worth me staying when a weather report called for more strong wind. In the end, I stayed, and fortunately the weather report was wrong. It made me realize, though, that we need to do a lot more to educate the public and equip them with the psychological and physical tools they need to Stay and Defend."

In Texas, the state has dispensed with the idea of Stay and Defend, choosing instead to make evacuation in the face of wildfire mandatory in some cases. It may seem strange for a government that cites freedom, along with family and faith, among its core values. But consider that Texas has—in its management of the Edwards Aquifer, which serves the water needs of more than two million people and protects several endangered species—North America's finest groundwater management program. In the ongoing efforts to conserve that water in times of drought and climate change, the Edwards Aquifer Authority employs more than eighty scientists to monitor water quality, water levels, and the fate of those endangered species. It has enlisted the support of municipalities, newspapers, and television and radio stations to convey the need to conserve in times of drought. Chances are good that a taxi driver will inform visitors of the need to take only short showers when they check into a hotel. A bylaw officer will ticket people who water their lawns in similar dry conditions. Visit the pristine pools and streams that percolate from various sources of that aquifer, and you do so at your peril if you put a bare foot or hand in. In Texas, no one messes with the management of groundwater or wildfire.

Whichever way one looks at it, it's clear that the "business as usual" approach is not going to be successful, as Tom Zimmerman has advised. Cerro Grande (2000), Thirty Mile (2001), Hayman (2002), Lost Creek, Glacier, Banff, Jasper, and the Okanagan Mountain Park fires (2003), Taylor Complex, Alaska (2004), and the long list of severe wildfires that led up to Fort McMurray in 2016 are bellwethers of what is coming. So, too, are the winter fires that torched the High Plains states of Texas, Oklahoma, and Kansas in March 2017, killing seven people and thousands of cattle, and the 1,900-acre (770-hectare) early spring tundra fire that ignited in the Selawik National Refuge in Alaska a month later.

A dizzying number of northern forest climate change scenarios coming out of the Berkeley Lab (2013),[5] SNAP, the Scenarios Network for Alaska + Arctic Planning, Centre d'Étude de la Forêt, Université du Québec à Montréal,[6] Mike Flannigan and members of the Fire Management Systems Laboratory in Canada, NASA's ABoVE program, and many other universities and institutions point to wildfires continuing to burn bigger, hotter, and faster in ways that will result in dramatic landscape changes and ecological and social challenges. One study that created a buzz in 2017 was led by Pennsylvania State University scientist Michael Mann. In a paper published in the journal *Nature*, he and his colleagues came as close as any group of scientists has in demonstrating a direct link between climate change and a dramatic increase in extreme weather events such as wildfire, heat waves, and flooding. When the paper was published, Mann cited Arctic warming as playing a key role in altering the flow of the jet stream, which drives many of these extreme events.[7]

Keeping up with the scientific literature on climate change is, as US Forest Service scientist David L. Peterson said, akin to drinking from a fire hose. Under the business-as-usual model, there is almost no way of taking it all in to make full sense of it in a meaningful way. What we can say is what scientist Monica Turner has been saying for some time: severe fires like the one that burned a third of Yellowstone in 1988 were not the ecological catastrophes that many people assumed they would be. Yellowstone recovered quite nicely, as did Glacier, the Bob Marshall, Banff, Kootenay, Jasper, and other places that experienced severe fires in the years that followed. The grizzly bears, elk, and other animals in those places benefited from the crop of berries, aspen shoots, shrubs, and wild root vegetables that rose up in the days, weeks, and months following the fires.

But an increase in fire severity intersecting with insects, disease, drought, and other disturbances that come with climate change will lead to patterns of recovery that are much different than they were in the past. The watershed degradation that followed the Hayman and

Figure C-2 Drought and warmer winter temperatures, brought on by climate change, have resulted in tens of millions of trees being killed by insects and disease. The recent spruce bark beetle infestation (shown here) in Alaska and the Yukon is unprecedented in modern times.

Lost Creek fires is a testament to that. So are the scorched-earth scenarios that Ellen Whitman and Marc-André Parisien have seen in northern Canada, the invasive species that Lee Frelich sees creeping into the boreal of Minnesota following wildfires, and the hydrological changes that Gerald Frost and others are seeing in permafrost thawing that is taking place in the Arctic. The response from humans, then, can't be one of "business as usual" because it is not going to be successful.

Perhaps a more holistic approach to managing our forests is needed, as Harvey Locke at Yellowstone to Yukon, Rick Hauer at the University of Montana, Jeff Wells at the Boreal Song Bird Initiative, and others envision. The establishment of more protected areas and wildlife corridors would increase the likelihood that more of the vast stores of carbon in the soils and peatlands would stay there longer, decreasing fire suppression costs and the losses that result from the buildup of expensive infrastructure. Protected areas and undisturbed wildlife corridors would give wildlife and plants the best chance to adapt to climate change. They would also ensure that the vast majority of people in Canada and the United States who depend on forest watersheds for their drinking water would continue to do so in the years to come.

None of this will happen if meaningful investments are not made into scientific research, conservation, prevention, education, and a better understanding of how climate, wildfire, insects, drought, flooding, and invasive species are going to shape our forests in the future.

It's worth noting that the Cuyahoga River burned a number of times before it famously did in 1969. The City of Cleveland by then had made it clear that it had had enough when it issued a $100 million bond to clean up the river the year before. According to historian Michael Rotman, the river fire in 1969 was not so much the terrifying climax of decades of pollution; rather, it was the last gasp of an industrial river whose role was beginning to change.

Decision makers and the public need to begin looking at the northern forests, wildfire, and the environmental degradation that is taking place in them in the same way. Wildfire is an integral part of a healthy forest. But without an investment in scientific research and a holistic plan in place to deal with fires that are burning bigger, faster, hotter, and more often, we stand to lose the clean water we drink and fish from, the clean air we breathe, the birds and animals we hunt and take pictures of, and the jobs that forest environments produce.

Acknowledgments

Firestorm: How Wildfire Will Shape Our Future got an unofficial start in 2008 when I got a call from scientist Brian Stocks inviting me to come to Cold Lake, Alberta, where he and 120 scientists from around the world were participating in a $24 million NASA-led project tracking smoke from boreal wildfires. Recognizing that northern forest fires were burning bigger, hotter, faster, and more often than in the past, the scientists' aim was to determine how pollutants from these fires were being transported around the world and how the black carbon emitted from them might be further driving climate change. I had written extensively about the severe fires of 2003 and had been intrigued when Rob Walker, a Parks Canada manager, had suggested at the time that those fires were a harbinger of what was to come. Stocks's 2008 invitation alerted me to the fact that Walker had been right. My writer's antennae were up from that point on.

The book that was eventually written wouldn't have been possible without the support I received from the scientists, foresters, fire managers, and ecologists who invited me to participate or to observe at their research field stations and study sites. This long list includes Monica Emelko and Uldis Silins, who have spent more than fourteen years monitoring the recovery that continues to take place after the 2003 Lost Creek Fire; Erin Bayne, who arranged to have me join graduate student Elly Knight in a burned-out forest north of Fort McMurray where she studies nighthawks; Mike Demuth, who studies glacial retreat in the Canadian Rockies and Northwest Territories; John Pomeroy, whose research on water, glaciers, and snowpack might some day be used to predict wildfires; biologist Gordon Stenhouse, who has invited me to come along on grizzly bear captures in the Rockies five times in the past sixteen years; and Andrew Larson, who gave me several intense lessons in fire ecology in the Lolo National Forest in Montana. Thanks also go to Dave Smith of Parks Canada, who showed me what the mountain pine beetle would do to Jasper National Park before the beetle did some serious damage to the forests there. The speedy march of the beetle into the national park has been an astonishing one.

I am indebted to scientist Jill Johnstone, who took me on a 1,500-mile-long drive to visit fire-study plots throughout the Yukon and Alaska; and to scientist Ric Hauer, who flew me into the Bob Marshall Wilderness, Glacier/Waterton national parks, and the Flathead River valley. Hauer and Harvey Locke, a cofounder of the Yellowstone to Yukon conservation initiative, inspired me to look at wildfire in a way I would have not otherwise imagined.

Thanks go to Scott Rupp with the University of Alaska, who took a couple of days to show me what has been happening in his state, and to Robert Schmoll of the Alaska Division of Forestry, who described to me in detail what it takes to deal with a severe wildfire season with limited resources.

Memorable is the only way I can describe the hike I did with scientist Jeff Wells of the Boreal Songbird Initiative. He introduced me to one of the last boreal forest ecosystems in Maine. I thought I knew something about boreal ecology until I spent some time with him.

No one kept me busier than Cliff White and Ian Pengelly. The two veteran wildfire experts took two days to walk me through the history of fire ecology in Banff National Park. Parks Canada's Rick Kubian was generous in taking a day off to revisit the Kootenay fires that he, Rob Walker, and Jeff Weir were confronted with in the summer of 2003.

Among the many current and past Parks Canada employees who offered insights into this project, Mark Heathcott stands out for his digging deep to provide me with official records and insights into the history of wildfire in Canada's national parks. Heathcott's way with words is legendary, as readers will have surmised after having read this book. It was always a pleasure talking to him.

I can't thank enough the many very busy scientists who sat down and talked to me about wildfire and the book I was writing. Like Heathcott, Mike Flannigan stands out. With a heavy teaching load, many graduate students to supervise, and research of his own to pursue, Flannigan took several breakfast, lunch, and coffee breaks to offer insights and advice. Following the record-breaking 2015 wildfire season, I had thought that I had missed my timing for this book. He scoffed at the idea of that. Another big fire season will come along somewhere, he assured me. A few weeks later, the forests around Fort McMurray lit up.

Brian Stocks was busy with a report that he and others were writing on the Fort McMurray fire, yet he obliged whenever I called as long as my inquiries did not relate to the events that took place in northern Alberta in 2016. He was at the time bound to rules of confidentiality.

I would have liked to talk more to fire managers and fire specialists from the government of Alberta and the municipality of Wood Buffalo who dealt with the Fort McMurray fire, but the initial discussions I had were cut short, presumably by two official reviews of that fire. At the time this book was going into production in May, neither one of them had been released.

I was most surprised and delighted by the cooperation I got from the Royal Canadian Mounted Police (RCMP). The Mounties received almost no media attention during the Fort McMurray wildfire. I had assumed that they were under an order not to speak publicly about the event. When I called K-Division headquarters in Edmonton to ask about a photo of theirs that I was looking for, I realized that I was wrong. I was invited to come in to view a short video they were working on. That led to an invitation to go to Fort McMurray to spend considerable time talking to Superintendent Lorna Dicks and to RCMP officers who were on the front lines of that fire, acting heroically as most other first-responders had done. Sergeant Jonathan Baltzer sent me home with dozens of remarkable photographs that he took. The police rarely get thanked for the good work they do. Here are my thanks.

Several people reviewed parts of this book and offered insights. Among them were Monica Emelko, Mike Flannigan, Lee Frelich, Mike Fromm, Gerald Frost, Peter Griffith, Ric Hauer, Mark Heathcott, Ted Hogg, David Langor, Andrew Larson, Harvey Locke, Marc-André Parisien, Scott Rupp, Uldis Silins, Rob Walker, Jeff Wells, Cliff White, and Ellen Whitman. Thanks go to David Peterson of the US Forest Service, who cautioned me against using adjectives such as "catastrophic" when they weren't warranted and to greet with healthy skepticism scientists who suggest that they are on to something completely new in wildfire science. Thanks also go to historian I. S. MacLaren, who read through a couple of pertinent chapters, offering valuable insights and, most important of all, correcting my grammar.

No one was more helpful than Marty Alexander. His record of

achievement and experience in the world of wildfire is indomitable. He has contributed to several books and dozens of articles on wildfire during a long, distinguished career with the Canadian Forest Service, the Department of Wildland Resources at Utah State University, the University of New Brunswick, the University of Alberta, and other institutions. He has served as a member of the USDA Forest Service Wildland Fire R&D Program Review Panel (2007), the International Advisory Committee, the European Economic Commission sponsored FIRE PARADOX Project, and many other international initiatives. He has been called upon to be an external reviewer for PhD theses, promotion reviews of scientists and university professors, and U.S. Joint Fire Science Program proposals. And then I came along.

Had I paid Alexander for the hours he spent reviewing my book, talking to me at his home, on the phone, and via email, I would be a poor person. I'm sure he doesn't agree with everything I wrote, and he warned me to expect pushback about some of the issues I have raised. The important thing, he kept telling me, is to get the facts right. If there are mistakes in this book, they are mine, not his.

For the second time, I have worked with the multitalented Courtney Lix, an editor at Island Press. Once again, it was a pleasure building a book with her. Writers rarely say that the editing process is pleasant and constructive, but this one truly was. Editorial assistant Elizabeth Farry deserves a medal for being so organized and patient with me getting this book into production for Sharis Simonian, senior production manager at Island Press. Sharis laid out instructions and a timetable that was easy to follow. Copyeditor Kathleen Lafferty's razor-sharp eye for detail was much appreciated. And once again, my wife Julia Parker demonstrates that she is as proficient in correcting grammar and sighting inconsistencies in my prose as she is in practicing law. In addition, Lisa Adams, my wonderful agent, deserves a lot of credit for steering this book in the right direction before I began to seriously put pen to paper. Lisa was never more than an hour or two in responding to my emails whenever I needed advice.

Finally, thanks go to the many people in Fort McMurray and especially to Lucas and Adrien Welsh, who told me their stories. I didn't include them all because it would have ended in a book about that one infamous fire. Even now, a year after that fire, I still can't imagine what they and the first responders went through. It's a remarkable story.

Notes

Introduction

1. Jennifer K. Balch et al., "Human-Started Wildfires Expand the Fire Niche across the United States," *Proceedings of the National Academy of Sciences USA* 114, no. 11: 2946–51, doi: 10.1073/pnas.1617394114.

2. New Jersey State Hazard Mitigation Plan, New Jersey Wildfire Risk Assessment, accessed May 24, 2017, http://www.state.nj.us/drbc/library/documents/Flood _Website/NJmitigation/FEMAToolkito/2006draft/NJ_wildfire.pdf, 330–41

3. Tom Vilsack, US Department of Agriculture, "The Cost of Fighting Wildfires Is Sapping Forest Service Budget," August 5, 2015, https://www.usda.gov/media/blog /2015/08/5/cost-fighting-wildfires-sapping-forest-service-budget.

4. USDA Forest Service Fire and Aviation Management and Department of the Interior Office of Wildland Fire, "2014 Quadrennial Fire Review," May 2015, https:// www.forestsandrangelands.gov/QFR/documents/2014QFRFinalReport.pdf.

Chapter 1

1. CBC, *The Current*, interview with reporter Marian Warnica, July 27, 2016, http:// www.cbc.ca/radio/thecurrent/the-current-for-july-27-2016-1.3696707/fort-mcmur ray-fire-three-men-in-charge-recall-the-fight-they-will-never-forget-1.3696732.

2. "Quantifying Disaster," MacEwan News, January 20, 2017, http://www.macewan .ca/wcm/MacEwanNews/STORY_FT_MAC_ECON_RESEARCH_2.

3. Glenn McGillivary, "The Writing Is on the Wall for Future Wildfire Risk in Canada," June 10, 2014, http://www.insblogs.com/catastrophe/writing-wall-future-wild fire-risk-canada/1390.

4. Gary Filmon, "Firestorm 2003: Provincial Review," February 15, 2004, http:// www2.gov.bc.ca/assets/gov/farming-natural-resources-and-industry/forestry/wild fire-management/governance/bcws_firestormreport_2003.pdf.

5. Office of the Auditor General, British Columbia, "Follow-up of 2001/2002: Report 1, Managing Interface First Risks, and Firestorm 2003 Provincial Review (2005/2006: Report 2), May 2005, http://www.bcauditor.com/sites/default/files/publi cations/2005/report2/report/managing-interface-fire-risks-and-firestorm-2003-pro vincial-review.pdf.

6. "Five Years after the Filmon Report, Forest Minister Still Unable to Provide a List of BC Communities That Are Considered 'At Risk' for Wildfire," *Revelstoke Current*, September 28, 2009.

7. US Department of Agriculture, Forest Service, "The Rising Cost of Wildfire Operations: Effects on the Forest Service's Non-Fire Operations," August 4, 2015, https:// www.fs.fed.us/sites/default/files/2015-Fire-Budget-Report.pdf.

8. "Indicator: Forest Fires," Natural Resources Canada, last modified November 1, 2016, http://www.nrcan.gc.ca/forests/report/disturbance/16392.

9. Greg Baxter, "All Terrain Vehicles as a Cause of Fire Ignition in Alberta Forests," *Advantage* 3, no. 44 (October 2002), http://wildfire.fpinnovations.ca/39/AD-3-44.pdf.

10. Damien Asher, *Inside the Inferno: A Firefighter's Story of the Brotherhood That Saved Fort McMurray* (Toronto: Simon and Schuster Canada, 2017), 35.

11. David Matera, "Taming the Beast in Fort McMurray, Hale Borealis Forum, Alberta Health Services, October 18–20, 2016, http://haleborealis.com/wp-content/uploads/2016/11/Northern-Lights-Health-Centre_Matear.pdf.

12. "Fort McMurray Fire: Three Men in Charge Recall the Fight They Will Never Forget," *The Current*, CBC, July 27, 2016, http://www.cbc.ca/radio/thecurrent/the-current-for-july-27-2016-1.3696707/fort-mcmurray-fire-three-men-in-charge-recall-the-fight-they-will-never-forget-1.3696732.

Chapter 2

1. Cordy Tymstra, *The Chinchaga Firestorm: When the Moon and Sun Turned Blue* (Edmonton: University of Alberta Press, 2015).

2. Warren Cornwall, "Record Drought Hastens Dramatic Spread of California Wildfires," *National Geographic*, September 20, 2014, http://news.nationalgeographic.com/news/2014/09/140919-california-wildfires-king-fire-drought-climate-change/.

3. Richard C. Rothermel, "Mann Gulch Fire: A Race That Couldn't Be Won," US Department of Agriculture, Forest Service, Intermountain Research Station, General Technical Report INT-299, May 1993, https://www.nifc.gov/safety/mann_gulch/investigation/reports/Mann_Gulch_Fire_A_Race_That_Could_Not_Be_Won_May_1993.pdf.

4. R. P. Turco et al., "Nuclear Winter: Global Consequences of Multiple Nuclear Explosions," *Science* 222, no. 4630 (December 23, 1983): 1283–92.

5. R. P. Turco et al., "Climate and Smoke: An Appraisal of Nuclear Winter," *Science* 247, no. 4939 (January 12, 1990): 166–76.

6. Ian Stirling, Nicholas Lunn, and John Iacozza, "Long-Term Trends in the Population Ecology of Polar Bears in Western Hudson Bay in Relation to Climatic Change," *Arctic* 52, no. 3 (September 1999): 294–306.

7. Transportation Safety Board of Canada, "Loss of Control and Collision with Terrain," Aviation Investigation Report A15W0069, May 22, 2015, http://www.tsb.gc.ca/eng/rapports-reports/aviation/2015/A15W0069/A15W0069.asp.

8. "Missing Men List Now Numbers 400," *Idaho Press*, August 21, 1910.

9. Quoted in Gerald H. Williams, "Wildland Fire Management in the 20th Century," *Fire Management* 60, no. 4 (Fall 2000): 14.

10. Rothermel, "Mann Gulch."

11. Quoted in Stephen J. Pyne, *Awful Splendour: A Fire History of Canada* (Vancouver: University of British Columbia Press, 2007), 338.

12. Harry Wexler, "The Great Pall Smoke, September 24-30," *Weatherwise* 3, no. 6 (1950): 129–42.

13. "Forest Fires Cast Pall on Northeast, Canadian Drift 600 Miles Long, Darkens Wide Areas and Arouses 'Atom' Fears," *New York Times*, September 25, 1950.

14. "Forest Fires Cast Pall."

15. Norman Carlson, "One Sunday Night in 1950 the Sun Went Out," *Jamestown Post Journal*, January 3, 1987.

16. Carlson, "One Sunday Night."

17. "Alberta Smoke Covers Toronto," *Globe and Mail*, September 25, 1950.

18. Helen Hogg, "Blue Sun," *Journal of the Royal Astronomical Society of Canada* 44 (1950): 241–45.

Chapter 3

1. Aldo Leopold, " 'Piute Forestry' vs. Forest Fire Prevention," *Southwestern Magazine* 2 (March 1920): 12–13.

2. "Wildfires," Insurance Information Institute, 2017, http://www.iii.org/fact-statistic /wildfires;

3. Wildfire statistics were extracted from data recorded by the National Interagency Fire Centre, https://www.nifc.gov/fireInfo/fireInfo_statistics.html.

4. National Interagency Fire Centre.

5. Glenn McGillivray, "The Writing Is on the Wall for Future Wildfire Risk in Canada," *insBlogs*, June 10, 2014, http://www.insblogs.com/catastrophe/writing-wall -future-wildfire-risk-canada/1396.

6. G. L. Hoxie, "How Fire Helps Forestry," *Sunset* 34 (1910): 145–51.

7. David Douglas, *Journal Kept by David Douglas during His Travels in North America, 1823–1827* (London: William Wesley and Son, 1914).

8. Stephen W. Barrett and S. F. Arno, "Indian Fires as an Ecological Influence in the Northern Rockies," *Journal of Forestry* 80, no. 10 (1982): 647–51.

9. Henry Lewis, *A Time for Burning* (Edmonton: Boreal Institute of Northern Studies, University of Alberta, 1982).

10. William B. Greeley, " 'Paiute Forestry' or the Fallacy of Light Burning," *The Timberman* (March 1920), 38–39; reprinted in *Forest History Today*, Spring 1999, 33–37.

11. For insights into both essays, see Andrew Larson, "Introduction to the Article By Elers Koch, *The Passing of the Lolo Trail*," *Fire Ecology* 12, no. 1 (2016), http://fire ecologyjournal.org/docs/Journal/pdf/Volume12/Issue01/001.pdf.

12. Lewis, *A Time for Burning*, 4.

13. Hutch Brown, "Wildland Burning by American Indians in Virginia," *Fire Management Today* 60, no. 3 (2000): 29–39.

14. David Mazel, *American Literary Environmentalism* (Athens: University of Georgia Press, 2000).

15. Peter J. Murphy, "Homesteading the Athabasca Valley to 1910," in *Culturing Wilderness in Jasper National Park*, ed. I. S. MacLaren (Edmonton: University of Alberta Press, 2007), 71–121.

16. Ross Cox, *Adventures on the Columbia River, including the Narrative of a Residence of Six Years on the Western Side of the Rocky Mountains, among various Tribes of Indians hitherto unknown: together with a Journey across the American Continent*, 2 vols. (London: Henry Colburn and Richard Bentley, 1831), 2: 203.

17. Harrison E. Salisbury, *The Great Black Dragon Fire, A Chinese Inferno* (New York: Little, Brown, 1989).

18. Geoffrey York, "Smoke from 224 Forest Fires Threatens Manitoba Airports," *Globe and Mail*, July 25, 1989, 1.

19. Dan Whipple, "Yellowstone Ablaze: The Fires of 1988," WyoHistory.org, accessed May 8, 2017, http://www.wyohistory.org/encyclopedia/yellowstone-ablaze-fires-1988.

20. Jerry T. Williams, "Managing Risk in Wilderness Fire Management," *Proceedings: Symposium on Fire in Wilderness and Park Management*, ed. James K. Brown et al.,

General Technical report INT-GTR-320 (Ogden, UT: US Forest Service, Intermountain Research Station, 1995), 22.

21. I. S. MacLaren, "Cultured Wilderness in Jasper," *Journal of Canadian Studies* 34, no. 3 (1999); B. J. Stocks, "Federal Forest Fire Research in Canada: An Impressive Past, a Troubled Present, and an Uncertain Future," Wildfire Investigations Ltd., Sault Ste. Marie, ON, presentation to the Wildland Fire Conference, Kananaskis, AB, 2012.

22. "Managing the Impact of Wildfires on Communities and the Environment: A Report to the President in Response to the Wildfires of 2000, September 8, 2000, https://www.forestsandrangelands.gov/resources/reports/documents/2001/8-20-en .pdf.

23. *Fire Management: Lessons Learned from the Cerro Grande (Los Alamos) Fire*, Committee on Energy and Natural Resources, US Senate, July 20, 2000 (statement of Barry T. Hill, Associate Director, Energy, Resources, and Science Issues, Resources, Community, and Economic Development Division).

24. Keith Easthouse, "Park Service Unfairly Scapegoated for Los Alamos Fire," *Forest Magazine* (April 5, 2001).

Chapter 4

1. "Wildfires—Annual 2003," National Ocean and Atmospheric Administration, National Centers for Environmental Information, published online January 2004, retrieved May 8, 2017, https://www.ncdc.noaa.gov/sotc/fire/200313.

2. "Entire Going-to-the-Sun Road Open for Day-Use," National Park Service press release, August 5, 2003, https://www.nps.gov/aboutus/news/release.htm?id=397.

3. Bill Graveland, "Raging Forest Fires Force Evacuations in Crowsnest Pass Area," *Globe and Mail*, August 4, 2003, 4.

4. Gary Filmon, "Firestorm 2003: Provincial Review," February 15, 2004, http:// www2.gov.bc.ca/assets/gov/farming-natural-resources-and-industry/forestry/wild fire-management/governance/bcws_firestormreport_2003.pdf.

5. Quoted in Charles J. Hanley, "Researchers Link Wildfires to Climate Change," Associated Press, July 21, 2006.

6. M. D. Flannigan and C. E. Van Wagner, "Climate Change and Wildfire in Canada," *Canadian Journal of Forest Research* 21 (1991): 66–72.

7. Brian J. Stocks, "Global Warming and Forest Fires in Canada," *Forest Chronicles* 69 (1993): 290–93.

8. Michael Weber and Brian J. Stocks, "Forest Fires and Sustainability in the Boreal Forests of Canada," *Ambio* 27, no. 7 (1998): 545–50.

9. Filmon, "Firestorm 2003," 76.

Chapter 5

1. "Fears May Be Outpacing Reality in Colorado Fires," *New York Times*, June 16, 2002.

2. "Fears May Be Outpacing Reality."

3. P. J. Gerla and J. M. Galloway, "Water Quality of Two Streams Near Yellowstone Park, Wyoming, Following the 1988 Clover-Mist Wildfire," *Environmental Geology* 36, no. 1/2 (November 1998): 127–36.

4. M. B. Emelko et al., "Sediment-Phosphorus Dynamics Can Shift Aquatic Ecology and Cause Downstream Legacy Effects after Wildfire in Large River Systems," *Global*

Change Biology 22, no. 3 (2016): 1168–84; U. Silins et al., "Five-Year Legacy of Wildfire and Salvage Logging Impacts on Nutrient Runoff and Aquatic Plant, Invertebrate, and Fish Productivity," *Ecohydrology*, February 17, 2014, doi: 10.1002/eco.1474.

5. Richard Hauer et al., "Glacial-Bed River Floodplains Are the Ecological Nexus of Glaciated Landscapes," *Science Advances* 2, no. 6 (June 4, 2016), doi: 10.1126/sciadv.1600026.

6. Meg A. Krawchuk et al., "Topographic and Fire Weather Controls of Fire Refugia in Forested Ecosystems of Northwestern North America," *Ecosphere* 7, no. 12 (December 2016), doi: 10.1002/ecs2.1632.

Chapter 6

1. N. Evangeliou et al., "Fire Evolution in the Radioactive Forests," *Ecological Monographs* 85, no. 1 (February 2015): 49–72.

2. "New Wildfire Sends Smoke Billowing over Chernobyl Exclusion Zone," *RT*, June 30, 2015, https://www.rt.com/news/270658-chernobyl-exclusion zone fire/.

3. United States of America v. W. R. Grace et al., US District Court for the District of Montana, Missoula Division, CR05-M-DWN, https://www2a.cdc.gov/phlcourse/Docs/uswrgrace20705ind.pdf.

4. Nikia Hernandez, email message to Christina Progress, July 7, 2016, https://semspub.epa.gov/work/08/1772063.pdf.

5. Philip E. Dennison et al., "Large Wildfire Trends in the Western United States, 1984–2011," *Geophysical Research Letters* 25 (April 2014), doi: 10.1002/2014GL059576.

6. John Sandlos and Arn Keeling, *Giant Mine: Historical Summary*, Abandoned Mines in Northern Canada Project, August 8, 2012, http://reviewboard.ca/upload/project_document/EA0809-001_Giant_Mine__History_Summary.PDF.

7. Canadian Public Health Association, Task Force on Arsenic: Final Report, Yellowknife Northwest Territories (Ottawa: Canadian Public Health Association, 1977), 59–62.

8. H. E. Jamieson, "The Legacy of Arsenic Contamination from Mining and Processing Refractory Gold Ore at Giant Mine, Yellowknife, Northwest Territories, Canada," *Reviews in Mineralogy and Geochemistry* 79, no. 1 (2014): 533–51; Robert J. Bowell et al., "The Environmental Geochemistry of Arsenic—An Overview," *Reviews in Mineralogy and Geochemistry* 79, no. 1 (2014): 533–51.

9. Adam James Houben et al., "Factors Affecting Elevated Arsenic and Methyl Mercury Concentrations in Small Shield Lakes Surrounding Gold Mines near the Yellowknife, NT, (Canada) Region," *PLoS One*, April 6, 2016, http://dx.doi.org/10.1371/journal.pone.0150960.

10. Houben et al., "Factors Affecting Elevated Arsenic and Methyl Mercury Concentrations."

11. K. J. Reimer and W. R. Cullen, "Arsenic Concentrations in Wood, Soil and Plant Tissue Collected around Trees Treated with Monosodium Methanearsonate (MSMA) for Bark Beetle Control," report prepared for the British Columbia Ministry of Forests and Range, June 2009.

12. C. A. Morrissey, P. L. Dods, and J. E. Elliott, "Pesticide Treatments Affect Mountain Pine Beetle Abundance and Woodpecker Foraging Behavior," *Ecological Applications* 18, no. 1 (2008): 172–84.

13. National Orphaned/Abandoned Mine Initiative, *National Orphaned/Abandoned*

Mines Initiative 2002–2008 Performance Report, 2009, http://www.abandoned-mines
.org/pdfs/NOAMIPerformanceReport2002-2008-e.pdf; Environment Security Initiative, *Mining for Closure: Policies and Guidelines for Sustainable Mining Practice and Closure of Mines*, 2005, http://www.grida.no/publications/259.

14. *Exploration and Mining Guide for Aboriginal Communities*, 2013, https://www
.nrcan.gc.ca/sites/www.nrcan.gc.ca/files/mineralsmetals/files/pdf/abor-auto/mining
-guide-eng.pdf.

15. Colleen E. Reid et al., "Critical Review of Health Impacts of Wildfire Smoke Exposure," *Environmental Health Perspectives* 124, no. 9 (2016): 1334–43, https://ehp
.niehs.nih.gov/wp-content/uploads/124/9/ehp.1409277.alt.pdf.

16. George E. Le et al., "Canadian Forest Fires and the Effects of Long-Range Transboundary Air Pollution on Hospitalizations among the Elderly," *ISPRS International Journal of Geo-Information* 3 (2014): 713–31.

17. J. C. Liu et al., "A Systematic Review of the Physical Health Impacts from Non-occupational Exposure to Wildfire Smoke," *Environmental Research* 136 (January 2015): 120–32, doi: 10.1016/j.envres.2014.10.015.

18. "Canadian Wildfires Produce River of Smoke," *Earth Observatory*, July 1, 2015, http://earthobservatory.nasa.gov/IOTD/view.php?id=86151.

19. Gary A. Morris et al., "Alaskan and Canadian Forest Fires Exacerbate Ozone Pollution over Houston, Texas, on 19 and 20 July 2004," *Journal of Geophysical Research: Atmospheres* 111, D24S03 (2006), doi: 10.1029/2006JD007090.

20. Mark E. Brigham et al., "Lacustrine Responses to Decreasing Wet Mercury Deposition Rates—Results from a Case Study in Northern Minnesota," *Environmental Science and Technology* 48, no. 11 (2014): 6115–23, http://pubs.acs.org/doi/abs/10.1021
/es500301a.

21. E. N. Kelly et al., "Forest Fire Increases Mercury Accumulation by Fishes via Food Web Restructuring and Increased Mercury Inputs," *Proceedings of the National Academy of Sciences USA* 103 (2006): 19380–85.

22. Arctic Monitoring and Assessment Programme, "Mercury in the Arctic," Arctic Council, last updated August 28, 2015, http://www.arctic-council.org/index.php/en
/our-work2/8-news-and-events/321-mercury-in-the-arctic.

23. David A. Taylor, "Mercury: Forest Fire Fallout," *Environmental Health Perspectives* 115, no. 1 (2007): A21.

24. M. R. Turetsky et al., "Wildfires Threaten Mercury Stocks in Northern Soils," *Geophysical Research Letters* 33 (2006): L16403, doi: 10.1029/2005GL025595.

25. Arctic Monitoring and Assessment Programme, "Mercury in the Arctic."

26. A. Rappold et al., "Forecast-Based Interventions Can Reduce the Health and Economic Burden of Wildfires," *Environmental Science and Technology* 48 (2014): 10571–79, doi: 10.1021/es5012725.

Chapter 7

1. Steven C. Grossnickle, *Ecophysiology of Northern Spruce Species: The Performance of Planted Seedlings* (Ottawa, ON: National Research Council of Canada, 2000).

2. Timothy Egan, "A Walk in the Dead Woods," *New York Times*, May 27, 2016, https://www.nytimes.com/2016/05/27/opinion/a-walk-in-the-dead-woods.html.

3. E. H. Hogg, J. P. Brandt, and B. Kochtubajda, "Growth and Dieback of Aspen Forests in Northwestern Alberta, Canada, in Relation to Climate and Insects," *Canadian Journal of Forest Research* 32 (2002): 823–32; E. H. Hogg and P. A. Hurdle, "The

Aspen Parkland in Western Canada: A Dry-Climate Analogue for the Future Boreal Forest?" *Water, Air, and Soil Pollution* 82 (1995): 391–400.

4. Prairie Drought Initiative: white paper.

5. Environment and Climate Change Canada, "The Top Ten Weather Stories of 2002," last modified June 18, 2013, http://www.ec.gc.ca/meteo-weather/default.asp ?lang=En&n=7E0A416A-1#t1.

6. Personal communication, Colleen Biggs.

7. D. Sauchyn and S. Kulshreshtha, "Prairies," in *From Impacts to Adaptation: Canada in a Changing Climate*, ed. D. S. Lemmen et al. (Ottawa, ON: Government of Canada, 2008), 275–328.

8. Environment and Climate Change Canada, "Top Ten Weather Stories of 2002."

9. Gary Filmon, "Firestorm 2003: Provincial Review," February 15, 2004, http:// www2.gov.bc.ca/assets/gov/farming-natural-resources-and-industry/forestry/wild fire-management/governance/bcws_firestormreport_2003.pdf; David Phillips, "Top Ten Weather Stories for 2003," *Canadian Meteorological and Oceanographic Society Bulletin* 32, no. 1 (February 2004): 9–14.

10. Jennifer H. Carey, "*Pinus banksiana*," in *Fire Effects Information System*, US Department of Agriculture, Forest Service, Rocky Mountain Research Station, Fire Sciences Laboratory (Producer), May 10, 2017, https://www.fs.fed.us/database/feis /plants/tree/pinban/all.html#INTRODUCTORY.

11. D. M. Shrimpton, "Forest Succession Following the Mountain Pine Beetle Outbreak in Kootenay Park which Occurred during the 1930's," report for Forest Health, British Columbia Ministry of Forests, December 1994, https://www.for.gov.bc.ca/hfd /library/mpb/bib107981.pdf.

12. Garrett W. Meigs et al., "Do Insect Outbreaks Reduce the Severity of Subsequent Forest Fires?," *Environmental Research Letters* 11, no. 4 (2016), http://iopscience .iop.org/article/10.1088/1748-9326/11/4/045008/meta.

13. Martin Simard et al.," Do Mountain Pine Beetle Outbreaks Change the Probability of Active Crown Fire in Lodgepole Pine Forests?," *Ecological Monographs*, February 1, 2011, doi: 10.1890/10-1176.1.

14. Wesley G. Page, Martin E. Alexander, and Michael J. Jenkins, "Effects of Bark Beetle Attack on Canopy Fuel Flammability and Crown Fire Potential in Lodgepole Pine and Engelmann Spruce Forests," in *Proceedings of the Large Wildland Fires Conference*, ed. Robert E. Keane et al., May 19–23, 2014, Missoula, MT, Proc. RMRS-P-73 (Fort Collins, CO: US Department of Agriculture, Forest Service, Rocky Mountain Research Station, 2015), 174–80, quoted in "US Faces Worst Droughts in 1,000 Years, Predict Scientists," *The Guardian*, February 12, 2015.

15. Benjamin Cook, Toby Ault, and Jason Smerdon, "Unprecedented 21st Century Drought Risk in the American Southwest and Central Plains," *Science Advances* 1, no. 1 (February 12, 2015): e1400082, doi: 10.1126/sciadv.1400082.

16. John Pomeroy et al., "Sensitivity of Snowmelt Hydrology on Mountain Slopes to Forest Cover Disturbance," Centre for Hydrology Report No. 10, Centre for Hydrology, University of Saskatchewan, June 23, 2011.

Chapter 8

1. "Lightning Triggers Fires Across Alaska," Earth Observatory image, June 22, 2004, http://earthobservatory.nasa.gov/IOTD/view.php?id=4591.

2. Alaska Division of Forestry, "Alaska's First Wildfire of 2016 Reported near Delta

Junction," Alaska Wildland Fire Information, February 22, 2016, https://akfireinfo
.com/2016/02/22/alaskas-first-wildfire-of-2016-reported-near-delta-junction/.

3. Personal communication with Glenn Juday re: Claire Parkinson and William
W. Kellogg, "Arctic Sea Ice Decay Simulated for a CO_2-Induced Temperature Rise,"
Climatic Change 2, no. 2 (June 1979): 149–62, doi:10.1007/BF00133221.

4. "Scientists Discount Drought Tie to 'Greenhouse' Warmth Trend," *Los Angeles
Times,* June 25, 1988.

5. Daniel H. Mann et al., "Is Alaska's Boreal Forest Now Crossing a Major Ecological Threshold?," *Arctic, Antarctic, and Alpine Research* 44, no. 3 (2012): 319–31, http://
www.bioone.org/doi/abs/10.1657/1938-4246-44.3.319.

6. Eccentricity is the shape of Earth's orbit around the sun. Axial tilt is the inclination of Earth's axis in relation to its plane of orbit around the sun. Precession is Earth's
slow wobble as it spins on its axis.

Chapter 9
1. Climate Central, "Alaska Entering New Era for Wildfires," research report, June
24, 2015, http://www.climatecentral.org/news/alaska-entering-new-era-for-wildfires
-19146.

2. Ryan Kelly et al., "Recent Burning of Boreal Forests Exceeds Fire Regime Limits
of the Past 10,000 Years," *Proceedings of the National Academy of Sciences USA* 110, no. 32
(August 6, 2013): 13055–60, doi: 10.1073/pnas.1305069110.

3. Yongwon Kim et al., "Possible Effect of Boreal Wildfire Soot on Arctic Sea Ice
and Alaska Glaciers," *Atmospheric Environment* 39, no. 19 (2005): 3513–20.

4. The wilderness includes approximately 19.7 million acres (8 million hectares) of
low tundra communities, 760,000 acres (310,000 hectares) of unvegetated intertidal
mud and sand flats, and 2,550 miles (4,100 kilometers) of shoreline broken by twenty-
two large river mouths and thirteen bays. The extensive intertidal flats are adjacent
to about 2.27 million acres (920,000 hectares) of wet, sedge-grass meadows that lie
between the average high-tide line and the storm-tide line. See http://www.whsrn
.org/site-profile/yukon-delta-nwr.

5. Jennifer B. Korosi et al., "Broad-Scale Lake Expansion and Flooding Inundates
Essential Wood Bison Habitat," *Nature Communications* 8 (March 2017), doi: 10.1038
/ncomms14510.

Chapter 10
1. Scott E. Nielsen et al., "Environmental, Biological and Anthropogenic Effects on
Grizzly Bear Body Size: Temporal and Spatial Considerations," *BMC Ecology* 13, no. 31
(2013), https://bmcecol.biomedcentral.com/articles/10.1186/1472-6785-13-31.

2. US Fish and Wildlife Service, Mountain-Prairie Region, "Wildfires and Grizzly
Bears," June 2003, https://www.fws.gov/mountain-prairie/species/mammals/grizzly
/wildfire&bears.pdf.

3. T. P. Cobb, D. W. Langor, and J. R. Spence, "Biodiversity and Multiple Disturbances: Boreal Forest Ground Beetle (Coleoptera: Carabidae) Responses to Wildfire, Harvesting, and Herbicide," *Canadian Journal of Forest Research* 37, no. 8 (2007):
1310–23.

4. Monica Bond, Curt Bradley, and Derek Lee, "Foraging Habitat Selection by
California Spotted Owls After Fire," *Journal of Wildlife Management* 80, no. 7 (2016):
1290–1300, doi: 10.1002/jwmg.21112.

5. Oregon Fish and Wildlife Office, "Barred Owl Study Update," accessed May 10, 2017, https://www.fws.gov/oregonfwo/articles.cfm?id=149489616.

6. Quoted in Wayne E. Reilly, "Maine's Mystery: Where Did All the Caribou Go?," *Bangor Daily News*, November 23, 2014.

Conclusion

1. Alaska Dispatch News, "Jury Finds Anchorage Couple Not Guilty in Sockeye Fire Case," *Alaska News*, May 12, 2017.

2. Alan Westhaver, "Why Some Homes Survived: Learning from the Fort McMurray Wildland/Urban Interface Fire Disaster," Institute for Catastrophic Loss Reduction, March 2017, https://www.iclr.org/images/Westhaver_Fort_McMurray_Final_2017.pdf.

3. B. J. Stocks, "Federal Forest Fire Research in Canada: An Impressive Past, a Troubled Present, and an Uncertain Future," Wildfire Investigations Ltd., Sault Ste. Marie, ON, presentation to the Wildland Fire Canada Conference, Kananaskis, AB, 2012.

4. John Maclean has written an excellent book on the Yarnell fire, which caused the greatest loss of life of an organized fire crew since the Big Burn of 1910. For more information, see johnmacleanbooks.com/yarnell/.

5. Charles D. Koven, "Boreal Carbon Loss due to Poleward Shift in Low-Carbon Ecosystems," *Nature Geoscience* 6 (2013): 452–56, http://www.nature.com/ngeo/journal/v6/n6/abs/ngeo1801.html.

6. L. D'Orangeville et al., "Northeastern North America as a Potential Refugium for Boreal Forests in a Warming Climate," *Science* 352, no. 6292 (2016): 1452–55, doi: 10.1126/science.aaf4951.

7. Michael E. Mann et al., "Influence of Anthropogenic Climate Change on Planetary Wave Resonance and Extreme Weather Events," Scientific Reports 7 (2017): 45242, doi: 10.1038/srep45242.